THE INTELLIGENCE EDGE

Also by George and Meredith Friedman

The Coming War with Japan
The Future of War

THE INTELLIGENCE EDGE

How to Profit in the Information Age

George Friedman

Meredith Friedman

Colin Chapman

John S. Baker, Jr.

CROWN PUBLISHERS, INC.
NEW YORK

DEDICATED TO

W. Edward LeBard
Jonathan Friedman
Maximilian Chapman
Michelle Baker

Netscape Communications Corporation has not authorized, sponsored, or
endorsed, or approved this publication and is not responsible for its content.
Netscape and the Netscape Communications Corporate Logos are trademarks
and trade names of Netscape Communications Corporation. All other product
names and/or logos are trademarks of their respective owners.

Published by Crown Publishers, Inc., 201 East 50th Street, New York, New York
10022. Member of the Crown Publishing Group.

Random House, Inc. New York, Toronto, London, Sydney, Auckland
http://www.randomhouse.com/

CROWN and colophon are trademarks of Crown Publishers, Inc.

Printed in the United States of America

Design by June Bennett-Tantillo

Library of Congress Cataloging-in-Publication Data
The intelligence edge : how to profit in the information age / by
    George Friedman... [et al.]. — 1st ed.
        p.   cm.
    Includes bibliographical references and index.
    1. Business intelligence.   I. Friedman, George.
  HD38.7.I55   1997
  658.4'7—dc21   97-17567
                                                              CIP

ISBN 0-609-60075-3

10   9   8   7   6   5   4   3   2   1

First Edition

CONTENTS

PREFACE

This book originated from a series of intercontinental conversations over an extended period of time. The issue was deceptively simple: Do businesses actually know what they need to know in order to make decisions? One of the authors, Colin Chapman, is a longtime business journalist who has been collecting information on businesses for decades. Two other authors, George and Meredith Friedman, had just emerged from the thickets of collecting information on the military, during the course of which they had discovered new sources and techniques that had heretofore been inaccessible outside the national security community but which were now pouring forth into the public domain. The question arose whether the methods used in tracking information about national security and the techniques discovered while studying the military and intelligence communities could be fruitfully applied to the craft of business intelligence. We were particularly interested in the new technologies that permitted the intelligence professional to go beyond espionage to the efficient mining of the public domain.

One of the outcomes of this conversation was the forming of a business, Strategic Forecasting, L.L.C., which applies these techniques on a daily basis. The other result was this book, which draws both on our particular perspectives in hunting down information and analyzing it as well as our experiences operating a business intelligence service. It was because we were in business that we realized that any book on business intelligence that did not include a word from a counsel was incomplete. Thus, we invited John Baker to have the final say, making this a wholly realistic work. The purpose of this book is not to provide a comprehensive manual for business intelligence operations but to create a framework for thinking about the problem of transforming information into knowledge. We have also provided some representative anecdotes to give the reader a sense of the steps involved in this process. All of the episodes recounted here represent actual cases in which we have been involved. Since, however, confidentiality is a critical element in our chosen profession, particulars, including but not confined to industry and country, have been occasionally changed.

We would like to thank several people who have helped us in our collective effort, including Chris Treadaway, Matt Baker, and others of our staff at Strategic Forecasting who were indispensable in the research for this book. We are also grateful to a number of members of the staff of the World Economic Forum and its founder and president, Klaus Schwab. William Bradford Reynolds and Dave Marshall both read significant portions of the manuscript, and we thank them for their helpful comments. And finally, we thank Bob Grevemberg, who kept us from taking this too seriously.

THE INTELLIGENCE EDGE

INTRODUCTION

The Knowledge Crisis

Intelligence professionals have regularly regarded their calling as the world's second oldest profession. They've been modest. Intelligence is actually the oldest profession around. Long before the first hooker named her price, Cain killed Abel, striking unexpectedly. From that moment on, humans watched and waited, trying to figure out from where the next threat—or opportunity—would come. It is impossible to be human without, in some sense, mastering the craft of intelligence. From buying a house to selecting a car to taking over a multinational corporation, life is about collecting, analyzing, and acting upon information. Rather than being some peculiar specialty, intelligence is actually the most ordinary and common of activities. How odd, then, that business should find intelligence so exotic!

We associate intelligence with spy satellites, high-speed encryption devices, and, above all, with "Bond...James Bond." It is hard to think about garment manufacturers and first-time home buyers as part of the intelligence game. But, truth be known, government intelligence is usually about equally unglamorous topics that happen to concern matters of fundamental national interest. And the same can be said for business and personal intelligence—it's not glamorous, but it is about as close as you can get to life and death in everyday existence.

Frequently, we confuse intelligence with espionage—illegal

activities in the service of the state. But intelligence is much more than espionage. Intelligence is about information gathering and analysis. Illegally acquired information may be sexier than the legally acquired kind, but it is rarely more useful. The most secret, illegal information improperly analyzed is worthless, and the most commonly available information properly analyzed can be invaluable. Good intelligence is less concerned with where information comes from than with making sure that all information required for decision making is in hand, and that the information has been properly processed and analyzed.

Information management is at the heart of intelligence. By information management we don't quite mean what the data-processing department means; rather, we mean knowing what to do with collected information, knowing what is important and what is not, what can be discarded and what must be preserved, how to make certain that valuable information is accessible and not lost in the crowd. This is the core of the intelligence process—one that we can, in fact, learn a great deal about from national intelligence agencies.

Collection without analysis is like foreplay without orgasm—only more frustrating.

During the Cold War, the Central Intelligence Agency (CIA) and other national intelligence services were given an enormous task. They were told that their responsibility was to know everything going on in the world that could affect the interests of the United States. Now, since that covered just about everything in the world, it was inevitable that the CIA would fail. No matter how well they did their job, sooner or later they would miss something. It was the very vastness of their mission that caused the CIA and other intelligence-gathering agencies to recognize that their only hope was to master the information management process—to implement a systematic approach to information capture, management, and analysis. The systematic approach actually works better in business than in government, because business has the luxury of being more focused.

The hard-won lessons of the world's national intelligence services can now be applied to business, and not only large corporations. Any business that needs information about its operating environment—what we call situational awareness—can profit from these techniques. What we are proposing is the logical next step in the great global privatization wave under way since the 1980s: the privatization of intelligence.

In the simplest sense, everyone in business is an intelligence operative and analyst. Business is about locating opportunities and risks, analyzing possible responses and acting on that analysis. Business lives and dies by information collection, management, and analysis. The issue is not whether you will engage in business intelligence, but rather whether you will do it casually or meticulously, ad hoc or systematically. Obviously, we think systematic and meticulous intelligence is more profitable than casual, ad hoc intelligence. You may think otherwise. But doing intelligence is not a matter of choice. It is what business is all about, and it is getting harder, rather than easier, to do.

A WORLD GROWN TOO BIG AND MOVING TOO FAST

The world is awash in information. We can sit in New York and know what happened only a few minutes before in a boardroom in Hong Kong or a ministry in Brasília. Government ministries all over the world are recording, archiving, and allowing access to activities taking place throughout their societies. Highly skilled and specialized journalists roam the world looking for events to record and explain. Employees in your own company are accumulating knowledge about things that are vital to decisions being made by your company's executives right now.

More than ever before in human history, businesses need to know what is happening on the other side of the world as quickly as possible—as well as what the mail-room clerk has found out during his lunch break. Opportunities open and close in a matter of hours and new technologies emerge in weeks and mature in months. New regulations constantly blindside businesses. All too often, we are making decisions without enough information. Businesses are suffering from a profound lack of knowledge.

Here is the paradox with which we live on a daily basis: Although we have more information available today than ever before, we don't actually know that much more, as a percentage of the whole, than we used to. We'll make an even more sweeping assertion: The percentage of information being turned into knowledge today is far less than the percentage a century ago. For all of our technical sophistication, we are day by day falling behind the knowledge curve. And it is costing us dearly.

In order to understand this, let's begin by distinguishing between three things: data, information, and knowledge. Think of data as a single fact—for example, someone just bought a bar of soap in Chicago; the chairman of the board of General Motors is sixty-three years old; the Fed Fund rate closed at 5½ percent on Tuesday. These are all data. They are true, but, by themselves, they have only limited meaning.

Now, if we were to say fifty thousand bars of soap were sold in Chicago yesterday, an increase of 12 percent over the same day last year, we would have a cluster of facts—a set of data. More precisely, the data would have been manipulated and organized in order to yield insights that no single piece of data could provide. This clustered and manipulated data we'd call information. So, if we were to say that the average age of a Fortune 500 board chairman is sixty-one, down from sixty-two a year ago, or that the Fed Fund rate is declining, we would have taken data and pulled it together so that it became information. Information is data joined together in revealing ways so that a person can analyze and understand its implications.

Knowledge, on the other hand, exists only inside the heads of human beings. Entire libraries contain not a bit of knowledge. All they contain is information, ready to be turned into knowledge when someone reads, learns, and understands. The crisis of our time is that the deluge of information that we confront has made it even more difficult to acquire knowledge. Finding needed information amid the torrent around us is a difficult, sometimes even impossible, task. Analyzing and understanding that torrent is even more difficult. Yet without that understanding, neither data nor information have any value. This surge of valueless information is the crisis of our time.

Knowledge is what you are after. Information is the raw material you use. Intelligence is what finds and processes information.

This crisis has arisen because of a single innovation: the computer. Think of the computer as nothing more than an extremely cost-effective recording device. What has happened in business, as elsewhere, is that all sorts of events are constantly being monitored and recorded by computers. Every operation on the factory floor, every purchase, every sale, every trip, every paycheck, every illness, every…well, every everything, is recorded. This has made a vast universe of information *potentially* available to us.

Those of us old enough to remember giant mainframes in air-conditioned rooms—with less RAM (random-access memory) than the PC (personal computer) we threw out last year—will remember the huge printouts that used to be delivered on little wagons. Huge data dumps, containing everything we needed to know, yet totally inaccessible, were placed on our desks. Who could figure out what those numbers meant? Who could turn the data into information?

The computing industry has spent the last generation turning all of the data produced throughout the world by computers into usable information. The PC was one step. By delivering the data to our desks electronically rather than on paper, it became possible for us to examine sales reports, production figures, wage rates—or whatever we were interested in—much more efficiently. The next step, of course, was software, designed to turn that data into information. From the simplest word processor and spreadsheet to the most complex, specialized, and customized software package, the result of the personal computer on everyone's desktop was the transformation of available data into information: huge, giga-byte-disk full, terabyte servers full of information. It was a sea of information, more than enough to drown in.

In business today, we have had a massive breakdown in intelligence. To be more precise, the massive surge of information has so overwhelmed the traditional collection and analysis systems that businesses use, that most information is lost and wasted. Critically important information is rarely acquired and even when acquired rarely turned into knowledge. The information is out there somewhere, but businesses are still making critical and costly errors. Modern business is facing a massive crisis of knowledge, rooted in the failure of intelligence. To put it differently, businesses have become quite sophisticated in turning data into information, but they are not nearly as good at turning information into knowledge. This is rooted in the failure of businesses to approach the problem of knowledge with the same rigorous systems approach they used in creating first data-processing systems and later information-management systems. They have neglected to create intelligence systems and to turn information into knowledge.

One solution that companies are turning to, and has been widely publicized of late, has been the creation of knowledge managers. These people have been given a wide range of titles, from Chief Knowledge Officer to Chief Learning Officer to Director of Intellectual Capital and the like. This is becoming a widespread phenomenon, particularly in large companies that are experiencing the problem first and most intensely because of the size and complexity of their operations. These companies are not confined to the computer industry. They include Coca-Cola, Monsanto, Coopers & Lybrand, General Electric and others throughout the business spectrum. These people have a common task: to organize, control, manipulate, and exploit all of the information that has been created inside the company and turn it into knowledge.

Whatever you call these new people, their mission is the same as that of the head of any intelligence service: to maximize the efficiency of data collection, collation, and analysis. An intelligence agency is an organization dedicated to collecting information and turning it into knowledge. The reason a Central Intelligence Agency was created, for example, was the conviction, born of experience in World War II, that not only was there tremendous inefficiency in American intelligence gathering during the war, but a great deal of information that was gathered was dissipated because there was no central collection and analysis point for it. Nor was there a central distribution point designed to make sure that everyone who had a need to know would receive the knowledge they needed.

Today's knowledge managers have as their first mission getting control of knowledge inside their companies. That was the same task the CIA had on its creation: figuring out what they had and turning it into usable knowledge. As knowledge managers get control of their internal systems, they will, inevitably, turn their attention to systematizing information gathering, analysis, and distribution—the entire knowledge generation cycle. In other words, the knowledge officer will build an intelligence system for the company.

It is not that business has been indifferent to intelligence—many large companies have established competitive intelligence departments. Indeed, the sure sign of this emerging profession was the creation of the Society of Competitive Intelligence Professionals, to which at least one of the authors belongs. However, we think competitive intelligence has, in many ways, been too modest. Dedicated to introducing intelligence techniques into the world of business, competitive intelligence has focused on carving out a niche for itself within the various fiefdoms of the corporate world.

Our view is a bit more radical. From where we sit, carving out a new division is not only too modest, it is damaging. Business is already excessively compartmentalized. From our perspective, businesses do not need another class of professionals nearly as much as the existing professions and specialties within a company need to add an additional perspective and function to what they are already doing. From our perspective, intelligence, like the production of knowledge, must be a universal responsibility within a company rather than the domain of specialists. That is why our understanding of business intelligence systems is linked to the redefinition of businesses as systems of knowledge and the symbolic emergence of the office of Chief Knowledge Officers, Intellectual Asset Managers, and the like in companies as varied as Coca-Cola and Coopers & Lybrand.

This is not to say that large businesses don't perhaps require some specialists in the area. Rather, this argues that intelligence—the knowledge production and management process—cannot be confined to these professionals. Knowledge permeates a company, flowing into it and being synthesized within it. From capture to dissemination of analysis, the management of the process must involve the company as a whole. Intelligence systems cannot be created without creating a culture of intelligence. With that culture, professionals may or may not be necessary. Without that culture, professionals are a waste of space.

INTIMACY AND INTUITION

Now, there may be businesses that do not need to create intelligence systems. A business working with stable technology requiring only expected, incremental updates; a business working in a circumscribed geographic region, where the laws, regulations, markets, and personalities are well known and changing only slowly; businesses that are small enough that employees efficiently share information; businesses that operate in a stable environment where the unexpected rarely occurs and time-critical decisions need not be taken—such businesses, if they exist, would not need intelligence systems.

This is not intended to be ironic. There are, in fact, businesses where managers are so intimately familiar with their environment that they sense shifts almost intuitively. A real estate broker, operating in a fairly isolated market, is his own intelligence system. He knows the few banks in the area personally, as well as the members of the zoning board. He knows most of his clients personally—and when he doesn't, he has friends who know them. He knows every vacant lot, every developer, and knows when a house is likely to come up for sale, sometimes before the owner does. Someone like this doesn't need an intelligence system because he is his own intelligence system. His network of relationships, his recollections of facts about his market and industry, his understanding of the techniques of the realtor substitute superbly for any formal system of intelligence gathering.

Indeed, if all business was done in this realtor's circumstances, this book would be unnecessary. But consider how rare such situations are today. Consider all the events that might happen to render our realtor's system of relationships and database of memories insufficient or even irrelevant: the local banks are gobbled up by huge bank holding companies; a new plant moves into the community, flooding the area with thousands of new buyers; a federal agency issues new rules on testing for chemicals on resold properties. All of these things come from outside the neat, stable environment of our realtor, and any of these could decisively change the way he does business. If he isn't prepared to respond to these changes, he could be history.

In an ideal business, intelligence systems would be both unnecessary and irrelevant. Ideally, a manager should be intimately familiar with all aspects of his working environment, from technology to personalities to regulations. A manager should have such a degree of intimacy with his environment that his ability to turn information into knowledge appears to be intuitive. We are all familiar with successful managers and entrepreneurs who operate in this way. We are also familiar with people who operate in this way, have been extremely successful, but who suddenly and unexpectedly seem to lose their touch.

In fact, losing touch is frequently not sudden, even if it's unexpected. It is the result of relying on an intuitive understanding of the working environment when the needs of the business have spread beyond the reach of intuition. The surefooted decision making of the earlier days breeds a sense of security and even complacency. The business grows steadily. It is the very success of the business, its growth, that undermines the intuitive information gathering and processing into knowledge. As markets grow, personal knowledge of the customers declines. As new product lines are added, familiarity with technology weakens. And as the number of employees grows, the all-important casual gossip that was so efficient in sharing information becomes less and less frequent. Many employees are now strangers.

Suddenly, the entrepreneur is confronting a world where there is no intimate personal knowledge, and, lulled into complacency by success, he thinks that his old decision-making style will still work. Mistakes begin to pile up. New markets are entered and sales don't live up to expectations. Nobody within the company notices new technologies. In the end, the company enters a period of crisis. The crisis is simple: Intuition works extremely well when you are intimately familiar with your environment. When success brings you beyond the reach of intuition, knowledge declines and information isn't gathered. Increasingly, the business flies blind until it hits a mountain or runs out of fuel.

You know that informal intelligence systems won't do when you haven't played golf—or pinochle—with most of your customers.

This is increasingly the entrenched reality of the business world. The crisis has two roots: geography and technology. Geography—the growth in the size of your company and growth in the geographical scope of today's business—forces managers to shift from intuitive to systematic information-gathering and knowledge-producing techniques. As the network of suppliers and customers expands, less and less of the market can be knowable. Events completely outside the scope of a manager's intuition can have a devastating effect—a fire in a plant that supplies a key component to a customer that causes a cancellation of orders to your business; a takeover of a competitor by a large multinational corporation can cause coronaries at your own shop, even though none of you had ever heard of the multinational. Forces impinge from far beyond the realm of expectations. But then, it is rare to be destroyed by the expected and predictable.

This is one of the critical problems of modern business. Businessmen and -women are practical people. They focus on their own business and their own work and regard overconcern about the big world beyond as both extraneous and pointless—there's not much you can do about it. This is especially true of entrepreneurs and those in small businesses. During the 1960s, most auto parts manufacturers focused on producing what General Motors and Ford wanted. If someone went to them in 1975 and said, "Look, GM is borrowing money at 13 percent while Japanese companies are borrowing at 3 percent," they would probably not have thought it had anything to do with them. But they'd be wrong; it had to do with efficiency. At 3 percent money, Japanese car manufacturers could build new plants and facilities—and put U.S. auto parts manufacturers out of business by the thousands.

You might ask: What could have been done about this? The answer is plenty—from pressure on congressmen to business plans focusing on increased diversification to alliances with Japanese auto manufacturers. Being small does not mean that you are immune to global forces. Nor does it mean that you are helpless. Quite the contrary. The smaller you are, the more likely you are to be subject to those forces. And the smaller you are, the more likely you are to be able to do something to dodge them.

As companies grow, systems for gathering information in unknown terrain become critical. As companies become successful, a more sophisticated definition of information becomes essential. Today, geography is one of the driving forces behind the need for intelligence systems.

The other is technology, or more precisely, the increased rate of technological change and the growing esotericism of technology. Early in the industrial revolution, it was possible for one man to know all about the technology in his industry. He might even know all about the emerging technologies, since he was responsible for a lot of them and since the community of researchers was both extremely small and generally concentrated in a few places. Certainly, inventions could take him by surprise. An inventor in France might have no idea that someone was doing similar work in the United States. But there was little that could be done about this. The information was simply inaccessible.

Today, it is impossible for one person to know everything there is to know about even a small segment of an industry. Technology has grown so subtle and nuanced that knowledge has become tremendously segmented. Moreover, technology has become increasingly interconnected. Designing a jet engine or a lawn mower requires knowledge from narrow segments of metallurgy, petrochemicals, synthetic rubber, and so on. One person cannot know everything that is happening in these fields that might potentially affect his own business. Just as important, technologies designed to serve the jet-engine industry could, quite easily and unexpectedly, revolutionize the lawn mower industry. As the texture of technological knowledge becomes finer and more nuanced, the consequences of technology become less predictable. They also become more important.

As technology becomes more subtle, the rate of change increases in two ways. First, small technological advances wind up having substantial affects on business. Second, the time between substantial technological change decreases. If we take these phenomena together, it means that the direction from which technological change might come becomes less certain, in the simplest geographical as well as in a more complex technical sense, while the frequency of significant change increases. This means that business is both at risk from technological change and that technological change holds open great promise for any business in a position to take advantage of that change.

We can now define the problem. The geography of business has expanded beyond the reach of even well-connected and sophisticated businessmen. The best personal network in the world will not cover all the areas that are of concern to you, nor all of the social strata you need to know about, nor all the individuals who might interest you. Modern business is ultimately technology-driven, but the tempo of technological change has increased so dramatically, and the scope of potentially significant technologies has expanded so much, that even the most sophisticated business-man or scientist cannot, by his normal daily activities, know everything important that is going on. It has simply become impossible to master one's environment through casual, day-to-day systems.

You may not be interested in technological change, but technological change is interested in you.

Finally, because of the computer, much more information is now available than was the case before. This is an understatement. The world is pumping out information as a by-product of everything that everyone does, because the introduction of the computer as a facilitator in most human activities has made information a by-product of everyday life. In a competitive environment—and who isn't in a competitive environment—the ability to utilize this information better than your competitors can mean increased sales, new products to the market before others, effective joint ventures, avoiding regulatory threats and everything else that constitutes modern business.

The same type of business, in different locations, generates dramatically different needs in information. Consider the difference between the needs for information of a painting contractor, working in a small town in Utah with well-known and slowly evolving technology, who knows all of his customers and competitors, and the needs of a painting contractor in a suburb of Washington, D.C. In Washington, everything is on a larger scale with millions of potential customers and hundreds of competitors. Whereas the contractor in Utah knows his competitors and customers personally, the D.C. contractor needs to know how to identify potential customers, and how to find out what competitors are charging and paying for help. In a market the size of Washington, D.C., it is not easy to find out what new products are available, if any new environmental regulations affect contractors, or if there are new, related businesses.

If you're a painting contractor with two trucks and three workers, you are certainly not going to set up a complex intelligence service, nor are you going to hire an intelligence consultant. But you may want to think more systematically about the things you do need to know, and more carefully about how you gather and analyze information. This may take a little time, a little money, and some effort in learning a few new tricks, but one or two new contracts, one or two disasters avoided, and the effort will not only pay for itself but possibly save your business. So whether you are a large multinational corporation or a painting contractor with three employees, you need to turn information into knowledge.

An intelligence system does not mean an intelligence department. It means what it says: a system for doing intelligence.

With this, as with anything else, some skills are required. In most cases—particularly for entrepreneurs operating on a small and efficient scale—this is a do-it-yourself job. The last thing most of us need is another professional mouth to feed. But in either case, and regardless of whatever scale you do it on, the critical issue is this: Can you make more money using intelligence techniques? That's what this book is about. How to get a sense of how much money you're losing through intelligence failures, and how to find out how to make money through intelligence successes.

In business, time is intelligence's mortal enemy. The intelligence process—from deciding what information is needed to understanding its meaning—is time consuming. Knowledge a week too late is the same as ignorance. The problem we face in business is turning information into knowledge before the decision point has passed. With the tidal wave of information we face, this is a daunting task.

Paradoxically, the same technology that created the information crisis also provides us with some of the tools for coping with it. Computers, information management software, databases, the Internet, and all the other tools of the modern age are certainly part of the information-to-knowledge process known as intelligence. These tools, some as sophisticated as remote sensing from satellites, some as simple as learning to use America Online, are the front line in the struggle against time and ignorance. They are indispensable, and we will spend a great deal of this book trying to teach you how to use them profitably.

But all of the methods and all of the gadgets in the world cannot replace the essence, the core of the intelligence process: honesty, first and foremost, to yourself. The enemy of knowledge is not only time, it is wishful thinking. It is habit. It is inactivity. It is the million ways in which someone explains to himself why everything is just fine, and no exertion is needed. Intelligence works when it delivers information to a user, who then recognizes that something has happened—something that requires action. Perhaps some previous course was in error and has to be reversed. Perhaps a new possibility is opening up. Whatever the information contains, the user must have a will to believe, a will to honesty, a willingness to face potentially painful truths and exert oneself.

The mortal enemies of intelligence are time and wishful thinking.

In all of our experience in the intelligence process, this is what has always been most lacking. The will to honesty, the will to believe what the information shows, both in individuals and organizations, is the scarcest commodity in the military, in government, and in business. The ability to see the consequences of actions clearly, even when that perception runs counter to conventional wisdom, requires courage and a willingness to be alone. Sometimes it requires the courage to be wrong, for none of us is guaranteed omniscience. But the will to believe what the facts reveal, and the courage to act on those facts, is the foundation of success in all endeavors.

1

FROM THE AGENCY
TO THE COMPANY

The Business Intelligence Organization

The Central Intelligence Agency was nicknamed the Company by its employees. An odd name for an organization that appears to be as far removed from business as possible. After all, the CIA is about secrets and plots, moles and doubles, the stuff of Le Carré novels. Companies are about making money. Calling the CIA the Company is ironic, but in the irony of old agency hands, there is a glimmer of truth. The CIA in many ways looks like a corporation and acts like a corporation, a vast global bureaucracy dealing in information. It is an information conglomerate with one customer: the executive branch of the U.S. government.

The CIA's interests differ, obviously, from private, profit-making corporations. Its interest is in national security and its per-spective is limitless. That means that it is inherently inefficient from a financial standpoint. Since threats can come from anywhere, it must cover everything—and cannot be limited by cost. This, plus the fact that, as a government agency, it suffers from the defects of government agencies everywhere, means that the Company resem-bles companies in only one sense: It is a vast organization hungry for information. In feeding this hunger, the CIA has developed real expertise in gathering and analyzing information. In this sense, there is much to be learned from the CIA, and from the other great intelligence agencies around the world like MI-6 in Britain, the old KGB in the Soviet Union, and Israel's Mossad.

HOW NATIONAL INTELLIGENCE
AGENCIES ARE ORGANIZED

Intelligence has always been with us, but the modern intelligence *organization* really emerged during the last hundred years. The twentieth century saw intelligence gathering turn from an incidental activity carried out by diplomats, journalists, and travelers in the course of their other activities, into a systematic, focused process run by professionals for whom intelligence gathering was the main activity of their lives. The reasons for this development are rooted in two phenomena. Internally, the emergence of revolutionary parties meant that the state needed to systematically monitor the opposition in order to prevent or preserve the revolution. Externally, the age of total war meant that monitoring potential threats to national security required a systematic and focused approach to intelligence gathering.

Revolution and total war combined to give rise to an extraordinary phenomenon: the intelligence organization. Unlike anything before in history, the intelligence organization was a vast bureaucracy created for the sole purpose of gathering and understanding information of interest to the rulers of the nation-state. Whatever one thinks of the purpose to which any particular agency—or for that matter, all intelligence agencies—is put, the sheer scope, the sheer ambition of organizations such as the CIA is breathtaking. It had as its goal the ability to pursue all information relevant to a nation's interest—vast indeed—the ability to analyze that information, and the ability to transmit the analysis to decision makers in a timely and understandable fashion.

What is remarkable about these organizations is how well they succeeded. We of course hear a great deal about intelligence failures, although many of the failures, such as the Bay of Pigs, were less intelligence failures than political miscalculations. Yet the intelligence services of modern advanced industrial countries have provided their political masters, day in and day out, with unprecedented situational awareness. An American president or a German chancellor knows far more about what is going on inside or outside his country than ever before in history. Mind you, this doesn't mean that they are any better at ruling. A genius with limited information will rule better than a dunderhead with encyclopedic knowledge. Nevertheless, all other things being equal, the information provided by intelligence services proves historically to be of enormous value.

There is, therefore, much business can learn from these intelligence organizations. Business and government have this much in common: both prosper through lots of information properly analyzed and understood. Understanding how intelligence services organize themselves will not give us a blueprint for business intelligence—God knows that a local meat processor doesn't need the overhead of the CIA. It may, however, give businesses a first glimpse of what is possible through systematic intelligence practices.

Let's begin by considering what is not part of the intelligence apparatus: security. The guards at the gate, the locks on the doors, the bodyguards accompanying executives, even the firewalls protecting computers from hackers are part of an organization's security apparatus. They are certainly important and need to be done but are not, properly speaking, part of intelligence. Guards and intelligence agents are doing very different jobs with very different goals. Putting them together is not useful.

In almost all countries, the intelligence agency charged with collecting foreign intelligence—the nation-state's competitive intelligence—is kept very separate from the agency charged with stopping foreign intelligence agents from spying on them. In the United States, the two functions are divided between the Federal Bureau of Investigation (FBI), which does counterintelligence, and the CIA, which collects and analyzes foreign intelligence. In Britain, there is MI-5 and Scotland Yard and its Special Branch for internal security, and there is MI-6 for foreign operations. Israel has Shin Bet, the internal security and intelligence force, and Mossad, which runs the foreign intelligence–gathering operations.

There are two good reasons for keeping intelligence and security separate. The first is the nature of the people involved in each. Security personnel, from top to bottom, are cops. They may be very good at protecting property, penetrating criminal organizations, and identifying security threats, but cops know little, and could care even less, about matters of high policy. The FBI, under J. Edgar Hoover, succeeded in capturing the famous gangster John Dillinger, but had a great deal of trouble understanding the sub- tleties of Franklin Roosevelt's unfolding foreign policy. Hoover's best solution to the problem of Japanese intentions during World War II was to arrest every ethnic Japanese in America.

Cops enforce laws and arrest people. Political leaders, who are an intelligence agency's customers, are not nearly as interested in finding the guilty party as in understanding the capabilities of for- eign nations, who may be friends one day and enemies the next. Putting intelligence operations in the hands of the security people may catch enemy spies, but it won't get you the kind of intelligence you need to carry out a foreign policy. The two jobs call for very dif- ferent types of people.

The second reason you want to keep security separate from intelligence is to keep intelligence honest. By dividing the CIA from the FBI, MI-6 from MI-5, Mossad from Shin Bet, you provide a check on the honesty of the intelligence service. An intelligence service, when it operates properly, can be a political leader's eyes and ears—and sometimes his brains as well. That means it's in the interest of every enemy and competitor to blind you or make you stupid. The best way to do this is to subvert your eyes, ears, and brains—to turn them against you. This is the nightmare of every intelligence agency. By keeping security and intelligence separate, you spare your intelligence service from the responsibility of moni- toring itself, allowing the chief executive officer (CEO) to sleep much better at night. It's why you have both a chief financial officer (CFO) and a comptroller.

Knowledge is power. Power corrupts. Think about it.

So, we begin with two premises. First, intelligence is not about security. Second, intelligence must be kept separate from counter- intelligence. This first sketch of the architecture is important so we can begin defining precisely what might be useful to a business in conducting its own intelligence operations. Organizations are not shaped the way they are by accident—their form derives from func- tion. If we can sketch the form, we can understand the function.

GENERIC ARCHITECTURE OF AN
INTELLIGENCE ORGANIZATION

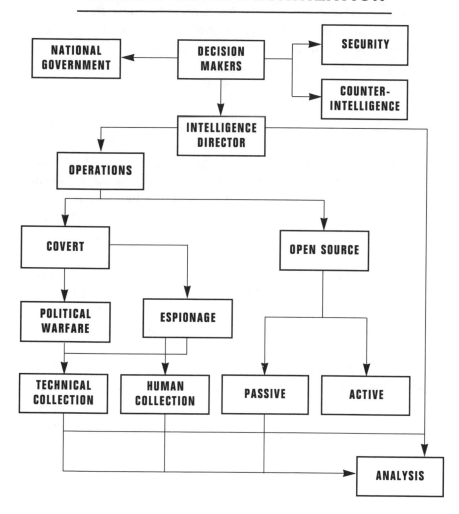

At the center of every intelligence agency's architecture is its reason for being: the customer. An intelligence agency's customers are the people who have to make decisions. The entire purpose of the intelligence apparatus, its only reason for existence, is to provide the decision maker with the information he needs to operate the organization he heads. One of the occupational hazards of the intelligence world is forgetting the customer. Intelligence people have an inherent tendency to believe that they are at the center of the universe. It is therefore very important that we pause now, take a look at that single, lonely box in the upper-left-hand corner of the chart on page 21 and realize that it is, in reality, about ten thousand times larger and more important than the complex of boxes below it. It is even more important than the decision maker. It is the task of the decision maker to operate that vast and complex box to his left and the task of the intelligence apparatus to support him in that task.

Intelligence directors sometimes forget that their prime reason for existing is to support the decision maker in his ultimate role of responsibility to the government and the nation. Even decision makers who become too fascinated with the inner workings of intelligence can forget that. A small entrepreneur who becomes overly fascinated with the intelligence process can quickly forget that intelligence is a means rather than an end. This has to be resisted at all costs.

There is an even worse condition. Sometimes, intelligence agencies decide that the decision makers aren't making the right decisions. People who do intelligence often suffer from paranoia and megalomania. The paranoia actually helps them do the job, part of which is to track subtle enemies. Paranoids don't have to be reminded of this. Megalomania is dangerous because, with the tremendous amount of information flowing to him, an intelligence director may develop the illusion that this information constitutes knowledge. He may believe he knows things about the world that the decision makers couldn't begin to imagine. There can be a compulsion to grab the controls away from the political leaders they serve. Unless an entrepreneur has some pretty interesting personality disorders, this at least is not something likely to come up.

Information isn't knowledge until it is in the hands of the man who knows what he wants to do and how to do it. In the hands of a person who has no real sense of the realities of decision making, information can appear to be knowledge, but it really isn't. Very few heads of intelligence agencies ever rose to lead governments. Yuri Andropov, the former head of the KGB, did, but he spent most of his reign in a coma, so we don't know how he would have done. George Bush headed the CIA for a while, but we wouldn't call him a professional intelligence director. Even so, many would argue that his presidency is hardly an argument for promoting heads of the CIA to supreme power. A real head of state can usually slap the director of intelligence down with little effort. The skills needed to run a government are different from those needed to operate an intelligence system.

There is another side to this. Ideally, the intelligence apparatus is not supposed to do anything but gather information and analyze it. How the intelligence is gathered—legally or illegally, open source or espionage—is immaterial. People who operate things, from government agencies to corporate departments, inevitably become advocates for their organizations. That is their job. Unfortunately, they inflate achievements and hide failures. Intelligence organizations must be indifferent to the outcome of their analysis. It must make no difference to them what actions decision makers take as a result of their information. When intelligence organizations run things, they are going to be sorely tempted to skew their reports to protect their operations. As a result, decision makers will not get clean analyses—and may make bad decisions.

We therefore have this paradox. Ideally, an intelligence agency should do nothing but look and think. But passive looking is sometimes not enough. It is frequently necessary to dig out information—sometimes a large, costly, and complex operation. These operations—spying—are the downfall of many intelligence agencies. Spies need to protect their operations just as everyone else does. And as we have seen many times, failed intelligence operations are frequently hidden from view by their sponsors—sometimes toppling governments in the process.

Operational intelligence gathering is an ailment that cannot be avoided. In the end, it can be fatal, but intelligence organizations can and do take steps to limit the damage rogue intelligence operations can inflict. Distinguishing between operations and analysis is critical. The analyst's task is to put the different pieces of information together, to recognize a pattern. For this he needs to have a deep historical sense, to know where things have been in order to recognize the patterns he's seeing. He also needs to have a clear understanding of the intentions, plans, and policies of the decision makers, for without that, he cannot recognize significant pieces of intelligence. The analyst does not need to know the source of information, but he does need to have all the information available. The analyst may not have the most glamorous job, but he is the pivot of the system. More than anyone else, he can damage the intelligence organization if he is turned by an opponent. He knows too much. Aldrich Ames was deadly precisely because he was an analyst.

Although analysts make up the bulk of an intelligence organization, collection operations is the part that most people associate with intelligence work. Here, too, in national intelligence services there is a division between covert operations and open source. Covert operations, in turn, divide into two parts: what might be called political warfare, and espionage. These have completely different purposes, but they are pulled together simply because those who gather intelligence covertly are also frequently in positions to carry out political operations.

Strictly speaking, political warfare is not part of the mission of an intelligence organization. In fact, as an operation that goes beyond information gathering, it directly contravenes the primary purpose of intelligence and tends to undermine its utility. All governments have goals and interests, some that cannot be achieved through direct persuasion or even the direct and open use of force. The available alternatives range from assassination to blackmailing or bribing foreign officials, from raising a rebel army to secretly arming the government. It makes sense that the same people who are adept at bribing foreign officials to provide secret documents are in a position to bribe them to stage a coup. Examples of political warfare abound: support of the Contras in Nicaragua by the CIA; the Mossad's counterterrorism operations in Europe during the 1970s; the KGB's support for Ethiopia's Marxist coup against Haile Selassie. Each was a covert operation, carried out secretly, regularly denied by the sponsoring government, even in the face of overwhelming evidence that it was taking place.

One of the great dangers any intelligence agent faces is falling in love—with a country, a source, an operation, an ideology, or a member of the opposite, or same, sex. Falling in love skews the agent's judgment by eliminating the paranoia and cynicism that is the healthy, well-adjusted condition of a field operative—that is, unless your name is Bond. In case after case, 007 can appear to fall in love yet not lose his judgment. For most agents, turning him into a political warrior turns him into a believer, if not in the cause itself then in the mission. At the very least, he understands that success or failure will directly affect his career. If he predicts it will fail he will be regarded as a defeatist and therefore will be held responsible for the failure. In any event, after working intimately with his network of agents to achieve an active end, he becomes, psychologically, part of that network. He ceases to be a critic and loses the distance required for sound judgment.

The Cold War is strewn with cases where intelligence agents who had been called on to engage in political warfare failed to provide decision makers with critically needed information. The CIA had been active in the Vietnam War, carrying out political warfare assignments such as Operation Phoenix, an attempt to destroy the Communist command structure through assassinations. Having been made responsible for executing the secret war, the CIA and its operatives naturally became positive thinkers—essential if they were to do the job they had been given. But they had another job: to collect intelligence so that the decision makers would have a clear idea of what was happening in Vietnam. The reality that the United States was losing the war was incompatible with the positive mind-set needed to execute the war. As a result, the CIA was instrumental in blowing smoke in Washington's face. National intelligence agencies should not be the guide in this area, as they are congenitally drawn into covert operations beyond what discipline and common sense would dictate.

Covert operations do have a clear place: to gather information that is vital to the national interest but not legally available. In some countries, this applies to virtually everything. In North Korea, for example, virtually all information is considered the property of the state and, therefore, a state secret. It is impossible to collect most information in North Korea without breaking North Korean laws. In other countries, like the United States and Western Europe, far more information is public than secret. For example, it is quite legal to take photographs at American or British airports, but try to do this in many countries in the Middle East, Asia, or even Italy or Greece. One cameraman we know was arrested and thrown into prison in the United Arab Emirates for trying to take some pictures of an Emirates Airbus taking off and landing, even though he was filming from a public place outside the airport perimeter.

The premise that if something is secret, or illegal to obtain, it's far more valuable than if it's publicly available, or legally obtained, is not true, especially when dealing with foreign countries. These are often merely cultural differences, although they have to be kept in mind when collecting information outside the United States and the United Kingdom. The public domain in most advanced industrial democracies is overflowing with valuable information. The problem is sorting through it all.

In most advanced, industrial democracies, intelligence work consists of sorting through the riches available everywhere. In the rest of the world, most of the effort goes into finding a few nuggets.

To a national intelligence service it can be a matter of national interest or national life and death to maintain a balance between open source intelligence and covert collections, since this controls what information is emitted into the public domain—and therefore what is available for capture. In business, however, covert operations are of little value. Quite apart from the physical and legal risks, the extraordinarily high cost of covert operations makes it a tool that is not for routine use in business. Any business, for example, that tried to routinely steal another business's research and development (R&D) instead of running its own R&D shop would very quickly go broke. It is frankly cheaper to do your own, good research than to pay the costs involved in stealing it. Obviously, there are specialized cases where direct corporate espionage might pay economically—crime sometimes pays financially if not morally. But we are drawn always to the lesson of the Soviet Union, which basically tried to use covert operations as a regular supplement to its own R&D. Occasionally it worked. In the end, the money spent on the KGB would have been better spent in research labs.

FROM NATIONAL INTELLIGENCE
TO BUSINESS INTELLIGENCE

The equivalents of political warfare—sabotage, assassination, organized uprisings—and espionage have no place in business intelligence. As a result, most business executives feel that intelligence is an exotic, but frankly irrelevant, part of their own business operations. This misconception derives from an overemphasis on these more sexy and glamorous popularizations of the intelligence structure. It fails to recognize that the heart of intelligence, the mining of open source data, is entirely applicable to business—and just needs to be put into an appropriate business context. A business intelligence organization chart would dispense with operational functions and focus on open source intelligence, containing technical and human intelligence gathering in an even more powerful form than most national intelligence agencies use.

The business intelligence service has as its customer the executive suite—the CEO, the chief financial officer, head of sales and marketing, heads of strategic planning, legal, mergers and acquisitions, and so on. Each has different needs, obviously, but they each have the same responsibility: the prosperity of the company. The only responsibility that the head of intelligence has is to gather open source intelligence—that is, information that is generally and legally available. Open source information is either fully emitted into the public domain or can be inferred from a variety of forms, ranging from formal publication to gossip. This is true of all intelligence organizations, but for various reasons, ranging from cost to the law, it is a fundamental rule for business intelligence.

Organizations constantly release information: sometimes planned and controlled releases, such as annual reports or press releases, and other times they are uncontrolled emissions, such as leaks to the press by discontented employees or subpoenaed documents. Sometimes emissions are forced during the normal course of business, such as material submitted to a government agency while seeking approval for a product or getting a patent. Information can also be released because of a completely legal, deliberate manipulation of the company by outsiders, like reporters or canny business intelligence specialists.

Sometimes companies don't emit information directly, but leave evidence of information that can be interpreted. Information sometimes leaves unintended, but unavoidable, hints of existence. It is much like an animal. Animals can be tracked by following the unavoidable, incidental consequences of being an animal—droppings, broken branches, warm grass, pieces of fur caught on bushes. The same is true of companies. The very process of being a company leaves unavoidable traces of information, if not the information itself. These traces usually lead to the information if they are followed and queried. In order to find out what another company

THE BUSINESS INTELLIGENCE
ORGANIZATION

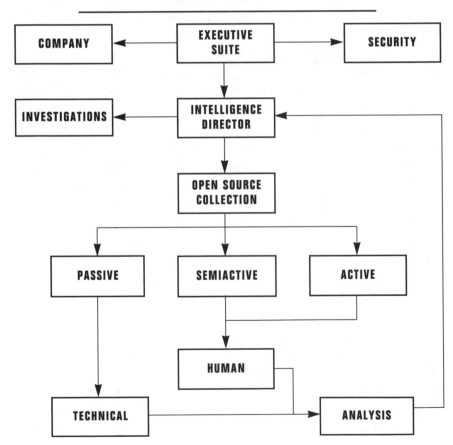

is doing in a particular R&D field, you may not be able to get copies of their research, but you could go to professional conferences where some of that company's staff researchers might present a paper on an aspect of their research. When traces left by funding organizations are tracked and show research grants given to this company in the same area of research, you have matched enough traces to safely calculate the information itself. This is not information in the fullest sense, but it is the traces that can be watched, tracked, and from which the real intentions and capabilities of a company can be inferred.

These emissions and traces are the quarry of business intelligence. Usually, like emissions from a smokestack, they are created, emitted, and dissipated into the air, with no one collecting them and thinking about what they mean. But when these emissions and traces are tracked down and collected and taken together, they can be interpreted and understood. Indeed, by being aware of what you are learning about your competitors, your company can learn to guard its own emissions and minimize your own traces as you go about your business.

Locating information is less a matter of sleuthing than of sorting. We live in a world of too much information rather than too little.

In tracking information, intelligence services divide their means into two sorts: active and passive. This is a critically important distinction. In order to understand the central difference between the two, think of how a submarine's sonar works. Sonar is essentially a listening device that indicates the presence of other ships by tracking sounds that propagate very efficiently in water. Sonar operates in two modes: passive and active. Passive sonar is nothing more than a microphone picking up the sounds that other ships inevitably make as they pass through the water. Active sonar, on the other hand, generates its own sounds, which the submarine emits and which bounce off other objects—large fish, rock formations, ships—returning as an echo. Anyone who saw the movie version of Tom Clancy's *Hunt for Red October* cannot forget the gripping tension of the American and Soviet submarines chasing each other around the Atlantic, each boat trying to pick up sounds from the enemy using passive sonar, and sometimes reverting to active sonar when there was no other choice.

With passive sonar, no one knows that you are out there listening; you have the element of surprise. It also keeps the submarine safe from counterattack. Its weakness is that it relies on the emissions of other ships. Active sonar, on the other hand, gives you control over the situation. No matter how quietly the other boat is running, no matter how carefully they control their emissions, active sonar bounces off their hull. The cost is that by pinging away, other submarines will be able to track down the location of your transmitter.

The difference between active and passive intelligence is the difference between actively going out and looking for information and capturing the information that comes to you. It is the difference, for example, between reading a newspaper or walking into a company, asking to speak to an official and asking him, point-blank, to answer a question. The first won't get you noticed, and you'll only learn what has been printed. The second may get you more information, but it will also get you noticed. In the past thirty years or so, the growth of technology has created an entirely new sphere of electronic information that is passive intelligence—information that makes its way to your door by itself. In effect, it captures emissions, uncovers traces, and delivers them to you.

All other things being equal, passive intelligence is much cheaper than active intelligence. Passive intelligence, like passive sonar, takes much less energy than active intelligence. It depends on effective receivers that are always cheaper than effective scouts. As soon as someone leaves the office to physically locate information, the clock starts running, the price goes up.

For practical purposes, we can divide passive and active intelligence between the kind of intelligence that can be carried out in your own office and the kind of intelligence that requires you to leave the office. In reality, we also use a third category we call semi-active, in which you reach out via phone or fax. It is still active—that is, you can be tracked—but not as active as driving around looking for things. And it is much less expensive than that most expensive—and rare—activity, the investigation.

In a way, the distinction between passive and active intelligence can be restated as the distinction between human and technical intelligence—so long as it is understood that these are not quite identical. Human, or active, intelligence is about spies and recruiting spies. Technical intelligence gathering, or passive intelligence, concerns the use of technology to peer, without being seen, into places that would otherwise be invisible.

Businesspeople might assume that technical intelligence has nothing to do with them. They see themselves as worlds away from the National Security Agency (NSA). In many cases they're right, but increasingly some of these techniques are becoming available and need to be considered. In the end, however, the safest and best intelligence that can make or break a business is what is called open source intelligence.

INTELLIGENCE TECHNIQUES AND TECHNOLOGY

Technical intelligence focuses on the means of collecting intelligence. There are, generally speaking, two types of technical intelligence gathering that were introduced by national intelligence agencies: photographic and electronic. Photographic intelligence, from satellite reconnaissance to airborne reconnaissance to some guy with a Kodak Instamatic, allows you to see physical objects, freezing them in time and space, allowing you to examine them at your leisure and alongside other information. Electronic intelligence allows you to intercept the electronic signals of the other guy. This means everything from monitoring his radio talk show to listening in on his telephone calls, mapping his radar, or tapping into his computer network—all of which the U.S. intelligence community does overseas.

Electronic intelligence is a huge task. Both the United States and Britain have created separate agencies to carry out electronic intelligence (the National Security Agency in the United States and

GHQ Cheltenham in the United Kingdom). The United States has created a new agency, the National Imagery and Mapping Agency (NIMA), which is part of the intelligence community but will also be a combat support agency to provide imagery and mapping for military purposes. It assumed the functions of obtaining and analyzing photographs from satellite imagery. The Central Imagery Office, the Defense Mapping Agency, and Defense Dissemination Program Office have all been incorporated in NIMA. Then, of course, all countries listen to open electronic emissions—radio and television. Once these are in place, it becomes possible to listen in on conversations without being physically in the room when the conversation takes place, and to see things without having someone on the ground, looking for you. The revolution in how we hear and how we see dramatically changed the process of intelligence collection.

It also changed the way in which we manage information. The electronic transmission of information had two effects. First, it dramatically increased the amount that could be known. Prior to the electronic transmission of information, conversations between two people were private, and hence never to be recovered except from the memories of the participants. Once they were electronically transmitted, or accessible—to put a nice turn of phrase to electronic eavesdropping—they could be captured by people who had never met either of the discussants. The conversations could also be retained.

It is still widely believed that intelligence gathering is restricted to governments and government agencies, such as the CIA or the Internal Revenue Service in the United States or MI-6, the Inland Revenue, and the Department of Social Security in Britain. Many do not see much evidence of it in business, and therefore cannot imagine surveillance being carried out against them.

But use of techniques such as wiretapping is widespread. In Britain it is estimated that more than a thousand wiretaps a year are carried out by the police officially. The government's plans to extend legalized electronic eavesdropping failed when, in 1997, they were defeated in their bid to give police power to enter anyone's home or office to plant listening devices or copy private papers if they believed the occupier may have committed a serious crime. But the debate in the United Kingdom continues. We can see that the retention of vast amounts of data by private and government intelligence services meant that new methods of storage and analysis had to be found.

This was the second effect. The agencies survived the deluge of information by using electronic methods of storage and, most important, by learning to manage that information. The National Security Agency, whose antennae listen in on tens of millions of conversations a day, retains the conversations forever in electronic storage media such as floppies, hard disks, tapes, and God knows what else. But this would be useless without a way of sorting through it all. The real challenge is recognizing which intercepts are worth listening to, which ones are important, and building up patterns of information. Storing and sorting data is the heart of technical intelligence. This is the key to business intelligence as well, and one of the most important things that businesses need to learn from the professionals.

The United States deemphasized human intelligence—or HUMINT, as the cognoscenti of intelligence call it—during the 1970s in favor of technical collection techniques, a move that has been a subject of controversy ever since. The argument in favor of technical collection—eavesdropping on phone conversations, tapping into computers, using photo reconnaissance satellites—was that it was cheaper and more reliable. Human beings are extremely expensive, and the more valuable the information they provide, the higher the price. Humans also lie, get confused, or turn out to be working for the other side—and worst of all for an agency's budget, they are in a position to know when they have really important intelligence in hand, and can shake the agency down for it.

On the other hand, humans are also more versatile. They can go places where there are no electronic emanations, and they can recognize valuable information directly, even if it isn't on a list of keywords provided to a computer database. There are obvious advantages under certain circumstances of using HUMINT. During World War I, the legendary Mata Hari, a Dutch-born erotic dancer, was recruited by the Germans as their top agent in France. She danced into the life of a French cabinet minister and became his mistress, acquiring much information for the Germans before being brought to court, convicted, and sentenced to death before a French firing squad. She was able to collect more information through her personal persuasions than any electronic means could have done. She was said to have all the ingredients of the glamour spy: a hedonistic love for life; intelligence; a powerful personality; a capacity for deception; and an ability to crack or even break men's hearts. The Mata Hari legend set a style for European intelligence work that was to last for more than three decades.

Another advantage of using HUMINT is the fact that they can network. Throughout the forties, fifties, and sixties, several thousand operatives—known as technology collection officers, working under assignment in various parts of the world undercover as diplomats, trade officials, technical assistants to international bodies like the United Nations, UNESCO (United Nations Educational, Scientific, and Cultural Organization), the International Labor Office, the World Health Organization, and UNCTAD (United Nations Conference on Trade and Development)—pulled in, quite legally, material from scientific and technological journals, used student exchanges to gather facts, and attended large numbers of conferences. Conferences were of particular benefit because attendance was upfront and legitimate. Apart from gathering and filing back official papers, they provided an opportunity for networking and identifying possible recruits for espionage. International trade union meetings were especially useful as a venue for establishing long-term contacts. The Warsaw Pact representatives often found political sympathizers among the Western representatives present. The Vietnam War during the 1960s, and its unpopularity among intellectuals and left-leaning trade unionists, was frequently used as an ice-breaker, allowing friendships to develop and documents to be exchanged.

Human beings can do something no technical means of collection can: provide nuance. In 1973, Syria and Egypt built up their forces on the Golan Heights and along the Suez Canal. Sharing the American fondness for technical intelligence, Israel knew precisely what the Arabs were doing. They used photo reconnaissance, signal intelligence, electronic techniques, and all the rest to map the precise location of all Arab forces. What they did not know, what they could not know from technical intelligence, is *why* the Arabs were doing it. The Egyptians and Syrians, fully aware of Israel's technical capabilities, carefully screened their plans. Nothing was transmitted electronically. All meetings were held in secured rooms where electronic probes were impossible. The Israelis did not have a spy who had attended the meetings and briefings or slept with a secretary on a general's staff; they did not have a spy who was in a position to pick up the gossip in the Presidential Palace in Damascus. Israeli intelligence knew what they were capable of doing but had to guess as to the Arabs' intentions and what they were actually going to do—and guessed wrong, with nearly disastrous results. The Arabs were able to mount a massive surprise attack in October 1973 that nearly overwhelmed Israeli defenses.

Despite these obvious advantages of HUMINT, it is clear that technical intelligence is here to stay, and this is why it is now possible to speak about spinning off some of those capabilities into the private sector. It is too expensive, time consuming, and in many cases illegal for businesses to be running strings of human agents or, for that matter, electronic and signal intelligence projects on their opponents.

Finding a human being who actually knows valuable secrets usually costs more than the secret is worth.

But technical intelligence is not only about intercepting messages; it is also about managing the vast array of information that is now available in electronic form. Photography and radio, with the ability to preserve images and the ability to transmit those images at great distances, changed the entire structure of reality. With the advent of these two technologies, it was possible to see what was happening as it was happening, to hear what people were saying without being there in person. More important, perhaps, it was possible to preserve the events in perpetuity. Still, this did not always clearly tell us what had happened. The mere fact that the Kennedy assassination had been photographed did not reveal the truth of what happened, as it was limited by the photographer's perspective. Nevertheless, we have certainly preserved events and transmitted their occurrence in ways that were utterly unanticipated a century ago. And today we have capabilities that wouldn't have been anticipated fifteen years ago.

All sorts of events are being recorded today that had never been recorded before. Every time a sale is made in a store, every time a product comes off the assembly line, every time a customer calls, the event is recorded and the record is maintained in perpetuity. One might say that it is the distinctive characteristic of our civilization that nothing is forgotten and everything is preserved. These techniques for the collection and preservation of information have been fostered by the world's intelligence agencies. These techniques are now diffusing even more widely.

Intelligence services became adept at taking pictures at great distances and transmitting those pictures globally. A critical focus of intelligence services from World War II until the present day has been the intercepting of electronic transmissions, from radio shows to telephone conversations, and they have done it very well. But the very process of electronically recording events by commercial media has overtaken the intelligence service's own ability to take photographs. Repeatedly, people at CIA headquarters in Langley, Virginia, have turned on the television to CNN to find out what is actually going on. Moreover, the systematic, even compulsive, recording of events in our everyday lives has found its counterpart in the systematic and compulsive reporting of summaries of these events. From the commercial media, to the statistical office at OPEC (Organization of Petroleum Exporting Countries), extremely accurate and revealing information pours into the public domain.

MANAGING THE PUBLIC DOMAIN

During the 1970s, the United States orbited a series of satellites known as Signal Intelligence, or SIGINT, platforms. The purpose of these satellites was to intercept the stray electronic signals that carried both publicly broadcast information—radio and television—and private telephone conversations that are carried by microwave communications as well as by communications satellites. These SIGINT satellites vacuumed up electronic signals and downloaded them to the National Security Agency in Laurel, Maryland. Huge amounts of data were captured, millions of hours' worth of communications daily. All of it was useless, unless the NSA devoted millions of man hours listening to conversations, like Aunt Natasha complaining about Uncle Boris's drinking, in order to uncover two minutes of unguarded conversation by a secretary at the Mongolian Ministry of Defense.

At about the same time that SIGINT satellites were being launched, the *New York Times* reached an agreement with the International Typographical Union. Under the agreement, the *Times* would be allowed to introduce computers. Previously, type had been set by hand, using machine-made lead slugs. From now on, reporters would type their stories into computers, the type would be set and edited on computer, and then the electronic code they had created would be fed directly into the printing press, producing the day's newspapers.

Suddenly, during the 1970s, information from such diverse sources as telephone conversations and newspaper stories found themselves housed in the same, still new, apparatus—the computer. This had tremendous implications for how we could acquire information, implications that were not at all clear then and are only fully emerging today.

Telephone conversations and newspaper stories exist in a computer as binary code. A sound, a picture, a sentence—all exist within a computer as a string of 0s and 1s. The binary code for a capital *A* in ASCII format is 10000001. The binary code for white is 11111111. Any sound can be expressed as code as well—as today's multimedia computers demonstrate. This was of enormous importance to NSA, which had millions of hours of sound to sort through. Having captured electronic emissions of analog phone conversations, it was possible to convert them to digital—or binary—form. Now, all of those conversations could be stored on computer tapes as vast arrays of binary code. Let's assume that people in the intelligence community were interested in knowing every time a phone conversation in Nicaragua mentioned the KGB. High-speed computers could scan through the binary code for all conversations captured in Nicaragua, until a match for KGB could be found—a process not nearly as simple as it sounds because of the complexity caused by variations in voices. Then, someone fluent in Spanish could listen to the entire conversation that contained the designated term. In effect, the NSA created vast databases of binary code that were searchable using search programs created by NSA.

The same process took place in the *New York Times*'s press room. By writing stories on computers—in effect, on the first word processors—every story appeared in analog form, as a string of letters on paper, and simultaneously, in electronic form, as a string of binary code. The intention was to save the *Times* money by simplifying the typesetting process. The unintended consequence, however, was that every word in every edition of the greatest newspaper in the world now existed as binary code, saved in electronic media.

This meant that the material could be scanned, just the same as the NSA scanned signal intercepts. Assume that you wanted to find every mention of the KGB in the *New York Times*. By loading all of the data that was already being created to print the newspaper into databases, you could, with increasing efficiency over time, locate every bit of binary code that spelled out KGB, call up the story in which the string was contained, and read it. Suddenly, the newspaper morgue, where detectives and intelligence agents spent their youth poring over old newspapers, was replaced by the computer terminal accessing a database of electronically formatted and preserved newspapers. What had taken days or weeks—if it could be done at all—now could be done in minutes.

Paper can store information for generations—and it can be used to wrap salamis. Electronic media can store information for generations and can be searched in seconds—but it doesn't do salamis. There are trade-offs everywhere.

In less than a decade every newspaper, every magazine, every company newsletter, literally everything was printed this way. This meant that if the material was saved into a database, all of it could be searched and accessed in minutes. Vast databases such as LEXIS-NEXIS, Dow Jones, FT Profile, and Dialog sprang up. All they did was provide containers for the electronic information that was a by-product of typesetting technology. They provided large computers, databases to hold the data and permit queries to be made, and modems so users could call in. Suddenly, the world of intelligence was transformed.

The printing press created public domain; the computer made public domain accessible. The huge volume of information existing in what constitutes the public domain is contained in newspapers, scholarly journals, corporate annual reports, and television and radio program transcripts. The problem is not the availability of the information, it is finding it. Visit the Library of Congress in Washington, D.C., or any other great archival library and try to find something. The catalogs are now, thankfully, computerized, rendering the old card catalog system obsolete. They tell you about the author, title, and the subjects under which the book is classified. But even computerized catalogs don't tell you anything about what the book contains.

Any knowledge worth having has some time and cost constraints imposed on it. Having access to material that will take two years and $100,000 to find is the same as not having access. Intelligence agencies had a choice of mounting an intelligence operation that had a 70 percent chance of finding the information in two weeks at a cost of $50,000, or searching through a library that may or may not have the material, which probably could not be found in under a year with costs that could double or triple the cost of the intelligence operation. It is no surprise that the CIA and MI-6 chose espionage over library research. It was more cost effective.

But the computerization of typesetting created a new and radically different reality. As with most of the computer revolution, its origins were in the space program. Spacecraft needed computers onboard to control the complex systems needed to carry out missions. The computers in use during the early 1960s were vast mainframes, many still driven by the vacuum tubes that had powered the early ENIACS and UNIVACS. Obviously, these could not be taken aboard spacecraft. NASA (National Aeronautics and Space Administration) needed to create an extremely small yet powerful computer. The solution was found in the microchip.

This deliberate creation of computers had another side effect. During the 1960s, NASA and its military counterparts came to the conclusion that they were falling behind the knowledge curve, that they were not accessing all the material needed to keep abreast of developments in the various scientific and engineering disciplines needed to create spacecraft. The Advanced Systems Division of the Lockheed Missile and Space Company, as it was known then, in Sunnyvale, California (later to be known as Silicon Valley), grappled with this problem starting in the mid-1960s.

The solution they proposed was a radical idea: create a database that would contain data on articles published in all scientific and engineering journals. Scientists working at Lockheed and in the space community would be able to call in queries using key words. Titles and abstracts would be searched and a bibliography of relevant articles would be generated. There were many problems to be overcome, ranging from data storage to the time it took early computers to search databases to user interfaces and so on. But in due course a database was created. In 1974, on the heels of the computerization of the printing industry, a new service was offered to the public by Lockheed: Dialog Information Services.

Dialog was a dramatic breakthrough in the way information was managed. For the first time, it was possible to skim articles—or at least parts of them—in order to locate items that might be of interest. This meant scientists could locate needed information more efficiently than ever before, with less risk of missing something critical. For the first time, the limits of the paper world were overcome electronically. Not insignificantly, the breakthrough came in a place noted for its secret "black" projects, including technical intelligence projects for the CIA and NSA—Lockheed's Sunnyvale, California, facility. Dialog created a new capability, but it was, at least initially, focused on a limited literature—scientific.

In the mid-1960s, a company named Data Corporation, based in Dayton, Ohio, was doing quick turnaround contract work for Wright-Patterson and Rome Air Force bases. By the late 1960s, it was foundering. At the same time, another Dayton business, a paper company named Mead Corporation, was looking for ways to off-set some of the downturns in the paper industry, and decided high technology was the way to go. Attracted by Data Corporation's Recon Central system for retrieving aerial reconnaissance photos and a new method for inkjet print, Mead bought out Data Corp.

Apparently, Mead was initially unaware that Data Corp. had contracted with the Ohio Bar Association to set up a full-text, computerized, legal research program. When it became aware of the contract, Mead hired Arthur D. Little, Inc., a management consulting firm, to evaluate the situation and was told that Data Corp.'s system was superior to any of the competition in computerized legal research, and that, in fact, there were no adequate systems currently available in this area. They also reported that there was certainly a profitable market for an advanced legal database and retrieval system. Upon Little's recommendation, in 1970, Mead's chairman decided to invest in the project, hired several of the consultants to manage it, and formed the corporation Mead Data Central. After a $14 million redesign, Lexis was put on the market in 1973. Although far surpassing the original plans of Data Corporation and the Ohio Bar Association, it is important to note that Lexis grew out of a company that was also involved with the military. Dayton is the home of Wright-Patterson Air Force Base, which happens to be the center of the U.S. Air Force's research and development program, and therefore one of the most technically sophisticated places on the face of the globe.

Lexis, and its later competitor Westlaw, revolutionized legal research. But from the standpoint of business intelligence, the great breakthrough came in 1979 with the introduction of Lexis's nonlegal counterpart: Nexis. Nexis stored the complete content of thousands of newspapers and periodicals on-line daily, and permitted the user to search every word in every article in a matter of seconds. Almost without notice, a vast universe of published information became easily and readily available. Once published and loaded into the database, the information could never be lost. The entire structure of the relationship of time to knowledge

changed, as did the precision with which information could be targeted and retrieved.

Mead Data Central became a multibillion-dollar company and
was sold to Reed Elsevier in 1994 for about $1.5 billion. By then, an
entire industry of on-line databases had sprung up. Both Dialog—
sold to Knight-Ridder in 1988 for $335 million—and LEXIS-NEXIS
had turned from creating their own databases to reselling databases
created by others. Other resellers had grown up, and database companies were swarming everywhere.

What we have seen in the past generation is both an explosion
in the extent and accessibility of the public domain. The geography
of business intelligence, as well as other types of intelligence, has
shifted dramatically as the focus of the intelligence world has also
been transformed from intelligence collection to management. For
the first time, a systematic and cost-effective approach to business
intelligence has become possible. Now the first search yields
enough for decision makers to make most decisions. Much more
important, the decrease in the time needed for information gathering, and the growing efficiencies of information management,
have increased the time available for understanding the material,
for hunting down the missing pieces, and for analysis, which is, after
all, the entire point of the intelligence process.

2

SPACE, TIME, MONEY

The Holy Trinity of Business Intelligence

The Book of Genesis tells us the story of Joseph, who has been given the gift of foretelling the future. This gift gets him into a lot of trouble; his brothers sell him to a band of wandering Arabs as a reward for being right too often. However, the gift also saves his neck, by making him invaluable to his masters. How valuable was he? In the first instance of commodity manipulation in recorded history, Joseph corners the grain market for Pharaoh by interpreting one of his dreams:

> Behold, there come seven years of great plenty throughout all the land of Egypt. And there shall arise after them seven years of famine....Now therefore, let Pharaoh look out a man discreet and wise and set him over the land of Egypt....And let them gather all the food of these good years that come and lay up corn under the hand of Pharaoh for food in the cities and let them keep it. And the food shall be for a store to the land against the seven years of famine....And he gathered up all the food of the seven years which were in the land of Egypt and laid up the food in the cities....And all countries came unto Egypt to Joseph to buy corn; because the famine was sore in all the earth.

Joseph is subsequently hired by Pharaoh as a commodities broker. Knowing the future with enough time to react, and having the resources needed to take advantage of his knowledge, Joseph buys corn on the spot market and actually takes delivery. Absorbing storage overheads into the low price, he holds until the predicted crop failures hit. He then turns around and sells in a series of government-to-government cash deals, not only creating tremendous wealth and shifting the balance of power in the region but also taking some incredible commissions in the process.

Every businessman is a fortune-teller. Unfortunately, few of us have Joseph's gift from God. Few of us can discern the future by interpreting dreams, looking at tea leaves, or even from looking at technical charts of corn futures. What little the rest of us can glean about the future comes to us from the past. It is not that history repeats itself in some simpleminded way but that history does in some sense hold sway over us. After all, most basic structures of the human condition do remain constant, even as their details change: agriculture is agriculture, industry is industry, finance is finance, and so on. These basic structures operate by their own rules, and while wild variations do occur, life is not, as Macbeth in his madness would have it, "A tale told by an idiot, full of sound and fury, signifying nothing." If it were, Henry Ford the car magnate, Warren Buffet the well-known financial investor, and the famously wealthy Rothschilds would never have succeeded in finance and industry. But they did. Each of them could somehow predict the future when it came to knowing how to make money.

In order to be a successful fortune-teller, a businessman has to recognize old and unprecedented patterns, and know how to take advantage of each. He must be able to identify, almost intuitively, things that appear to be familiar and therefore may point the way to what the future might hold. We think about the future through analogies and metaphors. Things remind us of something; this product reminds us of an older product; this technology is as new as some other, successful product; that guy reminds us of a super guy we once knew. Successful businessmen reason by analogy, but they also know its limits, dangers, and pitfalls. Analogy alerts us to possibilities and dangers, but the devil is in the details, and only mastery of the details can provide us with the knowledge we need to attempt to predict, and influence, the future.

Having mastered the past, businessmen need a constant flow of information about the present. And they need this information on two levels. First, they need information on the broad sweep of things in a constant, unprompted flow from all sources. Second, they need access to the smallest details on demand, in order to confirm whether their instinctive read was correct or not—and to determine how best to take advantage of the situation.

Successful businessmen are information junkies—and great historians. You can't spot a trend without the data.

THE GEOGRAPHY OF INFORMATION

Intelligence is always a matter of space and time: Where can information be found and how long will it take to find it? In the particular case of business intelligence, there is a third variable: money. Every step of the business intelligence process is defined by these three things. The ultimate luxury would be to find what you need instantly, on top of your desk, for free. Life rarely makes it so easy. More often, information takes a long time to find, especially if it's on the other side of the world, costing so much that it is just not worth going after. The core problem of business intelligence is to develop the knowledge and skill to find information quickly and easily, for as little money as possible.

Businesses and other organizations emit information. Often the emission is intentional and planned; sometimes it is simply the uncontrollable by-product of other activities; sometimes it is accidental. Each emission has a trajectory, originating in certain places, traveling in a certain way, arriving in a certain form. Sometimes it dissipates and disappears. Sometimes the information congeals, say into a magazine article, and finds a permanent home in libraries. Information has a life cycle. It may take a particular form early in its existence, and over time, change form and location. Information that is first emitted as gossip may become a confidential internal document somewhere else. It might then be made available in some informal way, and finally be published in a newspaper and then made available via an on-line service.

The information capture process is, therefore, extremely dynamic and complex. We can begin with a basic rule of thumb: the closer the information, the faster and cheaper it is to obtain. In planning business intelligence operations, optimizing space is the basis for optimizing time, which in turn minimizes cost. This means that a business intelligence system must be built around a geography of knowledge and a method of optimizing the use of time—and both must be related to price and potential rewards. This is not an academic exercise. It is a necessary part of focusing a business's attention on the costs of intelligence.

For many businesses, the apparent cost of doing formal intelligence appears prohibitive, often because there is no clear understanding of the steps involved in controlling costs. If intelligence is carried out in an uncontrolled fashion, then the question "where should we look" is always answered with "wherever it takes you"; the question "how fast do you want it" is answered "as soon as possible." Answers like these are certain to sour any business on intelligence, because "do whatever it takes to find it as soon as possible" guarantees that the price will be astronomical. Some projects are worth this, but not very many.

The geography of information is not quite like a map of New Jersey. Information exists in a variety of domains, some farther away and harder to access, some closer and easily accessible. Television, for example, is part of the electronic domain that comes to you. At the other end of the scale are competitors' proprietary secrets, that not only don't come to you but are in a domain so far away that it is almost impossible to get to them from where you are. Geography can also be in a more conventional form, such as a particular piece of information being located in Helsinki. However, assuming that the information is on a web site in Helsinki, or available via fax, the actual location is less relevant today than the domain. If you can sit at your desk and access the information, it is in a very practical sense "closer" than information physically located in a company next door.

So we must draw a peculiar map to describe the geography of information, charting the zones or domains in which information resides.

INFORMATION ZONES

- **Electronically formatted information:** This is the first and most easily accessible layer. Today's databases contain vast warehouses of readily searchable information, ranging from obscure industry reports to national newspapers. As time goes on, this domain will become richer and richer. Its weakness is that most databases contain information from no earlier than about 1980. All of them are accessible with a personal computer, a modem, and some training. As the world wide web develops, more and more of this information will be accessible via the Internet.

- **Paper formatted information:** If information cannot be found in the electronic domain, the next layer to search is the paper domain. Paper is an excellent, cost-effective storage medium, and until the advent of the electronic domain, all published information was formatted on paper. Information on paper, once located, is in many ways the most readily accessible—easy to read, to make notes on, and so on. Its weakness is finding it. While most electronic information originates in and remains available as paper, not all paper is available in the electronic domain. In fact, the vast majority of information produced today is available only on paper. In the United States, where computers have penetrated most intensively, electronic information constitutes the largest percentage of all types of currently produced information. In the rest of the advanced industrial world—Europe, Japan, a few other countries—electronic information is being produced, but not at an equivalent rate. Outside the advanced industrial countries—this is most of humanity—paper is still the primary storage medium of information. This makes the task of business intelligence more difficult, but still doable.

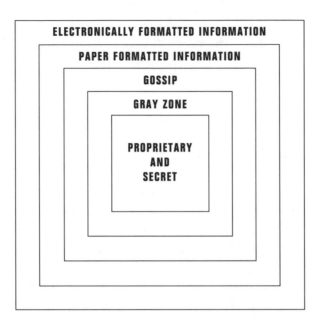

- **Gossip:** As we know in our own businesses, a tremendous amount of information is known and passed about by word of mouth, but much of it is never actually recorded and preserved. For want of a better term, we'll call this domain "gossip." It is hard to quantify how much information is contained in this domain. There is a certain type of information here that is extremely valuable, which might be called early warnings and unofficial truths. Information is frequently known before it is published, so monitoring this domain can be complex and demanding. Techniques for acquiring gossip range from the schmooze to debriefing the sales force.

- **Gray zone:** Between gossip and the world of secret and proprietary information—as much a legal concept as an operational one—there lies a vital, intermediate zone that we call the gray zone. This is an area filled with information that has been formally recorded and is technically available but cannot be accessed by formal means. In other words, it's there for the asking, but no one knows that it's there, and therefore no one knows it can be requested. This is a zone that can best be accessed from one of the outer three zones: a casual mention in an article, gossip over drinks, a blind phone call—any of which can reveal the existence of information of the exact type that you need but would have never found without working at it.

Typical information in the gray zone might be a government report, such as a U.S. Department of Energy internal study of the future of the natural gas industry in Tunisia. The study hasn't been published, and only five or six copies exist. However, it is not secret, and the author, who has never received any recognition by anyone at all, would probably be delighted to find that someone cares enough to request a copy. The problem is finding out that it exists in the first place. Similar situations occur in the private sector, where everything from scientific studies to marketing reports is available, sometimes for free, sometimes for a lot of money (and not necessarily with any correlation between cost and value), but only to those who know, or find out, they exist.

- **Proprietary and secret:** This is where open source intelligence ends and espionage begins. Every organization, government, business, and family has its secrets. Sometimes these are extremely valuable. Sometimes secrecy is used to make the person who knows the secret feel better about himself. However, the mere fact that something is secret doesn't mean that it is valuable and an enormous amount of time, money and risk can be allocated to getting hold of a secret document only to find out that it contains nothing that could not have been gotten out of the *Wall Street Journal.* Moreover, it is frequently possible to infer what is going on deep inside a company by studying the things that have emanated out into the public domain, and figuring out the thinking that went into producing that, and other, information.

The five domains of knowledge are each connected. A search of an electronic database reveals the existence of a published, paper document. Reading that document gives you the name of a key researcher. You call and chat, get together for drinks, and he shares gossip about another researcher who has developed some interesting studies. You call the other researcher and he agrees to send you a copy of some of his work. In reading his reports, and some other material you may have, you suddenly realize in what area a competitor of yours is doing research and development. The life cycle of every bit of information is unique. Some exist in different domains simultaneously, while some exist in only one. Some are permanent, others ephemeral, passing away with surprising rapidity. But all exist in one of these domains, and mastering them is vital to doing business intelligence. And of all the skills of mastery, none is more important than speed, since time really is money in business intelligence.

THE KNOWLEDGE CURVE

The purpose of business intelligence is to make money. It does this by providing information about some aspect of the business environment, supplying the business with four advantages. First, it must provide significant information, information that is not otherwise known. It must produce something that surprises you.

Second, it must be actionable information—providing the business with opportunities for action, information that allows a business to dodge a bullet. This kind of information costs money. This question must always be asked: If I knew a particular set of facts, would I be able to exploit the situation? Would it matter?

Third, the information must be timely. It must be delivered prior to the event, and it must be provided to the decision maker with enough lead time for him to respond. For example, a telegram ordering a war alert was delivered to Admiral Husband E. Kimmel at Pearl Harbor three hours after the Japanese launched their attack. The information was certainly significant, but it was not delivered inside a time frame that was actionable—making it not only useless but downright embarrassing. The precise definition of timely depends on the context. Sometimes it simply means knowing before the event. Sometimes it means knowing before competitors know about it. Sometimes it means knowing information so that other information can be understood, and so on. But this much is clear: Intelligence can be a wasting asset, and its acquisition must be measured by time.

Fourth, the information must provide a value greater than its cost. If it costs $100,000 to get information that is significant, actionable, and timely but with an added value of only $50,000, it will not take long for intelligence "coups" of this sort to take a company down.

All intelligence operations must be put to a rigorous test that measures these four variables: Would the knowledge gained in this operation be significant, actionable, timely, and cost effective? As with many things in business, it is easy to imagine that these things would be easily quantifiable, but in fact they are not. It is difficult to know the precise value of information. A particular piece of information, by itself, may provide little or no value. Its value is in the context of pieces of information the existence of which is as yet unknown. For example, knowing that two people had lunch yesterday may have no intrinsic value beyond the pleasure of gossip. But taken together with a piece of unanticipated information from tomorrow's newspaper, which tells you that one of the lunch's participants filed for bankruptcy, and knowing that the other luncher was a banker, might tell you something of the financial position of that company, which may or may not help you, depending on your position. So, information can have unanticipated and serendipitous value. But most information does not, and collecting information on the off-chance that it will become valuable is something that will quickly undermine both the bottom line and your sanity. So, while it may not be possible to rigorously quantify the information, some careful valuation prior to acquiring it is necessary.

It is important to understand what you are buying when you create an intelligence system. But in most cases, the information you are buying will eventually come to you anyway, as you read the newspapers, talk to colleagues, or just live a normal life. It's kind of like standing in Times Square, as the old saying goes: Everyone you know will eventually pass by. An intelligence system is designed to get you information when you need it.

Libraries are loaded with information, most of it free. Intelligence costs money, because it's about time rather than information.

Information is cheap if you don't care how long it takes to get it. But time is expensive, and each successive unit of time purchased tends to cost more. In terms of our geography of information zones, the deeper you go, the more expensive it gets. Now, those zones pass from published to nonpublished areas of knowledge. Accessing published information is obviously cheaper than accessing unpublished or nonpublishable information. This is so if for no other reason than that published information was intended to be accessed, and was provided for that purpose, while gossip, the gray area, and proprietary information don't give themselves up nearly so readily. Therefore, the price of acquiring additional warning time rises dramatically as we push the access point back to prepublication zones.

In thinking about the relationship between information, time, and money, we can begin to see clearly the questions involved in the intelligence process. The most important question is: How much information is enough? A knowledge curve emerges:

THE KNOWLEDGE CURVE

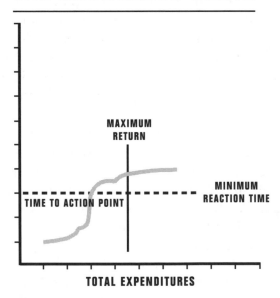

MAXIMUM
RETURN

MINIMUM
REACTION TIME

TIME TO ACTION POINT

TOTAL EXPENDITURES

The time/money/information curve is an S-shaped structure, representing early and late inefficiencies in information gathering. The curve intersects with two other lines. The horizontal dotted line represents the minimum amount of time that needs to be purchased in order to permit decision makers to make a decision. That defines the zones that have to be penetrated and the techniques that need to be used. The solid vertical line represents the maximum value of reacting to the information—reflecting both the benefits of success and the costs of failure.

The knowledge curve is that segment of the time/money/information curve that is above the reaction line but to the left of the maximum expenditure line. It represents both the minimum amount of time that has to be secured—the last point at which the information can be utilized—and the maximum amount of money that can be spent. It is the area where intelligence operations can turn information into knowledge, and where knowledge can precipitate action.

Every acquisition of information, therefore, has a unique curve, defined by the time that is being purchased and the maximum amount of money that can be spent acquiring that knowledge. If acquisition falls outside of this area, it is impossible. It is within this area that the information gatherer has choices to make, including the critical one: Where does he want to be on the knowledge curve?

The core decision in every intelligence project is: How much time do you want to buy—where do you want to be on the knowledge curve?

That, of course, depends on the mission. He can save money, buy less time, and take longer to acquire the information. He can spend more money and buy more time. How much time and how much money are both described in the curve, which, in turn, is defined by the idiosyncrasies of the particular piece of information, as well as the geography of knowledge—where within the five zones the knowledge is to be found. This is the point—the intersection of space, time, and money—where the intelligence specialist defines his project.

CONCLUSION: BUYING TIME, CONTROLLING SPACE

The knowledge curve is, obviously, highly stylized. Its primary purpose is to call attention to the peculiarity of intelligence. It is less about information than about time. In the end, almost anything important becomes known. But the end can come after a business has buckled from a catastrophe. The purpose of a national intelligence agency is to provide intelligence that can be acted on—what is called actionable intelligence. In a world where an intelligence failure can cause almost limitless and catastrophic damage, cost is no object. So, if you were looking at the CIA's knowledge curve, it would lack the vertical line. It is no accident, therefore, that the CIA's budget runs into the tens of billions. The earliest point on the curve must be the access point.

For businesses, where the primary mission is making money, the vertical line is critical. It represents the limits of effort. It is obviously easier to assert these limits than to calculate them ahead of time. In later chapters we will discuss techniques of costing intelligence operations. Estimating reaction time is no easy matter either. But the knowledge curve is the point on which business intelligence must be fixated. The goal must be to spend enough to get hold of information while it is still useful without spending so much that the project's value is destroyed.

When looking at the knowledge curve, you can begin to understand more clearly why business intelligence is possible today in a way that wasn't possible even ten years ago. Imagine that Zone 1—electronic information—didn't exist. The steep slope after start-up would not exist. Information accumulated in this zone would have to be back-loaded into other zones—paper, gossip, gray, and proprietary. Without the efficiencies of the electronic medium, the curve would slump down and to the right. In most cases, the entire curve would wind up below the reaction line and to the right of the maximum return line. In other words, business intelligence would be impossible.

The efficiencies of the electronic zone, which allows a tremendous amount of information to be accumulated very quickly and relatively cheaply, make it possible to use the other zones more efficiently, targeting missing, needed information rather than using these zones to accumulate baseline information. In short, the system works only because of the powerful advent of Zone 1.

As we said earlier, making money in business depends, to a great extent, on fortune-telling. So far, we have not discussed the reading of tea leaves or even, for that matter, the gathering of tea leaves. We have discussed the *need* for tea leaves and have marveled at the new varieties that have become available. In other words, we have been setting the stage for the real work.

That begins now. The real work is to master the techniques and skills needed to mine the five zones efficiently so the intelligence process can hit the knowledge curve. But as we get down to the nitty-gritty, it is important to bear in mind the core of intelligence: time. Time to react. Time to think. Time to foretell the future. Mastering intelligence is mastering time, in a world where time is money.

3

PUTTING IT TOGETHER

The Practice of Business Intelligence

The foundations of intelligence are discipline and an imposed honesty. An intelligence collector or analyst who lies, particularly to himself, may as well not begin the process. Two of the deadliest lies consist of hope and confidence. This is an odd thing to say, since a positive attitude has always been regarded as one of the keys to success in business. But, in intelligence, as opposed to business in general, a positive attitude is dangerous. Optimism tends to skew your judgment. The businessman or intelligence specialist doing the intelligence work always wants to report positive, hopeful things. No one wants to walk into a meeting and announce that he has just discovered that a new technology by a competing company has destroyed a project his own company has been working on for two years. Yet this is precisely the sort of news the intelligence specialist all too often must report.

As a member of the team, you begin with shared enthusiasm for a project. It is the intelligence specialist's job to lose his enthusiasm first, to doubt—to be right when no one wants him to be right, even when the careers of others are at stake. Pessimism is a much harder discipline to maintain than optimism, especially in a business environment. Yet few things have helped companies more than doses of truthful pessimism at strategic moments.

Another mortal sin of the intelligence specialist is self-confidence, which can be akin to self-destructiveness. The ultimate discipline is to question your own doubts; to constantly ask if your facts are sufficient, if there are any facts available that you haven't collected that would blow your analysis apart, if your analysis itself is correct, and if your recommendations are on target. If you are going with the consensus, you must question if you are doing it for the sake of being one of the crowd. If you are going against the consensus, you must wonder whether you are taking that stand to be ornery or to show off. And having taken a position, you must wonder continually whether it was the right one—and continue to collect information and evaluate it even after filing your report.

Ultimately, like an auditor about to file a troubling report, the intelligence specialist has to have courage. Most of us, under pressure, are unpredictable. Accountants range from being Rambo to being wimps—and sometimes we won't know which until the chips are down. But when the chips are down, the accountant can fall back on an accounting process that has enough precision in it to be looked at and evaluated dispassionately—it squeezes out hope and misplaced self-confidence. The process even substitutes for courage. Right or wrong, the process gives the practitioner something to hold on to. It disciplines, guides, and ultimately controls him. Therefore, to be successful, we need a process to encourage the ability to be appropriately negative.

Unlike accounting practices that have evolved over centuries, business intelligence, as a formal discipline, is in its infancy. Therefore, the world of business intelligence will not have a body of rules like those that support a lawyer or accountant. At this point, however, we can provide a fairly clearly defined, step-by-step approach that can guide the intelligence process—and that can serve as a reality check. The intelligence process is not intended to be a straitjacket. Nothing is ever as neat as a flowchart would lead you to believe. But it is intended to help clarify the process—and to move us from the theory to the practice of business intelligence.

This chart could have been complicated ad infinitum, and by the time we finish, it will be more complicated. For now, we provide a fairly simple schematic of the process (see page 58), and describe a case we worked on showing how it fits into this process: the case of the magnetic water treatment device—our first example of a complete business intelligence project.

THE INTELLIGENCE PROCESS

```
┌──────────────┐      ┌──────────────┐      ┌──────────────┐
│    DEFINE    │      │ IDENTIFY THE │      │  DEFINE THE  │
│     THE      │ ───► │  KNOWLEDGE   │ ───► │  KNOWLEDGE   │
│   MISSION    │      │     BASE     │      │    CURVE     │
└──────────────┘      └──────────────┘      └──────────────┘
                                                    │
                                                    ▼
┌──────────────┐      ┌──────────────┐      ┌──────────────┐
│   ACQUIRE    │      │    SELECT    │      │    TARGET    │
│ INFORMATION  │ ◄─── │     THE      │ ◄─── │     THE      │
│              │      │    METHOD    │      │     ZONE     │
└──────────────┘      └──────────────┘      └──────────────┘
       │
       ▼
┌──────────────┐      ┌──────────────┐      ┌──────────────┐
│ OVERLAY ON   │      │    RETASK    │      │ OVERLAY ON   │
│ KNOWLEDGE    │ ───► │     THE      │ ───► │ KNOWLEDGE    │
│    BASE      │      │    SYSTEM    │      │    BASE      │
└──────────────┘      └──────────────┘      └──────────────┘
                                                    │
                                                    ▼
                      ┌──────────────┐      ┌──────────────┐
                      │   ARCHIVE    │      │    FINAL     │
                      │     AND      │ ◄─── │ ANALYSIS AND │
                      │   DATABASE   │      │  EVALUATION  │
                      └──────────────┘      └──────────────┘
```

THE CASE OF THE
MAGNETIC WATER CONDITIONER

A client came to us who had put money into a company that manufactured and sold magnetic water treatment systems designed to reduce the buildup of calcium scale. The company was having problems and he wanted to know if there was any point in putting more money into it or if he should just cut his losses and run. He understood that this was an intelligence problem, because he felt that he just didn't know enough about the deal to make an intelligent judgment.

In preparing for our first meeting with him, we did a very quick check on the idea of water magnetism. In doing such checks, we rely heavily on an electronic database service we've already mentioned: LEXIS-NEXIS. NEXIS, the side that covers news and other sources extensively, goes back for about fifteen years with decreasing coverage. As a Zone 1 resource, it is fast and efficient. By inputting the term *magnetic water treatment,* we quickly got back a group of stories that would allow us to prepare for the meeting. LEXIS-NEXIS can appear quite expensive. Running down a single, simple story can cost hundreds or even thousands of dollars, so it is not for the casual user. But spending a few hundred dollars familiarizing ourselves with a topic prior to meeting with a client is a small investment. If it is a client worth going after—or an issue of fundamental importance to your business—it is worth the financial investment, and of course, the investment of staff and your own time.

Unfortunately for our client, the news wasn't good. We found that magnetic water treatment had been around for a while and was asserted, by its supporters, to be a way to reduce calcium scaling in water. Scaling is a serious problem in anything that uses water over an extended period of time, such as boilers in industrial plants. Scale buildup leads to rust in the ballast holds of ships or automobile radiators. The usual treatments are various chemicals, draining and scraping the container, or letting the buildup continue until the vessel is changed.

The theory was that by treating water with magnetism, it somehow reduced scaling. There was, however, a problem. The general consensus of the scientific community was that this was junk science, that it straight out didn't work, and that those who claimed it did were frauds. But we found a lot of anecdotal evidence, some from people with good reputations, claiming that, despite the consensus, magnetic water treatment did indeed work.

Our client apparently believed in his desalination system. After all, he had put good money into it. Since we had no basis on which to form any opinion, and really didn't have expertise in this area, we neither believed in it nor disbelieved. By trade we are pessimists—most promising technologies that no big company wants to touch are usually not worth touching. At first glance this seemed a case where an investor, not himself a specialist in the field, had taken a plunge and lost. It happens.

We went to the meeting in a suitable frame of mind—skeptical. More than anything, this was a last-gasp meeting: Was there anything to be done before he pulled the plug? In such cases there is a temptation to keep up the investor's hope; after all, hopeful investors write checks to intelligence companies while hopeless ones do not. This is a temptation we try not to indulge. To skew an analysis in order to make money would not only sully our reputation, and the industry's, but in the long run will cost more money than it earns. But let us not fool ourselves that these thoughts do not cross our minds; the important thing is to realize their danger.

Always open an intelligence operation in a neutral to negative frame of mind. It's marketing's job to lead the cheers, not yours.

Our client was enthusiastic enough for both of us. This was fortunate, as we only had to sell our skills and not the value of the project. The conversation turned to the core issue: validation. This product had the reputation of being fraudulent partly because of the involvement of a string of scam artists. To determine whether or not to put more money into it, or write it off to experience, our client needed to go back to reexamine the foundations of the business. That was our job: to gather the information he needed to make his decision and to support his decision making with our analysis. His initial investment hadn't been enormous. But if he could produce and sell this product, the calcium buildup problem he'd be solving would be sufficiently widespread to provide impressive multiples—and lots of money. And so we began our process.

Step 1: Defining the Mission

It was time to get down to work, and all work begins with clearly defining what exactly we were going to be doing about the magnetic treatment of water. Most intelligence operations suffer from vagueness and vastness. "Tell me everything" guarantees two things: The mission will fail, and accounting will go ballistic. No one can find out "everything," and even trying and failing will bust the budget. We were once asked by a company to find out everything about another company—and to do it fast. We tried to explain that what they were asking for was not only impossible but the bill was likely to be astronomical. The company they wanted to learn about operated in Russia, England, and the United States. They waved our warning away and told us to proceed. We probably didn't find out everything—what does everything look like and when do you know you've found it?—but we found out an awful lot. When the bill arrived, they were…well, it wasn't a pretty sight.

Any intelligence operation must be finite. If it doesn't have a clear and limited goal, it will fail, literally by definition.

The first step is to honestly and clearly define the mission: What do you need to know and why do you need to know it? If you can't define this with some precision, it usually means you have not thought through the entire project clearly enough. Indeed, a full accounting of what you need to know in order to proceed is a general business discipline, and that ought to go hand in hand with financial accounting. Unfortunately, accounting deals with a relatively simple variable—money—while information is complex and subtle. This increases the need for information accounting, and controlling it becomes all the more vital in order to focus business operations in general and intelligence operations in particular.

If you are asked to provide information on another company, the first bit of information you need is not about that company but about your own client. The reason your client is interested in that company defines the mission. If the CEO is doing his own intelligence work this should not be a problem. He should know what he is after and where his interests lie. But it is a critical issue in larger businesses where the intelligence function might be carried out by someone other than the CEO. All too often, this guy is kept out of the loop. He gets requests for information without being told why anyone is interested in it. As a result, he often doesn't know what he's really after. Like the poorly trained dog, he keeps fetching everything but the master's slipper. In the end, he is held responsible for the intelligence failures when in fact the real responsibility lies with the CEO for not communicating honestly with his intelligence manager—or worse, not trusting him. Basic rule: If you don't trust the guy running your intelligence operation, why is he still working for you? Keeping your intelligence people in the dark makes as much sense as keeping your lawyer and accountant in the dark.

Never accept an intelligence task where your client or boss won't or can't let you into the inner circle—unless you really need the job.

Define the mission and define your intelligence needs according to that mission. What was our client asking us to do? Well, he knew the product worked—it had been tested over and over again and it did what it was supposed to do. He knew a lot of people could save a lot of money using the product, but he also knew that hardly anyone would buy the product.

The mission: Explain why people wouldn't buy the product and what could be done about it.

The first part was easy. The problem was no one was buying the product because the company had no hard proof that it worked, only assertions. The industry was filled with sleazy hustlers who had developed a reputation for making fabulous claims that never panned out. The issue, therefore, was how do you prove that this product works?

Our mission definition looked like this:

MISSION
1. Locate a pattern for validating technologies similar to magnetic water treatment.
2. Determine what, if any, serious scientific work had been done in the area of magnetic water treatment that could be drawn on for validation.

3. Determine if there was actually any interest in a product like this *if* validation were achieved.

4. Estimate the cost of validation and the probability of successful validation.

In short, we were going back to the drawing board—to what ought to have been done in the first place—to see if the project could be quick-started.

At this point it was a knowledge problem. The investor didn't know things: Mainly, he didn't know how to get validation. He didn't know how much, if any, scientific information backed him up or even if there was any real interest in the product, save his own intuition and impressions. And he had no idea of the sort of costs involved. What he needed was information. For example, if he knew which scientists were involved in the field, he might be able to cut a deal with them and make them his research and development team. But first, he needed them identified. Intelligence comes in early in the process, defining the parameters. It then hands off to others.

This was, therefore, an intelligence project focused on technology. Our job was to find out about the science behind the process: What science had been done and who had done it? Also, we were to determine how scientific research in this field could be used to reverse the bad image of magnetic treatment of water, thereby convincing people that buying our client's product was a good idea. What we were doing wasn't quite science and it wasn't quite marketing; it was a little of both.

The intelligence professional gives the appearance of being a dilettante. The appearance is accurate. Business intelligence specializes in the general.

The intelligence methods part of the mission was now defined: Find out how new products with radical approaches to problems become validated. With that in hand, we could define our tasks and get on with the intelligence operation.

Step 2: Identify the Knowledge Base

The truth of how much the corporate executive actually knows rests somewhere between a desperate sense of ignorance and smug self-assurance. It is critical to understand exactly where you stand—what it is that you already know and what it is that you need to find out.

Businesses are tremendous repositories of information. Every employee, every mail delivery, every telephone conversation contains potentially valuable information. But most companies make no effort to retain and organize this information and, as a result, much of the information that passes through a company is never captured. This is not dissimilar to accounts receivable casually tossing aside checks at random. Failing to capture information means that, when the need arises, you will have to go outside the company to find what a few months ago you had in hand.

We were once involved in a defense-related project where we discovered that we badly needed information on the precise tonnage of material consumed by a U.S. Army division. The information existed somewhere, but we couldn't find it in the first three zones—electronic, paper, or gossip. So we had to go digging around in Zone 4, the gray zone. We finally found the information man-weeks later—a contact of a friend of a contact knew someone who had done a study that had never been circulated. There were other ways to find the information, but this was the one we found. A few days later, a new accountant on our staff wandered into an office and started talking to members of the team. It turned out that the accountant had left the army a month before, having served in supply. Apart from having a bunch of unclassified army manuals (always useful) he had the very numbers we had needed engraved in his soul. We had wasted time and money searching for something that was in the office down the hall.

This act of stupidity was not repeated. We put into place systems for organizing and accessing our own knowledge base. However, whether or not you have a system to access information, you must start any project by sitting down and taking inventory of what you already know. This is the only way to find out what you need to learn. In a one-man show, that consists of quietly thinking through and making a record of what you know about a subject. In a larger organization, the process becomes more complex. But a rigorous inventory of information is indispensable. Writing it down is important because it enforces a discipline that is badly needed at this stage.

Take the case of our magnetic treatment of water—this is what our information inventory looked like:

INFORMATION INVENTORY

Information from client

1. That the process works

2. Speculation about why the process works

3. A collection of odds and ends on the general theory of the process

Our own inventory

1. That the process, and the entire field, was regarded as junk science by most respectable scholars

2. An awareness of the potential importance of the process—if it works

3. An awareness, drawn from our experience in the defense area, that the U.S. Navy would be a likely customer if the process worked

It doesn't appear to be much to go on, but you play the hand you're dealt. Note a couple of facts from this list. First, the client provided the information that the product works. Barring evidence to the contrary, you've got to take the client at his word. This is not naïveté. He does not need to con you because it is in his interest to be as accurate as possible. In addition, even if he isn't an expert, he probably knows more about the field than you do. Trust him on this. Second, in mastering his field, the client has had a peculiar and idiosyncratic relationship with it. He was probably not systematic in collecting information, but he surely has more than he is aware of, so debrief him. Third, our own contribution appeared to be skimpy. We didn't really have any information on the subject, but we did have an insight derived from our knowledge—that the U.S. Navy sailed on the ocean and used lots of water in handling their ships. This brilliant insight would actually prove quite valuable.

The obvious is more likely to be true than the incredible. That's why they call it obvious, dummy.

Now, here is what we didn't but probably needed to know, based on the two core questions we had formulated:

INFORMATION REQUIREMENTS

Question: If this product works, why haven't others introduced it before?

Information required

1. Who is or has in the past worked in this field as researcher or manufacturer?
2. Has anyone used this technology in the past and what was their experience?
3. Who are the large users of water decalcification systems and what are they currently using to do the job?

Question: In this general area, how do new technologies become accepted?

Information required

1. Identify other processes in the same area as this one, particularly one that has come in from left field, and find out how it managed to get accepted.
2. Find out from potential users what they would like to see happen for them to get comfortable with this technology.

At this point, we pretty much knew what the mission was, and what questions we needed to have answered. Now we needed to know whether it was worth our while to answer these questions—

how expensive will this be, what is the potential payoff, and how probable is it that the payoff will occur?

Step 3: Defining the Knowledge Curve

Defining the position on the knowledge curve is the crucial step that makes or breaks an intelligence operation. What the knowledge curve does, as we discussed in the last chapter, is define the relationship between money, time, and information. How badly do you need the information? How much can you afford to pay? How much is it worth? Some of the answers are a matter of choice. Some are forced on you as a matter of reality—economic and intelligence. Defining your position on the knowledge curve is as much art as science, but it is never casual.

There are three sequential issues to address in positioning your project.

1. At what point must you act? How much time is there? How long do you have to gather and analyze the intelligence?
2. How much can you spend? What is the budget? What is the potential return?
3. In the segment between these two variables, where is the optimal position to shoot for? In fact, can the job even be done within the specified amount of time and cost?

In this case, the reaction time was set by the financial and legal position of our client's company. He had about two months in which to liquidate and litigate or to put in more money. So, we had, at most, five weeks to come up with the information he needed to make his decision, giving him a week to absorb the information, then about two weeks before the drop-dead date to select his course.

There are two types of curves that have to be distinguished, one of which might be called the discrete operations curve. As the name implies, this curve applies to an operation that has a discrete beginning and end. Here the starting point of the curve is the moment the operation is undertaken, with the closing point being either the final, usable date for the information or the maximum cost line. The other type might be called the continual monitoring curve. Here there is no starting point but rather an ongoing monitoring of the environment. In this case, the curve refers to the amount of time between the event's occurrence, the acquisition of information, and the amount of time needed to respond.

In this case we had a discrete operation with a starting date. The obvious questions were:

- How much time was there before the decision point?
- How far in advance did the user need to have the information in order to reach a conclusion?
- How much money was available for the project?

The hidden questions include how much flexibility was there in this time frame and how much more money was our client willing to spend in order to get answers earlier?

How much was this product worth? Current antiscaling technology relied primarily on chemicals added to the water, which was costly and did some damage to the containers themselves. But that technology worked and people were comfortable with it. So while the potential payoff for the new technology was large, so was the risk. This was in every way a high-risk, high-reward situation.

What had our client already spent on professional services, such as lawyers and accountants, in trying to keep this company afloat? How much would he have saved in legal fees if he had had decent intelligence in the first place? How much would he have to spend on lawyers in liquidating his company?

Remember, the purpose of intelligence is to take advantage of the knowledge and experience of others, avoiding the extremely high cost of moving up the learning curve on your own. It is a cost-avoidance, risk-control investment. Another approach to calculating a maximum expense level is to estimate the amount of money you could reasonably expect to spend in making mistakes in a start-up company, and assume that a certain percentage—say just 10 percent—could be avoided by drawing on the experiences of others collected by effective intelligence.

At the other end, assume that the entire start-up was a failure, but that you would not have invested in it if you had had the information that the entire project was doomed. Assume that 20 percent of all start-up investment is wasted on errors—an intuitive but conservative investment. Then, the most conservative expenditure on intelligence would be 10 percent of 20 percent—or 2 percent of total investment. At the far end, any information that avoids a total write-off is worth $1 less than the investment. Obviously, this is way too high, since spending intelligence dollars does not create potential value in the way that spending it on investment does. But it does give us a range for expenditures of investments—say from 2 percent on up, with the scale rising as the potential risk rises.

Intelligence is cheap thrills—living vicariously through other people's foul-ups. Compare the price of admission to the cost of throwing the party yourself.

Now what is the payoff? This can't be quantified, but it is potentially very large, as is the probability that no payoff at all will occur. Now, assume an investment of $3 million, which in various ways had been estimated as necessary to move this project along. Assume that there is a 10 percent chance of a $300 million payoff—a hundredfold payoff on a long-shot investment. An investment in intelligence ranging from 2 to 10 percent—that is, from $60,000 to $300,000—is certainly reasonable, with a 0.5 percent investment, or $15,000, being the bare bottom.

What was the client going to get for this money? Everything we could find out legally on the technology of the magnetic treatment of water, the key players in the field, their experience, and so on. The client had to clarify a space and time problem. How deeply did he want us to go, geographically, in terms of zones; and how quickly did he need the information? The latter question was simple to answer: He needed it in five weeks.

The geographical question was more complex. Like many business decisions, this one could be decided on the fly. Having fixed the time, and the initial investment in the intelligence work at about $30,000, we would be in contact with the client as the operation was carried out, giving him the option of whether to invest additional money for additional information.

Step 4: Targeting the Zone

There were two clusters of information that we had decided we needed in Step 2. The first was information on the technology itself. The second was information on the validation process. These were two separate but closely linked issues. We really didn't know much about any research that had been done in the field. Even our client didn't know of extensive scientific work in the area. This struck us as odd. Scientists will study anything. They'll study the hell out of a wart on an antelope's butt. It seemed to us extremely doubtful that someone, somewhere had not been given a research grant to study this. One of the great benefits of university tenure is the publish or perish system. Every professor wants to get tenure because it allows him to study subjects such as warts on an antelope's butt—under the cover of academic freedom. In order to get tenure, and later promotions, raises, grants, and other goodies, professors publish things—in fact, they'll publish just about anything, creating an absolute avalanche of incredibly useless stuff. The authors of this book won't bore you with examples of their own contributions to this sludge pile via the noted Journal of Irrelevant Studies.

However—and this is critical—within this pile are absolute gems. Buried in this pile is an article—in fact, a whole string of articles arguing with one another—on virtually any subject you can imagine. And once you find one article, you'll find that the helpful professor has done all your work for you. His footnotes and bibliographies contain practically everything ever written on the subject—that's how he proves he's done his homework. Those articles also contain everything he missed. Find just one article on your subject and you've found them all. So our first task was to target Zones 1 and 2: electronic databases and the good old library.

There are over 233,400 professors in the United States alone, studying every subject under the sun, every one of them

**publishing or perishing. Steal an idea from Microsoft and
prepare to die. Steal an idea from a professor, and it's called
research. But, as with diamonds, you've got to shovel a lot of
gravel to find the good stuff.**

Performing the first task—finding information on the technology itself—proved easier than the second task. Validation was a more amorphous topic. What did it mean, after all? Well, for us, what it really meant was how can we convince people that this gadget works and that they should buy it? Somehow we had to figure out how new technologies got to be taken seriously. The problem we had was that, unlike most new technologies, this one had acquired the reputation of being fraudulent. We needed more than ordinary validation—we had to dispel the reputation of fraud surrounding it.

On reflection, of course, we realized that this reputation was to our client's advantage. The big guys, like Westinghouse or General Electric, had not jumped into the game because the conventional wisdom was that magnetic water treatment didn't work. No one was motivated to try to overcome the reputation as they weren't hurting for business. That's what gave our client his chance—if he could get it validated, if it really did work.

We needed to find out what a big customer would require in order to buy this product. The biggest customer we could think of was the U.S. government, and in particular the Department Defense (DOD). What is particularly nice about the DOD is that they have rules on procurement; not clear rules, but they are, nevertheless, rules. If we could discuss this with someone, he could explain to us the rules under which this would be validated. And, of course, if the DOD bought something, it was validated. On the other hand, if you could land a Defense contract, who cared about validation? But nowhere in the tens of thousands of pages of federal procurement rules could we find rules on this. So we needed to go deeper, to Zones 3 and 4—gossip and the gray area—to find out whether or not the DOD had ever done studies on validation of, or bought, this technology.

We might find that the DOD had already tested this idea and that it was on every ship in the fleet. Or that they had tested the idea and the court-martial documents were available for the poor guy who lost his ship because of it. Either way, a foray into the first two zones was going to be the next step, followed by Zones 3 and 4, if Zones 1 and 2 justified it.

> **Always do the simpler work first. It frequently saves you having to do the hard work.**

If we found conclusive scientific proof that the process not only doesn't work, but that it can never work because it violates the laws of nature and nature's God, well, we probably wouldn't have to worry about the validation problem.

Step 5: Acquire the Information

Since we are going to devote most of the rest of this book to detailed advice on acquiring information, we don't need to go into it too much here, except as it affects our own little operation. First, of course, we took a careful look at the material we had in hand. It contained a few interesting articles—all of which contained footnotes. Those footnotes, in turn, yielded other articles from which we figured we might be able to learn some things. It was an important start.

The most important thing in these articles, however, was not facts or bibliography but language. Every field and subfield has its own language. The first task in any operation is to master the language—particularly the buzzwords that are used over and over again. In this case, terms like *rare earth magnets, flux fields, pressure gradients* all occurred and reoccurred. These were absolute gems for us, but not because they, by themselves, yielded anything intellectually—at least not at this stage. The value here was that they gave us keywords to use in database searches. There were three places in which we began our search, all in the electronic domain:

> **When in Rome, order in Italian. Every field has its basic vocabulary that you'll quickly locate because of sheer repetition. Those five or ten buzz words are your signposts.**

You don't have to understand them at first; just use them as mining tools.

- Dialog: We've mentioned this before as one of the first databases to use. Dialog is a database of other databases. There are literally hundreds of electronic databases that are searchable through Dialog. But Dialog has some drawbacks. It's fiendishly expensive—searches run in the hundreds of dollars and up—and you really should be a rocket scientist to use it. Still, it does contain a wealth of scientific and technical literature, or at least their citations, all searchable by Boolean operators, which means that in addition to recognizing whether particular words appear in the text or abstract, you can use terms like *and, or, but not,* and so on. That meant that we could say MAGNETIC AND WATER AND RARE EARTH BUT NOT ELECTROMAGNETIC, meaning that we wanted articles in which the words *magnetic, water,* and *rare earth* appeared, but not those that also used the term *electromagnetic.* Dialog gave us hundreds of potential articles to pursue.

- National Technical Information Service (NTIS): Everything owned by the federal government is free to the public. A little-known fact is that nothing that has been produced by the government carries a copyright on it. It's there for the taking. Since that was too simple, the government created NTIS, as a clearinghouse for information. NTIS, like Dialog, allows you to search using key words but not Boolean operators, which means that you can't exclude things. The search is free, but ordering articles through NTIS can run you from $10 and up an article. The article is free; the search is free. There's a service charge, but it's still not copyrighted. We didn't find too much here.

- Defense Technical Information Center (DTIC): This is the mother lode, but it's a little tricky gaining access. DTIC contains everything produced by and for the government in the defense area, which covers a huge amount of government-funded research and development. The problem with DTIC is that unless you are a defense contractor or bidding on a defense contract, you can't get at it…sort of. But a few calls, which we'll discuss later, will get you in, at least to the nonclassified sections. DTIC contains every study done over the years for the Department of Defense, and in our case, it told us what work, if any, the government had done in this field.

Our electronic data dump led us into the paper domain— Zone 2. A lot of the stuff we found on-line, or from the footnotes in articles we found on-line, were still available only in paper form for the full article. There is nothing, absolutely nothing, like a first-rate library, and a business that doesn't have people who know how to use a research library is a business that is operating blind in one eye. Our folks shuttled back and forth to the university library, which had another service worth mentioning: interlibrary loan. If the library doesn't have it, an on-line catalog called Online Computer Library Center, Inc. (OCLC), will tell the librarian every library in the country that does, and the interlibrary loan system will deliver it to you—though frequently not as fast as you would like. To avoid any delays, we maintain links with undergraduates and graduates at other universities. For pitifully small amounts of money, these folks will dig up the journals, copy the articles, and fax them to you, cutting down turnaround time.

We told you that intelligence work wasn't sexy. But our society is blessed with poorly organized, generally inaccessible archives containing the treasures of our civilization. Willie Sutton robbed banks 'cause that's where the money was. Intelligence types go to the library.

We piled up the journals and copies and read them. We had a couple of people on the staff who had scientific backgrounds, although not necessarily in this area. Expertise at this level isn't really as important as patience, intelligence, common sense, and an extremely high boredom threshold. What we were looking for at this stage was simple and twofold: (1) Who was doing basic research in this area?, and (2) What was the basic research finding?

Most of the articles were hot air—literature reviews of what other people had said, one-page articles by people selling the product, indictments against the people who hustled the products. We quickly separated out the noise from the basic laboratory research on the subject. That cut things down to size. We found that research had been carried out in only a few countries: the United States, Russia, Israel, Japan. We also found something interesting. Whereas the literature reviews were highly critical of the process, the basic research consistently showed that applying magnetism to water did indeed cut down on scaling, for reasons no one could explain theoretically.

The lab results—from some very solid universities and by some solid scientists—definitely showed that something was happening, although there was massive disagreement over exactly what. We had now achieved something important. We had enough information to say that our client's intuition was not wrong. Something was going on, although it wasn't clear what it was or why. It also pointed to a basic problem: In spite of the positive results in the lab, the noise in the scientific field remained negative. The key problem was the lack of theoretical consensus. In the sciences, knowing that something works is not enough. Having a theory about why it works tilts the balance.

Lists of research projects from DTIC also told us that for about fifty years the U.S. Navy had been experimenting with magnets to cut down on scaling—almost since World War II. Every experiment had failed. In fact, the coast guard had just concluded an experiment using magnets on pipes—it had failed. We now had an anomaly: The process tended to work in the laboratory, but it failed in field tests with the navy. What was going on?

Step 6: Retask the System

On the chart on page 58, retasking the system appears only once. This is because we were getting tired of drawing loops. Retasking is a regular process that repeats itself as often as needed. When you have completed one set of assignments, you stop and evaluate what you have, creating a new information inventory. At this point, ours looks like this:

INTERIM STATUS AND TASK REPORT

Findings

1. Research had been going on for fifty years.

2. Research centers were in the United States, Russia, Israel, and Japan.

3. Lab results were uniformly promising.

4. Field tests with the navy and coast guard were generally a failure.

Question

Why were lab tests successful and field tests a failure?

Task

1. Talk to the navy.

2. Talk to research scientists in the field.

We had completed our work in Zones 1 and 2. Our task now was to use the information we had developed to penetrate the fog we had generated for ourselves. In effect, the purely passive work we had carried out was over. Now our client had to approve a deeper foray, using what we referred to as semiactive means, which carried with it some of the advantages of passive intelligence. This was still relatively cheap, since it relied on phone and fax to ping the system in order to locate further information, but it was no longer purely passive. It could be detected.

This posed a dilemma for our investor—one that was inevitable. One of his advantages was the general contempt the field received from most people familiar with it. By being skeptical about it, they left it wide open for someone with enough imagination to see the possibilities and incur the risks. As soon as we went semiactive, we would be alerting people that someone with enough resources to ask the right questions was out there thinking about the business. With luck, we would be dismissed as loons. Without luck, it could start someone else thinking. The more active we became, the more likely we were to be noticed. The more we were noticed, the more likely it was that someone would figure out what we were up to. That risked competition. On the other hand, we could not begin to dissolve the mystery of the laboratory versus field tests without more information, and we had collected all the passive information available.

This is where the client must make the decision. It's not just his money, it's his risk. The move from passive to any sort of active intelligence is an extremely serious business decision. It has the potential to reshape the competitive environment. In many cases, the client focuses on the increased immediate cost. It's important to redirect his attention to the real potential cost—losing the element of surprise. In this case, the need for information, and the presumed protection provided by contempt, decided us on a semiactive attack.

> **Push the passive to the limits. It's not only cheaper, but it preserves the element of surprise until the last possible moment. The extra time bought could be the difference between an IPO (initial public offering) and being DOA (dead on arrival).**

We proceeded in two directions. The first was trying to find out what had happened in the navy tests and what was going on in the coast guard tests. We began by calling the offices that had conducted the tests. A Pentagon directory is handy and can be purchased. We made call after call—mostly to people who had no idea what we were talking about. But no call was a dead end. We insisted on a referral to their best guess as to who would be of use.

Remember, Department of Defense midlevel officials are civil servants. They are genuinely committed to helping the public. If you don't believe that, then believe this: They live in dread of a civilian complaint. Most civil servants go for years without getting a call from outside their department. So getting one is not a minor event. Getting a call from a civilian looking for information rather than trying to sell something is extremely rare. Getting a call from a civilian who is polite, firm, and seems to know about a study that was done by his department—in other words, someone knowledgeable—is extraordinarily rare. You will not be ignored.

The person at the other end will try to please you, first because it breaks up a boring day, and second because he wants you to go away and making you happy is the best way to achieve this.

> **On the whole, midlevel officials are more likely than not to be helpful if you let them know that you are not a crank, if you are polite, and if you behave as if you expect them to help you. Make it clear that you're not going away.**

We finally found the right official. He was in charge of bilge water for the navy. No joke. We couldn't make this up.

He knew everything there was to know about the navy's experience with magnets to treat calcification in water containers. He was the navy's institutional memory on this—and the coast guard's as well. They had clamped all sorts of magnets on pipes, but they had no effect. He mentioned several studies, most of which we had. He offered to send us some others. He was a delight to speak to and most helpful. We were polite and genuinely interested in his job.

He also told us that he wished the damned things would work, as the navy has all sorts of problems with calcification, and it costs a fortune to prevent it and repair the damage. But he also said that the navy was not going to fund any more research and development on the subject, and that the coast guard trials were the last as far as he was concerned. He said that from here on out, the navy would rely on private industry's validation of any new technology. He named several trade and professional associations with national reputations that conduct tests on new concepts. He told us that if one of those oversaw the tests, and the tests came back positive, they would give the product another try. But he said that he couldn't believe the successful studies we cited for him, since they had tried these magnets over and over and they never worked.

Second, we went to our literature and located the leading researchers in the area. Deciding that our client probably would not fund a trip to Japan—and figuring the Japanese wouldn't talk to us anyway—and that we really didn't want a trip to Siberia, where the Russian research team was huddling, we went to some American researchers. We found a couple of professors toiling away in a fine university who blew us away with what they knew. Delighted at getting a free lunch at a Holiday Inn, they told us about the work they had done in the magnetic treatment of water—and the magnetic treatment of other fluids as well. When we mentioned the navy tests they laughed. The navy had clamped magnets on the outside of metal pipes. What the hell did they expect? Metal screws up a magnetic field. They had never put the magnets on the inside, allowing water to flow over them. They went on to explain how and why it works. And on and on. See, no one had ever listened to them before.

They had been under contract to several small companies to do work in the area, they told us. They gave us the names of the companies. They showed us the contracts. They told us everything we needed to know, and many things that we really didn't need to know. In the end, we understood why the gadgets had worked in the labs, why the in-line magnets used by our client did in fact work, and why most other tests inevitably failed. We also learned about the kind of water the magnets would work in, and the kind they wouldn't work in. We learned about other uses, some of them mightily weird, some promising. And we learned that we were sitting across from the knowledge base of a new industry.

Step 7: Final Analysis and Evaluation

We now had a final report, that could have looked like this:

FINDINGS

1. Laboratory tests consistently provided positive results.
2. These tests were always carried out with in-line magnets.
3. Navy tests were conducted with clamp-ons, which don't work.
4. Fly-by-night companies sold clamp-ons or magnets inappropriate to the water conditions.

5. The navy would buy magnets if they were validated by an industry or professional group.

6. These are the names and phone numbers of scientists who would be happy to work with you.

EVALUATION

1. This is a valid product, but there is substantial risk, because further research and development (R&D) is needed to define the exact circumstances under which the product will work.

2. In addition to R&D costs, the client will need to underwrite testing and evaluation (T&E) for validation.

3. The danger is that with successful R&D and T&E, a large corporation will come in with its own product—leaving you to defend your patents against their deep pockets.

RECOMMENDATION

1. The only protection is to create and dominate a market before anyone notices.

2. Be prepared with full and substantial financing before beginning.

3. Protect yourself against R&D/T&E failure, then blitz on success.

Now, we could have handed in this one page and let it go at that. But clients don't like to pay five figures for one page. So we padded it out with really nice tables and charts, built an appendix, went down to Office Depot and bought an attractive cover—but this was the basic report. Either be prepared to blitz this with a lot of financing in hand, or figure that you'll get eaten alive by a big company who'll wait until you complete the research and development, see how the market develops, and if they like what they see, beat you to it. It is important to remember that months of intelligence work can sometimes boil down to just a single word, "yes."

There is no correlation between the amount of material provided and its importance or cost.

This left our client with a dilemma: Did he really want to take the risk? He approached us with a proposition. Would we take a piece of the business in return for our working with the scientists, developing the strategic plan, and so on. Well, it was attractive. And we were attracted. But this was a line we tried not to cross. It was the line between collection and analysis on the one hand and operations on the other. We were professional pessimists. Even in the midst of a successful report, we retained our naturally gloomy cast. If we were to get involved operationally, we would have to become optimists, cheerleaders—downright positive thinkers. And then we'd lose our edge. Pushing temptation aside, we declined.

We are, as a company, institutionally pessimistic. Businessmen are institutionally optimistic. We cross that line at our peril and that of our clients. This is why some of the authors of this book are intelligence people and some run businesses. It gives balance.

Step 8: Archive and Database

The project is not completed until every bit of information you've gathered is archived—put away somewhere—and databased—organized in such a way that it is accessible. This requires discipline. By the time you're finished with a project like this, you are usually utterly bored by it. The temptation is to chuck everything into a closet, lock the closet, and lose the key. It is often assumed that you'll never need the material again. It is absolutely surprising how often such material is needed under the most unlikely circumstances. For example, we never expected to be writing a book on business intelligence and never expected to use this as an example. The reason we could, and did, was that we shoved everything *else* into a closet and can't find the key anywhere. *This* information we archived and databased.

Archiving and databasing are made easier by the fact that so much of our information originated in electronic format or wound up in electronic format—after we reworked it, scanned it, or wrote it up. We will be dealing extensively with the database problem in coming chapters. For now, we will assert that our archives and databases are our institutional memory, and that, as the years go on, we need to do less and less because we have these archives to draw on. They must be part of any company's intelligence and knowledge management program.

CONCLUSION

In taking you through the intelligence cycle and the story of the magnetic water treatment, we wanted to pause and give you an overview of the intelligence project. This is, of course, a particular and idiosyncratic project. But that is the nature of every intelligence project. We found that we could not think up one that was both useful and generic. There is a generic process, but not a generic project. Every business intelligence project is idiosyncratic.

That is why the process itself is so important. The process, which obviously is not meant to be followed slavishly, is designed to provide a method that can be used as a general template. And it is designed to focus attention on some of the issues and trade-offs of the intelligence process. Now we will examine various types of information and how to find them.

And what happened to the product? Our client understood clearly what we were saying and bailed out. What we had said was that there was real potential and lots of risk—and that if you were going to be in for a penny you had to be in for a pound. He decided that he would rather put in pounds somewhere else, and he did.

We regarded this as successful work. More often than not, successful intelligence provides the decision maker with information that dissuades him from doing something that he is not really comfortable with. We had shown him the extent of the needed commitment, he evaluated his interests and resources and decided not to go. Our success lay in showing him what the total cost would look like before he took the plunge. In many business ventures, the total cost emerges only over the course of time, frequently wrecking not only the project but the finances of the principals. One of the things intelligence does is save you from mission creep, the nasty process in which a small hobby turns into a man-eating bear. Intelligence work is frequently more defense than offense. That's good enough for us. And the check cleared.

4

FIND YOURSELF

Tapping Internal Resources

The information explosion has left companies with a crisis of confidence. Companies of all sizes are aware of the enormous amount of information available, and are terrified of making the wrong decision because they missed an important fact. In a sense, this crisis of confidence was inevitable. The growing availability of information caught most businesses unaware. It was as if the sky had suddenly starting raining information, but there were no buckets to be found. Obviously, a three-man team with a makeshift bucket would grab more money than a hundred men without a clue as to what a bucket was.

The first reaction of many businesses was a stopgap measure—hiring consultants. When the Berlin Wall came tumbling down, opening up the former Warsaw Pact countries to democracy and Western investment, major multinationals immediately went seeking information about new and exciting opportunities. Most of them used major consulting firms in the belief that they had more intelligence and more insights. In many cases this proved not to be the case; in fact, the consulting firms were busy hiring former KGB officers or journalists to provide them with knowledge, much of it out of date. There was also a plethora of conferences, but few of them offered anything new. In the end, businesses would have to develop bigger and better buckets of their own so that the information flowing into a company could be captured and stored. And most important, a system would have to be put in place that would allow that information to be sorted, accessed, and turned into knowledge.

Any business intelligence system must begin by utilizing the information within the company that results from the normal process of doing business. This is not only the most cost effective information, but it is also the most precious and nonreplicable— such as a salesman's knowledge of another company, or a scientist's knowledge of a technology. Information is constantly pouring into your business, but most of it is lost, tossed away, or forgotten. In other cases, the sheer pressure of work on senior executives and entrepreneurs means that they have no time to keep a proper record of even significant in-house meetings.

The first stop in shopping for information is at home. Most of what you need to know is there. Finding material you already own, however, is sometimes more difficult than buying it again.

Finding information may be as easy as checking a computer file, a desk drawer, or a Rolodex. But if no one knows it's there, it may as well be on the other side of the moon. The larger the company the harder it is to locate the person who might have the information needed and also the knowledge to interpret it. The foundation of any intelligence system is a structure for making certain that information available inside a business is made accessible to decision makers.

Several examples come to mind:

- A company we know in the chemical industry had recently divested itself of a division that was a large part of the company. Being flush with cash, it was time to consider new acquisitions inside the industry. Obviously, the acquisitions it made would determine the focus of this company for a long time—it was a defining moment. Although the company was stocked with thousands of people who had done nothing but eat, drink, and sleep chemicals, the company turned to outside consultants for advice. None of the information, knowledge, or insight of these outside consultants came close to equaling the huge amount of information and expertise they had within their own company.

- Another company wanted to present itself to stock market analysts. It needed to maintain its share price in the light of some potentially unfavorable short-term results. So it decided to put together a very nice visual presentation, and hired PR consultants to do it. However, in getting the material on the company, the consultancy had to undertake a detailed internal study because senior management did not have enough information in hand to provide the PR firm.

- Yet another example was the subsidiary of a public company that heard that a much larger organization on another continent was seriously interested in a strategic alliance. The chief executive of the larger company, who was something of a celebrity, planned to visit with them. Over the years, the smaller company had amassed a great deal of information about the potential partner, most of it gained from a long-term, close working relationship. Yet when the day came to dig out this information, it had all been filed so chaotically that it could not be found, and executives had to engage in a mad scramble to learn the essentials.

There are always good and obvious reasons to go to outsiders. Among the better ones: to fill some defined areas of knowledge that your own company lacks; to serve as a reality check on your own reasoning; to deal with matters that involve extremely sensitive issues that must be kept secret within the business, such as a decision to fire everyone and shut down. But many businesses turn to outsiders for baseline information and knowledge. They are not filling in blanks or having a "B-Team"—a second team—to check their answers. They are using outsiders to provide information and knowledge on a regular basis. This is sometimes necessary because the company has downsized to the point of losing its own knowledge base, and they now have to rent an expert where previously they had one on staff. The problem of the outside consultant is a major issue in business today, particularly with downsizing. Internal intelligence systems may wind up cheaper in the long run—and be more effective—than hiring outside consultants.

CONTEXT AND NUANCE, DIFFUSION AND DISSIPATION

Every member of your staff, including yourself, is an intelligence gatherer. Indeed, your staff is the most efficient gatherer of intelligence, because it does so simply in the course of doing its job—or even when not officially on the job. A salesman having drinks in the hotel bar may not be selling much, but he may be picking up invaluable information. E-mail, phone calls, lunches, trade journals, high school class reunions, and illicit affairs can all cut into the amount of time your staff devotes to their primary activity. But these activities can provide a critically important stream of intelligence for your company.

Looking for and finding information is not nearly as easy as it might appear. There are two problems in retrieving information from within the company.

Problem 1: Not recognizing the significance of information.

A mail-room clerk at a local bank has a girlfriend who works in accounts receivable in a restaurant supply house. She calls him and says she has to work late that night—she's been ordered to generate a list of all outstanding receivables by the morning—so she won't be able to go to the body-piercing parlor with him that night. Bummer. Now, the local bank was working with a client who was preparing a buyout offer for the restaurant supply house. They had been working quietly, waiting for the right moment, not in any rush. The banker spearheading the project would probably like to know that the company needs to generate a financial statement by morning, including all receivables. This is not an everyday event. The stealth buyout is about to get blindsided.

The mail clerk is oblivious to the significance of this information. He has no idea that the bank is participating in a financing package for another group. All he cares about is his girl and body piercing. The vice president managing the deal doesn't know the mail clerk, and if he did, it wouldn't occur to him to ask the boy how his girlfriend is doing. So here we have a critical piece of information in the hands of a company employee who hasn't the slightest idea that it's important, and an executive who badly needs to know this fact but is not in a position to issue an urgent plea to all employees for information. First, this is a secret bid and asking would mean blowing confidentiality, and second, he would be deluged with information and wouldn't be able to extract what was important from the mess.

This is, in a sense, a classic problem of intelligence. The information is in the hands of a company employee, but light years away from the decision maker.

Problem 2: The important information can be lost in the diffusion of gossip.

Here is the paradox. Gossip is an extremely efficient method for gathering information but an extremely inefficient way to distribute it. Gossip basically represents the diffusion of information in a nearly undifferentiated soup. The mail clerk's conversation mentioned the late-night mission in accounts receivable, gossip about some friends breaking up, night classes at the local community college, and a report of an upcoming concert by Night Crawlers. And this is only one conversation of many in a day. A tremendous amount of information is transferred with very little overhead.

The inefficiency cuts in during the diffusion process. As you would expect, what is extracted depends on the interests of the discussant. Of the list above, the only thing the mail clerk cares about is the inability of his girlfriend to go and pierce body parts that night. So when the gossip is passed on from the mail room, the most important news, from the company standpoint, is lost, filtered out by the mail clerk's indifference. In the end, the low-overhead collection process becomes a near total loss to the company.

The problem is not in collecting information, but in organizing and controlling it once it comes into the company. Consider some examples:

- Every day, hundreds of ads are dropped on people's desks, delivered without effort to the business by the U.S. Postal Service. As a rule of thumb, almost none of the mail is of immediate interest to the recipient at the moment he gets it, so he dumps it in the trash. Yet almost all of it is of interest to someone in the company. One day, we needed a program that would allow us to show graphically how a decision tree branches—down to a level where there would be hundreds of thousands of nodes. We searched the Internet, called friends, pinged all the zones we could think of. It took us nearly a week to find a software package that would do. It was FedExed to us. As we were opening it, one of our staff looked at it and said, "Oh, yeah, that one. I got a flyer on that a couple of weeks ago. Looked interesting." We let him live.

- Every day, members of your company make phone calls. Each phone call provides information soup to that person. The more frequently a number is called, the thicker the soup, as relationships develop and information not directly related to the issue at hand is discussed. As important as information, context and nuance are created through these conversations. But content is retransmitted randomly, as interoffice gossip, stripped of its subtleties—if it is passed on at all.

- Departments within companies regularly take on projects focusing on some aspect of a problem. For example, our company's accounting crew once studied ways to bring down our extremely high, on-line service costs. They looked at what each service offered in order to locate the lowest cost provider or find acceptable substitutes for higher-priced services. A while later we were asked by a company to study their on-line information providers to make certain they were getting the best value. The research department was tasked with the study because it knew a great deal about the services. However, no one in research knew about the extensive accounting study, even though they had followed their recommendations, with the result that loads of man-hours were wasted in reinventing the wheel. All of the information was already within the company, along with a cogent analysis. Gossip hadn't alerted research about accounting's knowledge, and unnecessary labor—and lost profits—were the result. This wasn't supposed to happen to us. We learned from it.

- A company for which one of us once worked needed to invite fifty top European industrialists to a dinner. We knew their names and companies from a publication, but not their addresses. We did not own a directory, though there might have been one somewhere in the head office. Instead, we sent a researcher to a business library for half a day to copy out the addresses, whereas within ten feet of the secretary preparing the invitations was a computer terminal with an on-line European corporate database.

Each of these problems derives from an inherent inefficiency of communications within a company. Efficiency requires a division of labor in which there is as little overlap as possible. In a well-run business, people are hired to perform fairly specific tasks, and most employees are too busy doing their own jobs to do anyone else's. The result is minimal communication. Most communication is regarded as leisure—necessary overhead but not essential to the job. As a result, the efficient and focused organization tends to duplicate effort, reinventing the wheel regularly because of their very focus and efficiency.

Indeed, the farther apart two individuals are on the organizational structure—vertically or horizontally—the less likely information is to be successfully transmitted. Consider the example of the mail-room clerk and the vice president. The odds of the two of them meeting in any given week is minimal. The odds of them exchanging information is almost nil. The probability of the mail-room clerk having sufficient context to recognize the importance of his data and taking the initiative of transmitting it is similarly unlikely. There is even a low probability of two widely separated executives—say, the director of marketing for one set of products, and the personnel director at another company site—recognizing and transmitting information laterally.

As a result, information comes into the company and dissipates. Now, there is no perfect solution to this problem. Ideally, there would be a magic box into which everything known to everyone in a company would flow—with no additional cost to the company. Questions could be asked of the magic box and an answer would be provided. But the perfect magic box is not going to be created. The probability of the mail-room clerk having an important bit of information in a year is minimal, so the cost of debriefing him would probably outweigh the benefits produced and would cripple the mail room. Nevertheless, the magic box idea is useful as a tool for defining the problem and posing some less-than-perfect solutions. The focus of such a system is not on collection but on retention and distribution. This is the heart of the business intelligence problem, just as it is the heart of the national intelligence problem. Critical information is either not recognized as important or not transmitted to people who could act on it.

Consider one of the most famous examples. There were officials in Washington who had clear indication that the Japanese were going to attack the United States. These were not the highest-ranking officials, but relatively minor intelligence officers. First, they had trouble convincing themselves that the information was valid. Then they had the devil of a time getting the attention of senior officials in Washington. Then these senior officials were unable to transmit sufficiently clear orders to Pearl Harbor. The internal communication system, from receptors to decision makers to key outposts, was simply not geared for the rapid internal transmission of information.

Focusing on the collection system, spies and satellites and the other paraphernalia, is worthless unless the information they gather can be sent to the appropriate points, analyzed, and distributed. Frankly, if we had to choose between tripling the efficiency of collection or doubling the efficiency of internal dissemination, we'd easily go with the latter.

In creating efficient intelligence, increases in internal retention and distribution increase efficiency geometrically. Increases in collection increase efficiency arithmetically.

Imagine a particular bit of information and ask this question: Is that information more valuable in one person's possession or in the hands of five people? The answer is obvious. Now imagine five bits of information in the hands of one person or one piece of information in the hands of five people. Which is worth more? This makes the situation more complex. A single bit of information may have value, but its value increases as its context increases. Take the case of our mail-room clerk. The information—about his girlfriend working late—had very little value by itself. It became valuable only in the context of other information—only in the hands of someone who had perspective on the matter at hand and the authority and interest to do something about it. It is extremely difficult to predict the precise matrix in which a particular bit of information will have value. There really was no way of knowing, just by looking at that information, where value would be found.

This means that the probability of any bit of information being fully exploited increases as it is embedded in the largest number of contexts. One bit of information in the hands of five people yields five information matrices to provide information. Five pieces of different information in the hands of one person provides only one matrix to provide content—albeit a context enriched by five pieces of information. Let's say that five people have equal amounts of different information, with a value of N. Let's say that a piece of information is found with a value smaller than N: X. Now, in a very simple model, let's say that the potential value of X is its relationship with each individual component of N, which is to say that its value is in linking it to every other bit of information. This is not altogether true, because not every link will prove fruitful; but on the other hand, this ignores the increased values of links with combinations of information.

That would mean that the value of any bit of information inside a given matrix would be X^N—an exponential value. Exposing to multiple matrices, increasing the number of contexts it appears in—say, giving the information to five people, all with different information—would create a value of X^{5N}. Giving one person five pieces of information, on the other hand, would create a value of $5X^N$. If graphed it would appear as follows:

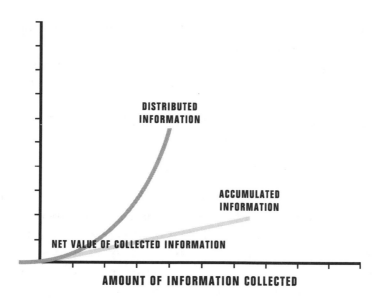

DISTRIBUTED
INFORMATION

ACCUMULATED
INFORMATION

NET VALUE OF COLLECTED INFORMATION

AMOUNT OF INFORMATION COLLECTED

All of which is an extremely pretentious way of saying that letting a lot of people look at a little information is better than having one person look at a lot of information. The key is in the efficient distribution of information—even more than it is on the collection of information.

Companies naturally accumulate information. The value of this information is rarely realized because the information realizes its full value only when it is embedded in other information. The more information matrices in which it is embedded, the more valuable the information becomes. Most information collected as a by-product fails to accumulate anywhere in the company. It is collected by a person who does not know enough to understand its value, and its life ends there. It rarely diffuses to enough people to maximize its value.

As a result of this, most companies look for information outside the company, not only for necessary information that is unavailable in the company but for information in general. Most companies might accept the premise that the people with the most substantial knowledge of the business and its needs already work for the company, but they also believe that internally accumulated information is so diffused that it cannot be harnessed efficiently.

Therefore, rather than building internal systems for distributing accumulated information, they turn outside.

This costs more than simply the cost of repurchasing information. It carries an additional price. Outsiders may have a richer collection of exogenous facts—about the industry, business in general, politics, regulations, or whatever—than insiders do. But outsiders, by definition, lack the same information set as insiders; their matrix is never as rich as those possessed by insiders. Why, you might ask, is this important? The crucial factor here is that context and critical nuance are missed. The reason this appears necessary to managers is the realization that this advantage derives from their focus on collecting information on these external events. Managers are therefore willing to buy this information—and analysis—outside, thereby sacrificing the finely textured context needed to apply it to the particular company. As a result, there is rarely synergy between the outside consultant's knowledge and the precise reality of the company. At best, two information sets—one from the consultants, the other from the executive—come together on one or a few desks. Most consultant reports land in a file cabinet, and executives continue to fly blind.

The key problem has been the inability of businesses to recognize the amount of information being collected and dissipated, along with a sense that it was impossible to accumulate and distribute this vast amount of information—or that the costs of accumulation and distribution, both in terms of time and money, would outweigh the benefits. Information controls, we would argue, are as valuable as cost controls or any other efficiency matters. The key is not to overreach. The goal is not complete, but increased, accumulation and distribution. And, as in many things, the first and simplest measures can show the greatest returns.

COLLECTION, INFORMATION, KNOWLEDGE

We've all seen movies like *2001* and *Three Days of the Condor,* or TV shows like "Star Trek." Each featured a magic box. You could ask virtually any question. It knew everything, including what it is that you meant when you asked a question. For example, on "Star Trek," a question such as "What is out there?" would be understood by the computer as referring to that strange object coming at you at the speed of light, and not the little particles of dust surrounding your ship or the stars all around you or the almost limitless other objects that "out there" could refer to. In reality, the magic box had the understanding and ability to provide context and nuance that a human being has, with the addition of a perfect memory and unlimited knowledge.

This defines the problem perfectly: Human understanding is indispensable for turning information into knowledge; on the other hand, human beings suffer from insufficient information and memory. A single human being cannot possibly absorb or store all the information needed to answer the questions put to the magic box. To put it in computer terms, a human being may have enough RAM, and even powerful enough programs to manage information, but he doesn't have nearly enough disk space, nor enough input devices to store the information.

Every company needs a magic box, but it is impossible to create a machine that knows everything. It is even harder than impossible to create a machine that can understand the question perfectly and can respond unerringly. But it is useful to keep the magic box in mind as a touchstone—an unreachable goal that can nonetheless serve as a standard and a measure.

If you wish to wait until artificial intelligence comes along to solve this problem, we suggest that you find a hobby to while away the time. We suggest watching glaciers move.

That does not mean we have to tolerate the perpetual dissipation of information. Certain computer-based and human-based systems can be instituted to decrease, if not eliminate, the dissipation. In our example of the mail-room clerk and his girlfriend, it is highly unlikely that any system can be devised that would make bringing that information to the vice president's attention anything more than a matter of luck. But creating routines for managing accumulated data can decrease the amount of luck needed and increase the probability that the right information can reach the right person.

For many, indeed most, of these tasks, we will want to use computers. But before we leap to computers, it is important to think about the process without computers.

One solution to this problem is to encourage everyone on your staff to think about the value of things that they've learned and voluntarily pass the information to those they think might be interested. This is certainly something that should be encouraged. Nor is it a trivial improvement. Creating an atmosphere that encourages the identification and dissemination of useful information is an obvious, simple, and rewarding first step. And if you aren't prepared to do that, you might as well forget the rest.

But there is a problem here. It is difficult to recognize important information from the limited standpoint of any single job, particularly those that are uniquely situated to collect information. You can encourage it, but given the limited amount of context, you risk a garbage dump. With the best intentions in the world, people lacking context, who take it upon themselves to bombard others with information they think is valuable, will quickly overwhelm the system with the trivial and the obvious with little benefit. Sometimes when we hire new people in our shop, they get enthusiastic and start dragging in articles from the front page of the *New York Times* or *Newsweek*. They just don't have the context. They're cute—for about a week.

This process needs to be brought under control, and this begins with identifying people in the company who are likely to be collecting information on a routine basis and encouraging them to think more clearly about what they are finding. This also requires context, but to a more limited segment of the workforce, for whom the time and money spent on creating a powerful contextual sense about the company is likely to pay off. This is due to their position in the company and the likelihood that they would remain with the company for an extended period of time, as well as peculiar personal skills that managers can recognize—like being gossips.

Some people, by nature or function, are natural collectors. Identify them and use them.

Every company has a different cadre that you might want to identify as prime collectors—it really depends on the type of business you're in. These people share certain characteristics:

- **Routine heavy exposure**—extremely high exposure to information and events outside the business in the course of their work. This refers to people who deal with large amounts of externally generated material. Salesmen and purchasing people are obvious choices. But a longtime accounts receivable clerk can have a sense of the ebb and flow of other businesses that is more powerful than even the CFO's sense. People who deal with maintenance and real estate issues are similar, and the person who goes to the bank every day picks up the damnedest information.

- **Multidepartmental activities**—people whose tasks involve more than one part of the business. Obviously, in small companies this will include everyone, which is one of the advantages small businesses have over large ones. In large companies, people who process information from various departments are particularly valuable collectors. For example, the clerks who process travel and entertainment vouchers are in a strategic position to recognize potentially valuable information because their position provides context by definition.

- **Longtime personnel.** Every company, at every level, has employees who have been with the company for years before the deluge of information began. These people frequently constitute the company's internal memory. In healthy companies, these people are recognized and rewarded, quite apart from the specific job they are doing, for that institutional role. It is fairly easy to spin that role into the intelligence collector role. If anyone can recognize context, these people can.

So the ideal candidate here is the thirty-year veteran of the purchasing department who takes care of company-wide needs at all levels, but especially in strategically significant purchases, who has seen everything, knows everyone inside the company, and outside as well. Getting this guy to pass along everything he learns that he thinks is of value will obviously be rewarding.

The second best solution is to identify strategic collection points in the company—those departments or segments of departments through which large amounts of information routinely pass. In other words, select departments first, then identify individuals within the departments you would trust with the task of keeping an eye out for significant information and passing it on. Ultimately, you do not want everyone in your company acting as a collector. What you do want is people at strategic points being tasked to act as collectors.

The percentage of people tasked as collectors within any department can and will vary. For example, the sales force is inherently intelligence-oriented. They are in constant contact with the market and are the most sensitive to what competitors might be doing. You might want to designate 100 percent of this group for intelligence gathering. In another department, say among routine assembly workers on an assembly line, the number might be extremely low or even nonexistent. It obviously varies by the type of business activities in which they are engaged. The focus must be on selecting your collectors to maximize the probability of capturing valuable information while minimizing the burden that collection places on your main business.

These people will constitute a relatively small fraction of the workforce who will be doing a value-added service as intelligence collectors. An additional selection criteria will be trustworthiness. They will have to be briefed regularly about what is happening inside the company, and trained and tested to make certain they keep their mouths shut. They will need this briefing in order to recognize what is and what is not important. They can also be tasked to carry out additional searches in their area of expertise.

You cannot have an intelligence service if you don't trust anyone. Certainly, some people will blab about what they've

**learned. But the amount of information you collect will
outweigh that blabbing by several orders of magnitude.**

Information gathering for intelligence is a cultural shift,
requiring a redefinition of value to include knowledge production
and making everyone part of that process. The cultural shift is
needed in order to allow employees to see their designation as a
collector as a reward—a new opportunity to add value to their positions—rather than as a booby prize to be avoided at all costs. The
job of information collector cannot be carried out without
rewards—whether these are immediate financial rewards, increasing the probability of promotion, or something quite different.
Collecting information for the intelligence department can be
incorporated into the general demands of the business, just as
many companies assimilated the idea that safety is everyone's job, or
that customer satisfaction is everyone's responsibility. The rewards
can be shared, too. In one bank we know of, workers in every
department are rewarded if someone brings in a new customer.

If you do not use everyone as an information collector, but
choose to designate only certain people, tensions can arise between
those who are doing their usual jobs and those who are doing both
their job and an added intelligence function. This is more likely to
happen in a department where, say, six people are doing their regular job and the seventh is designated collector of information on
top of his existing position. How do you reward the one who is
doing what is seen as the extra work? And how do you keep jeal-
ousies from arising in those who feel he is getting the more important, or sexier, role? It is important to recognize that you are not
using this person in a primarily intelligence-gathering position. His
primary function remains what it always was; all he's doing is thinking about what he's seeing in a broader context than his colleagues.
It is important not to overdo the sexiness of the task. He is just a collector of information.

There is a more delicate issue here—a paradox that in some
ways cuts to the heart of a business's identity. The more a particular employee derives his value to the business from his role as an
information collector, the greater his value to the intelligence sys-

tem, and the greater his reluctance to transfer valuable information into the company. His value to the company is his knowledge of what is going on in the marketplace. If a salesman is good, he knows his customers, their needs, his competitors and their product lines better than anyone in the business. He is naturally inclined to hold this information close to his vest, out of fear that by transferring it into the company's knowledge base, he would undermine his own value. If the company knew everything he knew, then maybe the company would decide they don't need him.

This is indeed a serious problem. Businesses that would use this transfer against their employees are clearly not going to develop effective intelligence systems. But frankly, companies that treat employees this way will have much bigger problems than lack of intelligence. A culture that would treat employees that way breeds systematic disloyalty throughout the entire structure. Everyone is guarding his own expertise against poaching. The only companies that flourish under this sort of regime are those where employees see themselves as independent businessmen operating under the general umbrella of a company. Examples are sales organizations like real estate companies, stockbrokers, or insurance companies, where salesmen are treated less as members of a team than as competitors and independent entrepreneurs trading part of their commission for a base of operations.

Reassurances and incentives must be made to information-rich personnel in order to induce them to pass information through to the general knowledge base. One of the assurances, particularly with people like salesmen, who are performance-oriented and measure performance in precise quantities, must be that the collection task will not cut into their primary function or that, if it does, suitable compensation will be made. However a company structures this compensation—contests, bonuses, estimates of percentage of time spent on intelligence and appropriate pay—this drives home a critical point. In order for an intelligence system to work, its cost must be rigorously controlled. The system must not become a burden, but be a value generator. It must therefore be kept simple.

Encouraging employees to turn over information requires that businesses resist the temptation to screw their employees.

> **Intelligence is a long-term proposition, and the value of collectors must transcend immediate advantage.**

MINING THE DATA LODE

Imagine that a magic box were a bulletin board by the coffee machine—not necessarily a bad place to post important intelligence—then the collector would have to write it down, carry it down the hall, and post it. Each step takes time. The same with loading the information into a database. Now, these steps might seem trivial, but multiply it by a small fraction of the information rushing at a business and it rapidly becomes a burden. Let's remember an inevitable principle of our era: Everything inflates. There is a natural tendency to think that everything is important, a fear that you might miss something critical. Intelligence inflation is real, and you want to resist it. That's why the first information you should collect and sort is the information you've already got.

Your business has perfectly ordinary, prosaic departments: customer service, ordering, maintenance, and so on. Nothing unique, nothing sexy. Yet, as we've argued, each of these departments, simply in the course of their everyday work, collects information. Your first task in building an intelligence system is using the information gathered in the course of this business to provide you with knowledge about what is going on around you. You are not going to be able to build an actual intelligence system from scratch. What you have to be able to do is to use existing systems in another way. You may use computers in this endeavor, but the real key is redefining the mission and indoctrinating the staff with the new ethic of intelligence.

British Airways is perhaps one of the best illustrations of the successful collection, retention, and distribution of information within a company. BA's success has been the creation of a system that involves all employees and staff in the collection and dissemination of information about their product: customer care in the airlines. Sir Colin Marshall, chairman of British Airways, is a great proponent of the argument that global communication and technology should not replace the human side in the ability of a business to practice professional customer care. He states: "The secret of success will always depend on the creativity that is put into the use of information."

British Airways now has one of the biggest information and communications systems in the world, with more than 200,000 terminals linked to mainframe computers. The airline employs 2,200 information technology staff, spending on it more than £150 million a year—about $245 million—the equivalent of two Boeing 747 aircraft. BA has many different databases, but they are turning toward data warehousing to create more specific use information centers to aid in analysis. BA is trying to create a system that is accessible and useful to the customer as well as the company internally.

Prior to its privatization and when in British government ownership, BA's knowledge of its customers and their wants and habits was almost negligible. After privatization, British Airways introduced a program called Putting People First, where they refocused the whole company around the customer and his needs. The BA staff are trained to work with their management to increase sales and customer loyalty. They collect information on the likes and dislikes of passengers, on their travel habits, and on how they rate their service on the actual flights. Senior managers get involved in customer-listening forums and listening in on phone calls from customers. Senior managers also discuss customer service problems with the customer relations department, which has set up a Care Line for customers to express their satisfaction or dissatisfaction with their service. It's always easy to listen to positive feedback from customers, such as when they call to report good service on a flight; the hard part is listening to them when they're unhappy or irate.

BA takes the attitude that the department of customer relations is the "customer champion" department, and its goal is to keep customers happy, thereby keeping their business. Good customers of the airline receive a birthday card on the appropriate date sending them the airline's best wishes, and informing them that, as a reward for being such good BA customers, they are being given an extra five hundred air miles. Essentially, the marketing tools have two purposes: One is to keep the customer happy; the other is to open a line of communication to the customer. This means that the customer service rep is a prime information collector—and one with potentially enough context and nuance to sort and distribute the information he collects.

Complaints are critically important intelligence. Just collecting complaints, however, is obviously not enough. It is most important not to let these complaints diffuse and get lost once they enter the company. BA has a system to collect, track, and enter information in its database—passenger complaints as well as habits and wishes. Instead of seeing complaints as a pain to deal with, or an area of failure, BA sees the customers as doing it a favor by reporting any problems they have had. How else are they going to know if they have unhappy customers? They also try to deal with them efficiently, responding as quickly as possible.

British Airways developed their own analytic side of the company that objectively evaluates the operations part. This B Team, called a marketplace performance unit, is totally separate from the marketing, selling, and operating part of the company. This unit views BA from the perspective of the customer, independently judging and measuring its performance. It was recognized that the operational side of BA—the crew and staff who interact with the customers—needed feedback on their service. But in the service business it is hard to get reliable data. Apart from evaluation and feedback from its B Team, BA gets customer feedback by handing out survey cards to all their passengers and taking random samples from those who have arrived at their destination. This gives a customer an opportunity to comment on his experiences flying with British Airways. The service director is the one in charge of the cabin crew, and he and the crew use the information from the filled-out cards to evaluate their strengths and weaknesses in meeting their goals for customer satisfaction.

British Airways uses its various clubs as collectors of information. What the British Airways Executive Club actually amounts to is a very extensive and useful database. The airline knows where and when you travel, whether you travel alone or with company, where you live and work, where you stay when you're away on business or pleasure, your nationality and passport number, the name and address of your travel agent, the identity of your secretary, the type of car you like to rent, and an assortment of other pieces of information, some of it useless but much of it relevant to route planning and customer service. The basic data is, of course, gathered from Executive Club application forms, which can be updated every time you make a reservation. From time to time, mailings or conversations with a trained reservations agent will elicit more detailed personal information, such as where you would like to go for a vacation.

A senior media person in a British company received a friendly letter from a computer posing as a senior executive of the airline, noting that he had often traveled in one direction on British Airways on any given trip but seldom in both directions. Was there something wrong? To give him incentive to use BA for both legs of any journey, the Executive Club offered him double air miles on his next round-trip. A few weeks later his secretary received an invitation to join the BA executive travelers' Personal Assistant association. This provided a monthly newsletter detailing changes in scheduling, a special reservations number, and the opportunity to win free trips.

The airline's success in establishing and using its database system is all the more remarkable because it has been achieved at modest cost. BA's chairman was astute when he recognized that the development of new technologies would give the airlines more competitive ability in real terms, at less cost, than they ever imagined. Everything is centered around the collection, storage, and analysis of information to provide better-quality service for their passengers, thereby ultimately increasing the company's profits.

As the British Airways example shows, data already being created are often primarily numbers being crunched—and that's extremely useful. What we are suggesting, however, goes a bit beyond that. What is being tracked here is knowledge before it gets loaded into computers, by tracking the traces of such knowledge. This material can serve as the core of a magic box into which a wide variety of material can be loaded.

Some of it is immediately usable, such as sales reports to track the sales of your product in various regions and in various product lines. But there is other information inside your company that you get regularly, use for certain purposes, and let go. For example, think about your phone bill. You receive regular itemized records of all your calls, either as a printout or, at your request, as computerized data. Accounting goes over the bills in order to make sure that it's coming in within budget, that people aren't calling Tibet on personal business, and to make certain that your phone company is giving you a good deal. This kind of prepackaged information comes in the door regularly and is available in formats that can be fed directly into your personal computer (PC).

This is information that is generally computerized to begin with, so there is little or no overhead cost involved in getting it loaded up. In most companies, these datasets are used only for their original purpose—accounting, sales, and such. They are rarely made accessible to people outside those departments. This means that while the direct utilization of information does occur—and occurs with a high degree of efficiency—the indirect use of information is neglected. Put a bit differently: We create information for a reason. But information can provide knowledge over and above intentions, if it is made accessible.

Consider a fairly simple and straightforward case. One of the biggest problems in any company is finding someone who knows someone. Let's say you have decided to try to sell something to a new company. Obviously, a cold call is not nearly as good as starting with someone with whom you already have some sort of relationship. Finding such a contact is a critical part of the sales process. Assume that no one on the marketing team has ever had any dealings with anyone at that company. In a large economy like the American or European, this isn't unusual. The next step is to find someone within your own company who has a contact. Sometimes this works. Sometimes, particularly in larger companies, asking around doesn't help.

The problem is the same as in our mail-room clerk/banker example. Information may be present in a company, written in someone's Rolodex, embedded in someone's brain. The owner of the information doesn't know of the need for the information. There may be somebody over in engineering whose closest friend is in charge of buying the stuff that the marketing people want to sell.

The engineer would probably love to pick up brownie points—and his friend would at least be prepared to give a hearing. It's a perfect situation except for the fact that the marketing folks never heard of the guy in engineering and that guy has no idea that his knowledge is needed.

Now, one way to solve this problem is to have everyone enter into a database everybody they know. Sounds good, but it will never work. Apart from privacy issues, people are just not going to keep these databases updated. Like many such postings, it sounds good, but the database would very quickly become stale. Positive feedback systems, systems that require active, voluntary cooperation by large numbers of people, simply don't work in cases where there is no clear use of any given action.

Databases abound. People who bother to use them are rare.

This is a place where the indirect use of information is important. Question: How is it possible to identify people with contacts in other companies, without having them actively identify themselves or without using informal means, like gossip. Answer: Look at the means that people use to stay in contact with other people. No rocket science needed: People stay in contact using the telephone. Friends stay in touch. Modern telephone systems can track even local calls, either internally or from telephone bills. Check them. The bills were not created in order to track relationships, but this is an extremely effective unintended use. If you want to know if someone has any contacts over at XYZ Corp. and asking your four closest colleagues doesn't yield anything useful, then find out the phone numbers used at XYZ Corp. and check your billing records. If you find an employee who regularly calls someone over at XYZ, you've got a pretty good indication that he knows someone over there. Maybe your employee can help you get in over the wall. Sometimes it's just a case of pawing through old phone bills. But since most of the information produced by the phone company and your own phone system is in digital form already, it can readily be loaded into a database and mined.

What we are really talking about here is constructing intelligence systems out of existing material to track expertise within your own company—and knowing people in the industry is very much a variety of expertise. Nothing is wasted more regularly—or more expensively—than expertise. People within your company have a tremendous amount of knowledge that goes far beyond their job description. Usually, this unexpected gold is found accidentally, or when you have a particularly aggressive and insightful employee. Usually it is never found.

The first and most important mission of an intelligence system is the location of information and knowledge within your own company. That is not as difficult as it may sound. People with knowledge and skills leave tracks. In this case, phone records can reveal that someone in your company has a contact in a company you want to sell to. Those same phone records will tell you if there is anyone who knows anything about a particular government agency, the stock market—anything that requires telephone contact. The phone call is the activity. The phone bill is the direct result, designed to get accounts payable to generate payment. But that same bill is a place where experts leave evidence of expertise—and they can be tracked, with or without computers. The phone bill allows you to infer things that are valuable.

Phone bills are just one example of traces inevitably left by experts that can allow you to locate internal expertise. Here are some other sources of information, found in most companies, that can be used to track expertise:

- Purchase orders, listing who purchased what and where can tell you who in your company knows about particular technologies. If someone has been ordering a lot of database software, he might be the one to discuss your own database needs.

- Travel and entertainment vouchers, listing where employees traveled and who they had meals with. You can use this as you use your telephone bills, but since the purposes of travel and entertainment are usually included, this is an even richer lode of information. By hooking this into a CD-ROM–based yellow pages, each person's company can be identified with an industry. Run a computer check for everyone who has had lunch with real estate specialists in Seattle and you might find someone in your company able to discuss expansions in that market.

- Interview records: Your human resources office is constantly conducting interviews and constantly collecting information on people. Entered into a database, the applications job-seekers fill out can contain valuable information. Let's say you have a sudden influx of people applying for jobs who previously worked for one of your customers. Worrisome— and definitely something you want to know about. Now, even four or five applicants from that company can be significant, but not if they're lost in a fairly large human resources department. Collecting these and analyzing patterns is not why you are collecting these files, but they are certainly an outstanding use.

All of these represent another use for an existing data source. It's cheap because you're collecting it anyway. The only thing you are paying for is the interrogation system—the mechanism that allows you to ask questions. The list of sources isn't exhaustive. Just look over the files you maintain in your own business to get a sense of what treasures you have. Then think through what other information could be inferred from those records and create a system— from a shoe box to a mainframe—to track what is going on in your own company.

So, for example, if we find that John Smith over in information systems called XYZ Corp. on average four times a month for the past year, traveled there once, took two XYZ Corp. employees to lunch, and purchased several of its products, the chances are that Mr. Smith knows quite a bit about XYZ. Before you make your cold call on XYZ, sales might want to chat with Mr. Smith. Mr. Smith might even be tasked to gather more specific information. But without what we might call an inferential data system (and doesn't that sound grand for some files in a shoe box), how will sales find out about Mr. Smith?

The most valuable data in your company, therefore, is the data

that you are collecting anyway—so that it doesn't cost you anything—and from which you can infer other useful facts. The most
important of these facts is always expertise. Tapping into the knowledge base of your company should always be the first step in an
intelligence operation. First, the answer is probably right there. Second, if anybody can find the information you need, it's the one who
already knows an awful lot about the system.

BUILDING THE MAGIC BOX

There are, therefore, two types of important information captured
by businesses. One is direct information—the kind of information
that can be captured directly by collectors. The other is indirect
information—from which unanticipated knowledge can be inferred. Both are being collected. The problem is that information
is not getting to the right people. The collectors frequently can't
recognize the value of the information that they've gotten hold of
and the decision makers don't know what information there is available or who has it in hand. This is not a problem of collection but
of organizing and providing access to collected information. Businesses simply need to continue what they are doing in order to collect it. What they need to change is what they do with the
information after they've collected it.

A systematic means of disseminating information is critical.
The system can be extremely simple or sophisticated, but it must be
able to achieve certain definite functions:

- The information must be disseminated quickly enough to
  permit action. It must be well positioned on the knowledge curve.

- The information must have some degree of targeting without
  losing the exponential advantage we have discussed. This is
  difficult to achieve, but important. You do not want to inflict
  a daily information dump on everyone, because important
  information will tend to get lost or the entire process will be

ignored. On the other hand, you want to achieve the widest, appropriate, distribution of information possible.

■ The information must be preserved in some archival form, so that it is retained for consultation over time.

■ The archive must be queriable—it must be organized in such a way that the information base of the business grows over time.

A basic, notional outline of the internal business intelligence would look like the chart below.

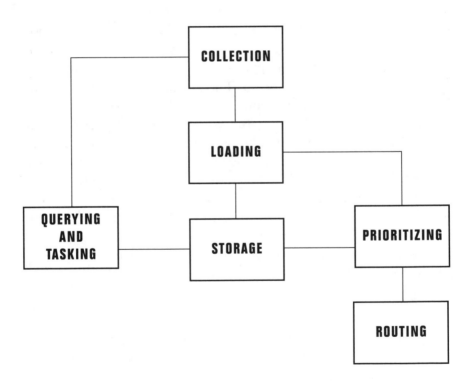

INTERNAL INTELLIGENCE MANAGEMENT

There are four general approaches to information/knowledge distribution:

- Send everything to everyone.
- Have the collector route the material.
- Have a central control on distribution.
- Create a pull system where information consumers decide what they want to see.

Each of these systems has drawbacks. The first gives us information overload, in the second the collector makes decisions he may not be qualified to make, the third increases overhead by creating a central office, the fourth assumes that the consumer will know what is available before he sees the material. Put simply, what is to be done with all the information accumulated?

The first, simpler, part is the question of what to do with the information by those who have sufficient context and sophistication to be able to recognize its true significance. This is a problem of knowledge management, since the information has already been turned into knowledge in the collector's mind. The second, more complex, issue is what is to be done with the pure information— information that has been collected but has not been recognized as valuable by the collector.

The first case is easier to manage, since the only question here is whether the knowledge should be directly forwarded to an appropriate recipient or whether it should be transmitted to a central point for prioritizing and routing. Although different, these two strategies are compatible. One of the advantages of a small business is that the collector who recognizes the value of the information he has found will be in a position to identify the optimal user of the information.

In the larger company, this becomes a much more serious problem. There is a point in the growth of a company where everyone is no longer familiar with everyone else. This normally begins with newer, junior employees being unknown to older hands. At the next stage, middle managers cease to know other middle managers, but can still identify senior management—although they might have declining access to them. In some companies, senior management ceases to have direct contact or even full knowledge of other senior management and their responsibilities.

The larger the company, the harder it is for information to flow. You can't swap stories with someone you've never heard of.

This process of growing managerial anonymity poses a tremendous challenge to the diffusion of knowledge and an even greater challenge to the diffusion of information and its transformation into knowledge. In large companies, the context available to collectors declines, and therefore their ability to transform information into knowledge declines. Most of the input into the system is raw, uncontexted information. But even where the information is turned into full knowledge, it is difficult to know who to pass it on to. And when the collector knows who to pass it on to, it may be extremely difficult to gain access to that person.

Current managerial doctrine calls for maximum openness in order to avoid this problem. Sounds good. But we've been there. In very short order, managers will be swamped with a huge quantity of information from those who think they understand context. The informal paths and relative intimacy of smaller companies increases their understanding of context sufficiently to allow collectors to screen out the chaff—with informal penalties for eager-beavers who keep dumping garbage and pretending it's the crown jewels. But in larger companies, both knowledge and information have to be managed.

In businesses that are large enough to achieve a certain degree of internal anonymity, the informal evaluation and transmission of information and knowledge used in smaller businesses would quickly create gridlock. Managers are users of information and creators of knowledge. They cannot simultaneously be evaluators, prioritizers, and information managers. Some minimal overhead system must relieve them of the information/knowledge management burden, while allowing them access to needed information. Indeed, even small businesses need a system for storing and retrieving information, since even the best entrepreneur forgets.

There has to be some sort of organizational system that achieves three goals:

1. Provides a means for collectors to input information and knowledge.
2. Provides a system for prioritizing and routing information.
3. Provides an information storage location that can be efficiently queried.

Obviously, this needs to be built around a computing and data-basing system that we will discuss more extensively later on. For our immediate purposes, the issue that needs to be discussed is the loading process—what is to be done with information collected by individuals. Storage, sorting, routing, and querying are all part of the general system. But what is a salesman to do with a nugget of knowledge once he's found it?

Mechanically, this has a great deal to do with the type of management system in place. We are talking about a computer-based system and some sort of information/knowledge database into which random bits of information can be loaded and which will both deliver information to appropriate users and allow users to query the system. But most important, this internal information must be merged with all the other, more actively sought information. After all, the user doesn't care where the gold was mined, only that it was gold. And the gold within the company must be merged with the gold outside.

MINING THE OPEN SOURCE

Passive Intelligence Gathering

In 1995, the CIA held a competition. The test: who could gather the most information on Burundi. The CIA had some of its own people enter the competition, along with companies from the private sector. The winner, leaving the CIA's own team in the dust, was a private company called Open Source Solutions. OSS, as it's called, produced, within twenty-four hours, a tremendous amount of information on Burundi, ranging from vital statistics to lists of scholars who should be read and contacted. The CIA team—dead last in the competition—barely produced more material than that contained in its own, quite useful but widely available, *CIA World Factbook.*

Apart from what this story tells us about private sector efficiency, the importance of the test was the coming-of-age of what is called open source intelligence. As we have discussed before, open source intelligence is material that is not secret information—neither treated as secret by the government nor as proprietary by private businesses. Open source information always dwarfs secret information. Indeed, much of what is treated as secret by governments can be found in open source material. There are legends about massive, covert operations that have managed to uncover vital secrets—only to find that *Time* magazine had published the same material six months before.

The advantage enjoyed by Open Source Solutions was that it had mastered the emerging electronic domain. The CIA, created in an era when the primary challenge was the location of information, used extremely complex and sophisticated techniques for capturing information. These methods were costly in terms of time and money, but, prior to the emergence of the electronic domain, were state of the art. Indeed, one of the great ironies is that the intelligence and defense communities had been instrumental in developing the electronic database systems that matured into today's on-line services. The CIA is the largest customer for some of these services, like LEXIS-NEXIS.

Paradoxically, having been instrumental in creating the technology, the CIA concentrated its attention on its own internal database development. These are undoubtedly powerful indeed. What they didn't take note of was that the external databases, taking advantage of the digitization of open source data, had become a superb source of material. There is a tendency, both inside and outside the intelligence community, to equate open source with trivial. Nothing could be farther from the truth. Intelligence agencies used to spend a substantial amount of their resources hunting down and collecting open source material. From regional Chinese newspapers to Bulgarian radio broadcasts to trade organization statistical publications, the CIA and all other intelligence agencies spent tremendous resources accumulating, organizing, and mining this data.

Once in house, of course, the information was no longer considered open source. This was reasonable. Bulgarian radio broadcasts were open source only in the sense that they did not originate as secret material. But they were effectively inaccessible to anyone without the CIA's Foreign Broadcast Information Service, which used listening posts to capture the broadcasts and teams of translators and analysts to translate and decipher their meaning. In effect, the fact that collection and interpretation facilities were uniquely in the hands of the CIA and could not be duplicated without great expense made this information "secret." It was inaccessible to people outside the intelligence community, except as the CIA chose to make it public.

During the 1980s, and then with increasing speed in the 1990s, much of this "secret" material was replicated in on-line commercial services. Masses of material were included that the CIA would not have regarded as directly pertinent but which were of tremendous value to businesses, making these new, open source databases priceless.

> **Even a *Time* magazine article digitized and databased has intelligence value in excess of its printed form because you can search and compare in seconds.**

Open source electronic systems have increased the quantity of material available while decreasing the amount of time needed to find and acquire that material. That's how Open Source Solutions beat the CIA. The question—find out about Burundi—was uniquely amenable to passive, Zone 1 searching. The private sector, by mastering these techniques, dramatically speeds up the time cycle for the first phase of intelligence. But it must be remembered that not all information is available in Zone 1 and that, as you pass into more complex realms, from the library to the gray zone, the old-time penalties reappear. Indeed, it would be fair to say that the CIA and other intelligence agencies will continue to dominate Zones 4 and 5, while they are increasing their mastery of Zone 1. The advantage Open Source Solutions had over the CIA was undoubtedly not permanent. Regardless of how well the CIA does its job, the growth of electronic resources creates a tremendous opportunity for businesses looking for information.

PASSIVE, OPEN SOURCE MATERIAL: THE ELECTRONIC DOMAIN

The definition of the electronic domain is, of course, that the material is maintained in an electronic format. That generally means that you need a computer to access the material. The structure of the electronic world is roughly as shown on page 117.

The electronic domain can be divided into three realms: commercial on-line services, the Internet, and CD-ROMs. In general, these three have more characteristics in common than differences.

ORGANIZATION OF ELECTRONIC INFORMATION

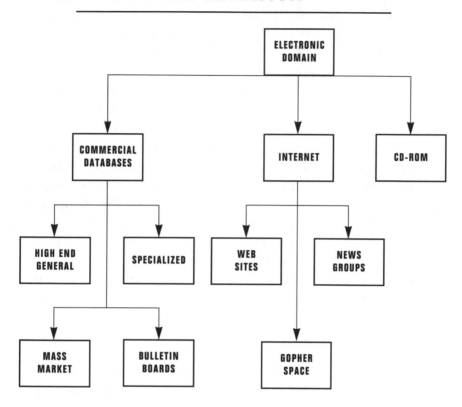

The data is in digital form. That means that in all three cases, the material is searchable using tools appropriate to each realm. Basically, in mastering the techniques needed for operating in one realm, you are mastering the techniques needed for all.

There are thousands of on-line services, hundreds of thousands of Internet sites, and countless CD-ROMs available. The fact is, however, that for 90 percent of the information you are going to need, a relative handful will suffice. The trick will be to locate the really useful ones as quickly as possible and to hone your skills for finding the 10 percent of information that you need that is not readily available. But basically, you can use this rule of thumb: About 60 percent of all information you need will be electronically available, with the best and most predictable sources of information being, naturally, the more expensive commercial databases and CD-ROMs. The other 40 percent will come from paper and other sources. Of that 60 percent, most will come from no more than a dozen sources, with five or six serving as your routine workhorse. A small fraction will require extensive searching.

All of this, of course, begins with the computer, and we need to say a few words about what is needed here, because the computer is going to be your core intelligence tool, for both finding and storing information. For most American businesses—and, increasingly, European and Asian businesses as well—the computer is already a staple in the office, so the primary need will be to make sure that you have good connectivity to the world outside. A wide range of computers is acceptable, but in general, we prefer IBM clones, running Windows, just because they are so commonplace. Some on-line services and all CD-ROMs contain search software that is specific to a particular platform. Virtually all are available for the Windows-Intel or Wintel world, while an increasing number don't bother to "port" themselves to the Mac. Thus, if you have a choice, we would urge you to select a Wintel system, simply to maximize your options in sites and CD-ROMs.

Your computer is going to be the workhorse of your intelligence system, as well as carrying the other burdens you put on it. While most computers will do, getting a fairly powerful one will pay in the long run. This is particularly true if you intend to do searches and downloading of information while using a spreadsheet, database, or word processor. Moreover, if you are going to be doing graphically intensive work—working with pictures, maps, drawings, or other graphical equipment—you are going to need both a powerful processor and plenty of disk space. This is not something you ought to skimp on. If you already have a computer, you will reach a point where you will want to upgrade. If you are buying a computer, consider the following configuration:

A minimum Pentium 75 processor with at least 16 megs of RAM

A video card with at least a megabyte of memory

At least a gigabyte of disk space

A 6X CD-ROM drive

A color bubble-jet printer

A 28.8 baud modem

The most important aspect of your computing system from the intelligence standpoint is your connectivity—how well you hook into the outside world. The simplest connection to the outside world is something called a modem, short for modulator/demodulator. A modem is simply a telephone that allows a computer to call and connect to other telephones. A modem can be purchased today for under $200, and Windows comes with built-in software to allow you to operate the modem. The modem's strength is that it is simple to use, uses existing telephone lines, and is therefore inexpensive.

A modem allows you to hook into another computer. The simplest computers to use are those provided by large, commercial vendors, like America Online (AOL), CompuServe, or Prodigy. Apart from information that is available on these services, like news, stock quotes, and the like, they also provide electronic mail, or e-mail, and connections to the Internet. These services provide their own software to use when hooking up with them, including e-mail software and software for connecting to and browsing the net. The modem can also be used to connect to other, higher-end, proprietary databases.

The modem connection is certainly a good, practical solution for the gathering of information. Its greatest weakness is speed—it takes forever to load images from the Internet via services like AOL. Somewhat faster are Internet providers that advertise in local newspapers. This doesn't save money, and it doesn't give you the other services that on-line services do, but it does simplify the Internet connection.

Another, higher-priced solution is some sort of dedicated, high-speed line running directly to an Internet service provider. In a small business, an Integrated Services Digital Number (ISDN) line can be purchased for a few hundred dollars a month. An ISDN line permits not only high-speed connection to the Internet—twice the speed of the fastest modem—but it also provides a much larger bandwidth than the ordinary telephone line. Think of a telephone line as a straw. One measure of the straw is how fast it draws liquid through it. The other measure is how large the straw is. A straw that is twice as fast and five times as large as another draws ten times as much liquid through in the same period of time.

If you are running an extremely small business with stand-alone computers, the chances are that a modem connection will suffice for you, unless you happen to be an extremely heavy user. However, if you run a somewhat larger company, particularly one that has created a local area network tying several computers together, a dedicated ISDN is the best solution. Having one means that all members of the staff that are connected via a local area network can use the line simultaneously. This does provide one savings: You won't need to provide every computer with its own modem and line. In the vast majority of cases, this system will allow you to access all available databases, since most permit both direct dial in via modem or Internet connection.

ORIGINS OF THE INTERNET

Let's begin with what we are all most familiar: the Internet. How good is the Internet as an information provider? The answer is it's OK, on average. But when we say average, we're reminded of the old statistics joke: A man is lying on the ground, his head is encased in ice, his feet are on fire. Asked how he's doing, he answers, "on average, OK." That's the Internet. There is some great stuff out there. And there is some incredible trash. The amount of time you're going to spend sorting through the Internet to find what you need will probably cost you more than going straight to proprietary databases. The Internet is certainly going to evolve into something critically important, but it isn't ready to support serious intelligence needs.

Let's begin by understanding what the Internet consists of. It originated as a Defense Department project in the early 1980s, funded by the Advanced Research Project Agency. Its purpose was to tie researchers' computers together so that they could exchange information rapidly. Because most of these researchers were at universities, the practical effect of the Internet was to tie together university computers using dedicated telephone lines. Now, in those days, most university computers were mainframes, or very large minicomputers like the Vax, that had terminals attached to them. Researchers would log into their accounts and have, as one of their options, the ability to send messages over the precursors to Internet like ARPANET—later expanded to include BITnet—to each other, as well as transmit files.

The Internet started as a tool for rocket scientists. For all its apparent simplicity, it still helps to be a rocket scientist.

Students realized sometime during its evolution that they could use the Internet to send personal letters to each other transcontinentally, and what began as a serious endeavor became a highway for ordinary and downright trivial communication. In fact, the system very quickly became clogged with things like electronic chain letters. The key to the ARPANET and BITnet was that they were free. The universities provided the mainframes, terminals, and accounts, and later underwrote the cost of connecting to nodes— major university computers that served as switching centers. Since it was free, it wasn't rationed. By not being rationed, it grew like crazy.

About the same time, independent of the Internet, another phenomenon arose, centered around the new personal computers: the bulletin boards (BBS). Hobbyists dedicated all or part of their computer disk space, a modem, and a telephone line to creating BBS that others could call in to. These BBS contained, depending on the systems operator (SYSOP), anything from useful programs and technical support to on-line Dungeons and Dragons or pornography. These BBS were text-based and totally anarchic. Numbers of BBS were listed on other BBS, and folks called, sometimes long distance, to find out what the BBS had available.

A critical point emerged with something called FIDOnet.

Build around Digital Equipment's computers, FIDOnet linked individual BBS together. SYSOPs would regularly log onto other BBS and transfer messages, download new programs, exchange bulletin board messages, and so on. FIDOnet was followed by other BBS networks, all built around slow—1,200 baud—modems and telephone lines. The result was a delightful anarchy.

At a certain point, the BBS system and the Internet system merged. The critical moment was the introduction, at the University of Minnesota, of something called a gopher—after the school's mascot. A gopher was a BBS that could be accessed via the Internet. Among other things available on the Minnesota gopher was the university library's card catalog, now digitized, and a load of other interesting stuff. Soon every university was creating gophers, with on-line books, programs, and everything else. Then McGill University in Montreal, Canada, introduced Archie, which searched Gopherspace for material you might want. Later, a more powerful search engine, Veronica, came on line, and soon the University of Minnesota and every other sane university was considering shutting down access.

Then came the breakthrough from text to graphics, and from mainframes back to the old BBS idea of PC-based nodes, or web sites. By now, commercial vendors had come in to provide connectivity and anyone who had a PC and wanted to build a web site could. This ability increased after a company called Netscape, with one of the more bizarre and effective business plans in history, emulated the old SYSOPs and gave away software for building graphical, PC-based web sites, and software for accessing or "browsing" those web sites. The net result was the world wide web.

To call the web anarchy understates the matter. The web is a zoo, and the animals have become the keepers. The key problem is that no one really has control of what is on the web. In fact, since it costs very little to get on the web, everyone has his or her own web site. A complex and extremely worthy company web site has to compete for attention with Cousin Mathilda's shrine to her lost love. The cheerful anarchy is not nearly as cheerful when you actually need to find something. But there are nuggets there to be found.

USING THE INTERNET

Using the web for information gathering requires a browser—software for searching the net—a search engine, and exquisite patience. People are putting information on the web. The number-one reason: self-promotion, marketing. A great many business-oriented web sites are little more than digital brochures. The web has become an extremely low-cost marketing tool. That means that you need to sort through the hype, the come-on, simple errors, to find what you are looking for. But the web does have one advantage: Looking is free, and so is most of the information.

The key to using the web is using the web search engines. Normally, when you click on the search icon from either the Microsoft or Netscape browser, you'll be brought to a window that allows you to choose among various search engines.

Netscape offers access to twenty-one search engines, as well as an add at the top of the page. These search engines are what allow you to look for the information you need. All of them search by matching the terms you select with the terms used in the sites that are contained in the database. This can lead to some hilarious results. Inputting Sahara in search of information on a desert can

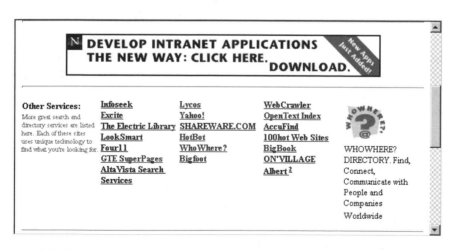

lead to locating the web site of the Sahara Strip Club and Harry Sahara's personal web page showing pictures of his pet lizard. That's the weakness of search engines—they're stupid. All they know is the term you've selected, which they see as a string of 0s and 1s. All they can do is locate identical 0s and 1s. Every search engine is working to overcome this difficulty, and each does it in a somewhat different way. Search engines change so quickly that some of this will be outdated by the time you read the book. You can find a list of search engines, and our evaluations of them, in the appendix.

The best way to master the net and the various search engines is by actually searching for something. Let's assume that you are someone interested in getting involved in the pager business and need some information on the technical aspects of pagers—just what they do. How would you go about finding information on the net?

The first step is to select the search engine. Let's begin with a general search engine, like Infoseek.

When we asked Infoseek to search for information on "pagers," what we got is shown on page 125. The first two were ads for free pagers—clearly companies hawking pager contracts. Then there came two Motorola Bravoplus free pager offers. Then a free pager marketing opportunity, and so on. As you can see, we didn't find what we wanted here. Now, there were many more pages we could look at, and buried among the come-ons there might well have been information on pager technology useful to us in making a decision on investment. But finding that would require a tremendous amount of time.

Notice that Infoseek, like most search engines, ranks sites by what's called "relevance," which sounds more useful than it is. Infoseek ranks for relevance according to whether the query term is found near the start of the document or in the title; how many times the term appears; and whether the term has a "high weight," which means that rare terms like *interstitial* have a higher weight when they appear than the term *pager.* This shows that relevance means, on the whole, nothing, but it is the best that programmers can come up with to screen the soup. The highest-ranking documents we found had values of 34 percent, which meant that *pager*

Your News		
Premier News	Free Pager! 34% (Size 2.7K)	
related news:	Free Pagers 34% (Size 6.6K)	
	Motorola Pagers Bravoplus Accessories Motorola Accessories Pager	
Paging	34% (Size 7.3K)	
New Web Services & Home Pages	Motorola Pager Bravoplus Free Pager Offer! Features Of Bravo Plus! 34% (Size 6.9K)	
	Free pagers 34% (Size 4.1K)	
smart info	SPS Free Pager Marketing Opportunity 34% (Size 6.1K)	
company profiles:	Bergman Jewelers Antique Watches Gold Diamonds Rolex Jewelry Necklaces 34% (Size 15.8K)	
Dial Page, Inc.	FREE Pagers - 80.00 Value 34% (Size 5.8K)	
Paging Network, Inc.	FREE PAGERS! 34% (Size 2.1K)	
	Pager - GSM - Pagers - Cellular - Phone - - Telephone Directory 34%	
MobileMedia	(Size 7.3K)	
big yellow	Make Money Giving Away Free Pagers Work at home Opportunity	

Reprinted by permission. Infoseek, Ultrasmart, Ultraseek, iSeek, Quickseek, Imageseek, Ultrashop, "proof of intelligent life on the net" and the Infoseek logos are trademarks of Infoseek Corporation which may be registered in certain jurisdictions. Other trademarks shown are trademarks of their respective owners.

was a common word, appearing not all that frequently in the text—which means nothing. Relevance on the net is a case of false precision.

On the Internet, nothing is more irrelevant than relevance.

Obviously, this first search yielded little. We shifted our search to an engine called Savvysearch. This is what is called a metasearch engine, which searches about twenty search engines simultaneously—in other words, rather than going to one search engine after another, you can just have the metasearch engine do it all. Now, you might think that by searching twenty infoseeks simultaneously, the data dump would increase. But Savvysearch and the other metasearch engines do two extremely valuable things. First, they merge together similar categories. For example, the multiple hits on "free pagers" that swamped our first search are merged into one single entity. You can choose to click on that line and wade through the free offers if you want. But you can also ignore them.

The second thing that the metasearch engines all allow is something called a Boolean search. These are extremely important and not quite as boring as they sound. Basic search engines allow you to search for key words. Be sure to check the tips given when using a particular search engine to see if it is case sensitive—some are, some aren't, and it could make a difference. So, if you were to input John Kennedy, every site where the terms *John* and *Kennedy* showed up would be listed—not very useful since you'd probably find ads for Bill Kennedy the john cleaner in a non-case-sensitive engine if you didn't specify. Boolean searches allow you to gain greater control. You can specify, in the best engines, the distance from each other that two words have to be—so that you are only interested in John Kennedy when they occur next to each other. They can specify that you are interested in John Kennedy and Lee Harvey Oswald, and only those sites containing both names will appear—or you can say that you are not interested in any site containing both names, in which case John Kennedy will only turn up when Oswald isn't mentioned.

Between merging output and Boolean searches, the meta-search engines are much more powerful tools. What we got when we input pagers this time is shown below. The first thing that shows up is for an electronic mosquito repellent! We spent precious minutes looking at that because...well, you've just got to, right? And that's one of the real problems on the net. The ratio of inter-

V&M Distributors presents Electronic Mosquito Repella... (WebCrawler)

wireless (WebCrawler)

Pagers & Voice Mail (WebCrawler)

Motorola in Deutschland, Aktivitäten 1995 (WebCrawler)

Pager Sales & Service (WebCrawler)

B&B Services,Free,Pager,Web,Scan,900,MLM,vitamins,bus... (WebCrawler)

Pager Automation (Yahoo)

InterNet **Pager** (Yahoo)

Weather Watcher **Pager** Service (Yahoo)

Reprinted with permission of SavySearch.

esting but useless information is so high that you are inevitably going to stop to look at the weird things that turn up. But some other things turn up as well—each with the search engine that found them listed to their right.

We clicked on pager sales and service, which gave us, among other things, the home page of a pager company in Vermont (see below). Rare among business "brochures," this page gave us at least some minimally useful information on pagers, including what they do and linking us to manufacturers. Of course, while more useful than other sites, we still haven't learned much that we didn't know before—or to put it differently, if we didn't know this stuff already, we had no right to be interested in the industry.

Anyway, as you can see, we were getting nowhere fast on the net. We turned our attention to another, somewhat less well known part of the Internet, called newsgroups. Newsgroups predate the world wide web graphical home pages, evolving out of the old bulletin boards. Basically, these are places to post messages. There are currently about fifteen thousand newsgroups, with the number growing continually, each located on someone's computer somewhere, and each accessible through various Internet tools—and each dedicated to some topic, from bestiality to quantum mechanics to everything in between. The Usenet Calculator estimates over

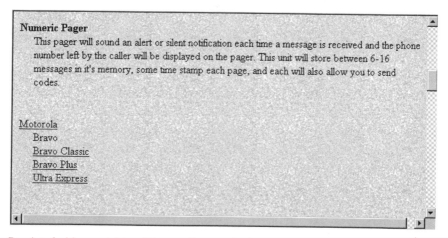

Numeric Pager
This pager will sound an alert or silent notification each time a message is received and the phone number left by the caller will be displayed on the pager. This unit will store between 6-16 messages in it's memory, some time stamp each page, and each will also allow you to send codes.

Motorola
  Bravo
  Bravo Classic
  Bravo Plus
  Ultra Express

Reprinted with permission of Contact Communications.

eight hundred megabytes, or the equivalent of eight hundred hefty, four-hundred-page novels, and is posted to Usenet newsgroups every single day of the year. This amount has, in recent years, been increasing at the rate of 100 percent (i.e., x2) every year. That's a lot. Chances are, what you're interested in is discussed in excruciating detail somewhere in Usenet.

When the president's press secretary rails about conspiracy theories being published on the web, when Pierre Salinger talks about an intelligence document he found on the web, when we talk about neo-Nazis using the web, what we are really talking about are the newsgroups. These can be searched in the same way, and with similar engines and tools, as the web sites we started looking at. We used a search engine called Dejanews. Looking and working very much like other engines, it searches through this mass of rubble.

Well, there may have been something useful here (see page 129), but we couldn't find it. What we did find was a mass of pagers for sale and requests for programs that would crack pager control systems. There is an awful lot of junk here. But these discussion groups do provide one thing of value: They point to people who might be interested in the same thing you are and give e-mail addresses. All of these hackers trying to find pager program crackers probably know an awful lot about pager technology. If you're really up against it on a project, it's not a bad place to try—assuming you're careful about who you're dealing with and how much you give away.

We pushed the search one step farther. We refined the search from "pager" to "paging industry," using another metasearch engine called Motherlode Insane Search, which in our experience provides some of the better results by ranking things a little more accurately (see page 130). We clicked on the second line, Industry Links, provided by Lycos, and that took us to another page, and another. What was finally yielded is shown on page 131. This contained an extraordinary collection of information on the technology of pagers by someone who used to work for Motorola and now worked for a company called Real Time Strategies. We also found, from VHF Communications, a brief history of wireless communications, all culminating in the pager. From Pagetrac, we found an

Date	Scr	Subject	Newsgroup	Author
1. 97/02/06	027	WTB: Pager Interface (PI	tnn.comm.pager	rbarnett@trav
2. 97/02/06	027	PAGER	pl.ogloszenia.sprze	guc@ibib.waw.
3. 97/02/06	027	AS/400 Pager support	comp.sys.ibm.as400.	cer793w@ursa.
4. 97/02/05	027	ignore: Re: A Pager Busi	akr.freenet	red@redpoll.m
5. 97/02/05	026	Pager Gateway	comp.groupware.lotu	JMPL87B@prodi
6. 97/02/05	026	A free $80 pager	tnn.comm.pager	twinspetes@ao
7. 97/02/04	026	Pager advice - numeric o	soc.culture.singapo	lukym@hotmail
8. 97/02/04	026	Motorola pager for sale	tnn.comm.pager	"M. Etchamend
9. 97/02/04	026	Need Pager program crack	alt.2600.crackz	Voyager1@my.n
10. 97/02/04	026	Need Pager program crack	alt.cracks	Voyager1@my.n
11. 97/02/04	026	Need Pager program crack	alt.crackers	Voyager1@my.n
12. 97/02/04	026	±,⅛-ÁˣÀĪ,¦ ¾Æ⅛¿ã?	han.misc.misc	"Perious" <ds
13. 97/02/04	026	NEED A PAGER $AVE	alt.cellular	"acs" <acs@li
14. 97/02/04	026	FREE.....$80 pager	misc.industry.elect	twinspetes@ao
15. 97/02/04	026	pager	pl.ogloszenia.sprze	"inez" <inez@
16. 97/02/04	026	Pager Control	comp.lang.basic.vis	Peter Nguyen
17. 97/02/04	026	pager program	uvm.general	"Joesph L. Ro

Reprinted with permission of Deja News, Inc.

offer to sell—for $1,200—a study on Consumer Trends in "paging." And we found most of the corporate web sites.

In the end, we found a great deal of information, all of it for free—save the one study being offered that we didn't have to buy. But the free information came at a high cost. It took us about six hours to carry out the search and about two hours to sort and organize the material. The search required someone with enough sophistication to distinguish the significant from the insignificant, so it was far from minimum-wage work. A day to nail down the information that we found means that it cost us a few hundred dollars. Now that wouldn't be bad if we had found everything we needed, but what we found was quite spotty—certainly not enough information to make any sort of decision on whether or not to invest in an industry or a company.

And that's the problem with the Internet. There are certainly valuable things to be found, but it is unlikely that you will derive a comprehensive situational awareness—one sufficiently robust to allow you to make a significant decision. Nor can you predict what class of material you'll find on the web. The web's chaotic nature means that, from industry to industry and from time to time, you literally might find anything—or nothing. And that nothing can cost quite a bit, considering the amount of time it takes and how much that time costs.

World Wide Web

- VHF Communications, Inc. - A Brief History Of Wireless... *(Webcrawler)*
- Industry Links *(Lycos)*
- Memtecs Global Markets - Annual Report 1996 - Extract from the 1996 Memtec Annual Report showing Memtec's Global Markets *(ALIWEB)*
- sandag wireless communications facilities issues paper *(Webcrawler)*
- Association Publications *(Lycos)*
- Transit Industry Software - Information on CSI's capabilities for the Transit Industry including computer-aided dispatch, communications and schedule management. *(ALIWEB)*
- Special Reports *(Webcrawler)*
- A Independant Telecom Consultants extensive site for '96 p *(Lycos)*
- Hotelbuyer.com - HotelBuyer.com is designed to be an electronic meeting place where Hospitality Industry related business people can come together to find leads for and offer products to others in the Hotel Industry. We list vendors who sell to the Hospitality Industry.

Reprinted with permission of USWeb.

The Internet is free only if your time's value is zero.

That's why, for us, the web is rarely the first stop. Unless your time doesn't cost much, or the project is not that significant, we tend to shun the web—until the end, when we're just looking around for things we might have missed. In our experience, a high degree of confidence in knowing where to find what you need more than makes up for the money that must be spent on that confidence. One day the web may be a good place for intelligence, but right now, we prefer the commercial, on-line services.

ON-LINE SERVICES

On-line services are peculiar creatures. They are not, themselves, information providers. Rather, they are middlemen. They provide outlets for information producers. They provide the equipment—the computers and phone lines and so on—as well as the market. In return, they take a fat percentage off the top. Sometimes they buy a single source, like a newspaper, and sell access to it. Sometimes they buy entire databases, like the Hoover Directory of U.S. Businesses. They also provide the search engine, which, in many

Reprinted with permission of Bradley F. Dye.

cases, allows you to search for information across several data sources simultaneously. Rather than having to search each newspaper individually, the search engine allows you to search all of them simultaneously. That simultaneous search capability represents a fundamental increase in analytic power. It is also something you pay for.

Anyone wanting to do business intelligence must master the tools of the trade. The basic tools of this trade are the on-line services. There aren't that many good general ones, but each has its strengths and weaknesses and the serious practitioner must know when to use each.

One of the most popular and powerful databases is LEXIS-NEXIS, whose origins we have already discussed. LEXIS-NEXIS provides a tremendous amount of resources. When you log on to LEXIS-NEXIS, you are provided with a host of options (see page 132).

This is the first menu page on LEXIS-NEXIS for the NEXIS side. The LEXIS side is primarily of interest to lawyers and need not interest us here. Note that NEXIS is divided into what are called libraries. The libraries divide between general news libraries and specialized topics ranging from industries to various geographical locations. There is a substantial overlap between the sources in each library. A particular publication might appear in the News Library, as well as

```
Please ENTER the NAME (only one) of the library you want to use.  To see the
description of a particular library, type its page number and then press the
ENTER key.

NAME   PG NAME   PG NAME   PG NAME   PG NAME   PG NAME   PG DNAME   PG

----------- Types -----------      ---------- Topics ----------     - Int'l -
 General                            BANKNG  3          Medical      ASIAPC  7
 -- News - - Legal -                BUSFIN  3          GENMED  5    CANADA  5
NEWS    1 LEGNEW  1                 CMPCOM  3          EMBASE  5    DUTCH   7
REGNWS  1 LEXPAT  4                 ENERGY  3          MEDLNE  5    EUROPE  7
TOPNWS  1                           ENTERT  2                      GERMAN  7
                                    ENVIRN  2                      MDEAFR  7
                                    INSURE  3          Political   MEXICO  5
 Financial                         MARKET  1           APOLIT  6    NSAMER  7
ACCTG   2                           PEOPLE  2          CMPGN   6    UK      5
COMPNY  2                           SPORTS  2          EXEC    6    UKCURR  5
NAARS   2                           TRANS   3          LEGIS   6    WORLD   7
                                                                    Assists
                        Reference                                 GUIDE   8
                        BUSREF  3                                  TERMS   8
                                                                   PRACT   8

For further explanation, press the H key (for HELP) and then the ENTER key.
```

This chart and those on pages 133 and 134 are reprinted with the permission of LEXIS-NEXIS, a division of Reed Elsevier Inc. LEXIS and NEXIS are registered trademarks of Reed Elsevier Properties Inc.

in World, UK, People, and so on. You cannot search all of NEXIS simultaneously. You must, rather, choose a particular library.

Each library is subdivided into individual files. These files can be searched individually or collectively—although sometimes some files are excluded. Assume that we were interested in information on particular companies. We would go into the Company Library, which is reproduced on page 133. This gives you a series of options from which to choose, including everything from bankruptcy reports to mergers and acquisitions. You can also choose to search for everything simultaneously.

Let's assume that we were to do a search on our pager problem in NEXIS. We would go, for example, into Alnews and do a general search on pagers. We were informed that over a thousand articles would be available with the term *pager*. We therefore narrowed the search a bit to "pager manufacturer," which still gave us 485 stories (see page 134).

Notice the mix of press agency stories and industry media. It now takes time and patience to sort through these stories, which are full-text, and find what you are looking for. It is important to understand a little of how this works, because watching a computer sort through literally millions of individual articles looking for the word or combination of words you've put in, and then calling up the story in well under a minute, is a pretty remarkable thing—and the

```
Please ENTER the NAME of the file you want to search.  To see a description
of a file, type its page number and press the ENTER key.
          FILES - PAGE 1 of 16 <NEXT PAGE for additional files)
 NAME   PG DESCRIP          NAME   PG DESCRIP          NAME   PG DESCRIP

          ----- C O M P A N Y   L I B R A R Y -----
   Company Reports By Type  ----- SEC Filings -----    ----- News & Business ----
 BDS       1 Bankruptcy Rpts  FILING  1 SEC Full-Text  ALLNWS  1 Company News*
 EXECDR    1 BUS Bio Reports* EDGARP  1 EdgarPlus      ALLABS 15 Company Abstr*
 USCO      1 US Co Rpts       SECOL   1 Sec Online     BUSOPP 15 Intl Bus Opps*
 INTLCO    1 Intl Co Rpts     ACCESS  1 Access Disclo* -------- Assists --------
 ALLMA     1 M&A Reports      ---- U.S. Companies ---- GUIDE  16 Descriptions*
 SEC       1 SEC Filings      USPRIV  2 US Private Cos
 STKRPT    1 Stock Reports    USPUB   2 US Public Cos
 PRESS NEXT PAGE FOR ADDITIONAL SOURCES.  Files marked  *  may not be combined.
```

NEXIS Service

core phenomenon of our time. In effect, every word in every article and every database is entered into a master database. Each word, in turn, has entered after it identifications that point to articles in which that term appeared. Every time an article is entered into the database, it is broken up into words. Where a word already exists, an entry is made stating that such and such an article also contains that word. If the word doesn't exist, it is created with the appropriate notation. So, when we enter the word *pager,* the computer instantly goes to that alphabetical entry, finds all the articles that have the word in the title, and lets the user know that the article exists and offers to call it up for him.

All of this is, of course, expensive. Our search on pagers cost about $725 on a per-use basis. Now, you can get a flat rate on LEXIS-NEXIS for $4,250 a month—plus print costs, which run about $2 per document. Obviously, we try to control our LEXIS-NEXIS costs. It is basically a trade-off between labor costs and search costs.

An alternative to LEXIS-NEXIS is Dow Jones news service. This comes in two flavors: a web-based service called DowVision, which focuses on feeding real-time news to you, and the dial-in service Dow Jones News Retrieval, which is more of an archival service, although there is a great deal of overlap between them. Dow Jones tends to have more detailed financial information than LEXIS-NEXIS, but the breadth of its global news retrieval is not up to LEXIS-NEXIS standards. When we searched for pagers on Dow Jones, we

```
                    LEVEL 1 - 485 STORIES
1. The Associated Press, February 3, 1997, Monday, BC cycle, Domestic News, 9491
words, ATLANTA
2.    AP Online, January 31, 1997; Friday, Financial pages, 2654 words,  AP
Financial News at 9:10 a.m. EST Friday, Jan. 31, 1997
3.    Computergram International, January 31, 1997, No. 3090, 107 words, BANKS
STAND BY BANKRUPT PAGER MOBILEMEDIA, IAC 06231375
4.    Newsbytes, January 31, 1997, 610 words, MobileMedia Files For Chapter 11
Protection 01/31/97, IAC 06231040
5.    Agence France Presse, January 30, 1997, Financial pages, 200 words, India
approves foreign projects worth 57 million dollars, NEW DELHI, Jan 30
6.    AP Online, January 30, 1997; Thursday, Financial pages, 667 words,
Statistic Freedom Wins Over NBA, LARRY NEUMEISTER, NEW YORK
7.    AP Online, January 30, 1997; Thursday, Sports, 867 words,   NBA Loses
Statistics Lawsuit, LARRY NEUMEISTER, NEW YORK
```

NEXIS Service

found overlap between many of the more recent articles, but found that LEXIS had a stronger historical base. Dow Jones is a good choice if your needs are focused on fairly recent material—and it is substantially cheaper to use than NEXIS-LEXIS.

There are alternatives to LEXIS-NEXIS and Dow Jones that are powerful and cheaper. Eye Q is a smaller but still powerful on-line service that focuses heavily on business needs. For a fee of $39 a month—plus $3 per article retrieved—Eye Q provides a scaled-down version. Eye Q's business menu (shown on page 135) gives you a sense.

Notice the simplified user interface. While generally desirable, we find that simpler interfaces frequently gloss over the fact that the search engine is less powerful or the data contained on-line is less extensive. Powerful search engines and large, yet focused, libraries seem to require complex interfaces.

When we ran our search on pagers, we found that we did not get the kind of coverage that we got from NEXIS, although we did get decent information at a fraction of the price. One strength in Eye Q: market reports that were not available on NEXIS. We spent about $125 to $150 looking for pager information. Our results are shown on page 136.

Among the cheapest sources and an interesting approach to initial screening is E Library, which is primarily a newspaper and

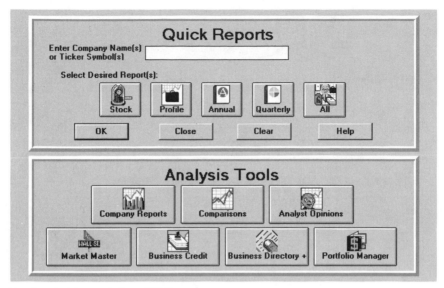

Reprinted with permission of UMI.

periodical archive going back to about 1990. It allows full Boolean searching and is divided into libraries (see page 137). Its great advantage is price: $9.95 a month, unlimited access, unlimited downloads. At that price, we think it's a powerful tool indeed. When we ran our pager search there, we found only about one fifth of what NEXIS gave us, and perhaps one tenth of what we did have could not be found in NEXIS. But it did provide us with some basic, useful coverage.

IAC Insite consists of six different databases: ranging from the top-of-the-line Market Insite, which covers a wide range of current publications, news wires, press releases, and so on, down to the highly focused Health and Wellness Insite. Market Insite allows you unlimited access for a year—for a hefty $5,995. For that you can access data from about two years. One of the nice aspects of IAC is that it contains brokerage firm reports and summaries of companies that are usually not available on LEXIS-NEXIS or Dow Jones. It does not have industry periodicals—a substantial lack. IAC allows you to access information much more easily than the others, and includes hypertext links that are not available elsewhere. Its flat rate

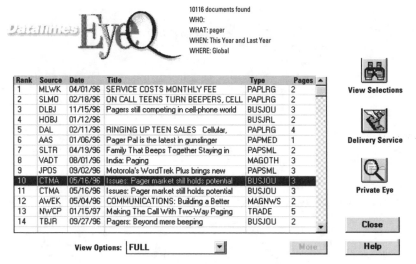

UMI

sounds steep, but compared to LEXIS-NEXIS, it's a bargain. It gave us many of the recent stories on pagers that we got in LEXIS-NEXIS, but not all of them.

Profound is accessible as a dial-in service. A base package is offered for a fee of $198 a month. But many of the files you'll want cost extra. Profound is heavily focused on company and market news. It gives good graphics and therefore provides excellent charts, but it has relatively little news outside of this: New technology, which is what we are interested in, is not emphasized, except where it impacts on companies. This is a great place for people playing the stock market or for companies needing quantified information, but it won't do for more general searches, and the price can add up.

There are other services. Proquest is an extremely expensive, relatively sparse database that can be avoided. In fairness, it did give us a great article on the European pager market, but we finally found that elsewhere and cheaper. FT Profile is similar to LEXIS-NEXIS in price but not in breadth and is both difficult to access from the United States and lacks (although this is said to be changing) powerful search tools. Others spring up and drop out regularly. But starting a database service takes time. The established databases

Reprinted with permission of Infonautics, Inc.

have a tremendous advantage over new services: They've already stockpiled a huge database. So, while others will be entering the fray in niche markets, we expect fewer rather than more business databases.

There is another class of on-line service that you should bear in mind when looking for information—what we call the general, mass-market on-line service, like America Online and CompuServe. Both are intended for multiple functions, including providing e-mail and Internet access, general education and entertainment, travel planning, and so on. While each contains business information, we find that CompuServe is far and away the more powerful business service. CompuServe provides a service called Executive News Service (ENS) for $10 over the regular monthly subscription of $24.95 plus $1.95 an hour over twenty hours. ENS is an electronic clipping service. You can input a word or a company and anything appearing in up to twenty-four news services will be delivered to you.

Perhaps more important are the additional-fee business services available via CompuServe (see page 138). While some of these services, such as Dun and Bradstreet Reports, can cost a bit, others, like Hoover, cost little or nothing. We find ourselves regularly using specific services on CompuServe, simply because they are not easily available elsewhere.

Reprinted with permission of CompuServe.

AOL is attractive because it carries a great deal of material from Dow Jones. Some of this is identical to the material contained in Dow Jones's own business databases but is included in AOL's base price. A CompuServe and AOL account will actually give you a great deal of current business information. What you won't have is a great deal of archival information—stuff from five years ago. You also won't have powerful search tools. But having the two accounts will cut down the research you have to do on more expensive databases. But neither AOL nor CompuServe yielded very much on pagers. Once we had companies we were interested in, like Motorola, both could provide us with some basic, useful information for very little time or money.

A word about MSNetwork from Microsoft. It is really geared to family and home. It has some personal investment information but very little for business. This is likely to change, but at this point, we wouldn't class this as a business investment.

Now let's pause for three other on-line sources that are heavily focused on technology: Dialog, National Technical Information Service (NTIS), and Defense Technical Information Center. The last two are actually run by the federal government while the former, discussed before, is currently owned by Knight-Ridder. These are great places to find technical information on anything, but they are all costly. Not surprisingly, the two government databases are the hardest to access, the hardest to search, and quite expensive for information that is supposed to be free. Dialog is notoriously hard to use and expensive as well. But we found a wealth of information on paging technology, much of which was so technical we weren't capable of following it.

Finally, let's remember libraries. A great on-line source is Colorado Alliance of Research Libraries (CARL), run by the University of Colorado. This is accessible over the Internet (via Telnet) and archives abstracts of recent articles in popular and not-so-popular journals. The search is free. They will also fax articles to you for about $10 a throw, but you can usually pick up the same article at a local library or university for free. CARL is not useful for very current material, but it's great for historical articles. And this brings us to the final point: libraries. In the end, you've got to go to them. But their catalogs will come to you—and you'll find an awful lot there. The appendix gives you a list of the better on-line library catalogs— almost all of them free.

In the end, we found an article on pagers on LEXIS-NEXIS from the *St. Petersburg Times*. The article was about a local company that had made a fortune in pager repairs. The article pointed out that pagers are made to last about two years. After that, they need to be repaired. This one little article led us to Dialog, NTIS, and then to the library for an answer to the question. If you want to get into the pager business, think about pager repair and refurbishing and stay away from sales.

CONCLUSION: REMEMBERING THE TRIED AND TRUE

In the end, the most extensive and cost-effective sources of information are the vast research libraries that until recently represented the sole information archive of our society. These libraries—and the books and journals they contain—remain and will remain the foundation of our society's knowledge base. Paper remains a powerful storage medium. It is durable and user-friendly. The great weakness of paper is accessibility, and that is a problem difficult to overcome.

Electronic sources can be searched by the word. Paper sources cannot. It is impossible to know what is contained in a book or article without reading it. Titles may or may not provide the needed information. Subject headers hint content, but they are rarely exhaustive and can even be inaccurate. Even author-prepared abstracts of articles may not reveal information in which the author was not interested but in which you might be. That is the crucial problem with paper. Regardless of how powerful the cataloging system might be, it only catalogs information about publications and not the publications themselves.

There are plans to change this. Project Gutenberg is an academic project designed to digitize great books. The Library of Congress has a program under way to digitize its collection. All of these will ultimately fail. Even today, far more information is being produced on paper than is being produced electronically, and the transformation of the historical archive into a digital form will outstrip society's resources for a long time to come.

Businesses must, in their passive intelligence, master libraries the way they are. Fortunately, the cataloging system for books and periodicals has changed tremendously over the past twenty

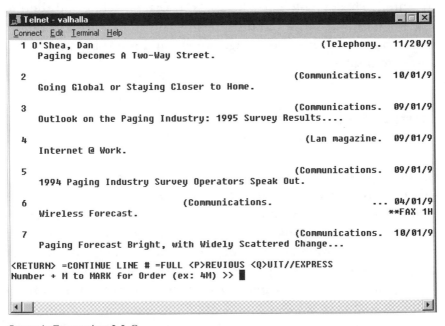

Strategic Forecasting, L.L.C.

years, permitting imperfect but useful searches of the paper domain.

Indeed, one of the advantages of digitization is that it allows you to locate material even if you are located in Podunk. We can recall in our early days having to make trips to the Library of Congress in Washington, Harvard's Hollis Library in Cambridge, New York's 42nd Street Library, and so on. Today, you don't have to go to New York, Washington, Boston, or other large cities with archival libraries in order to search their catalogs—you can do it from home in Podunk. You never have to leave Podunk.... This is real progress, we suppose.

In the appendix is a list of libraries that we like to use. They are all libraries accessible via the Telnet function on the Internet (we provide addresses) and were selected for ease of use, size, usefulness, and so on. We have not included the finest library in the country and possibly the world—the Library of Congress (locis.loc.gov)—because its search engine is so bad that only the federal government could have created it. Still, if you can figure out how to use the search engine—and you are better folks than we if you can—a world of riches will open up for you.

WORKING THE SYSTEM

Semiactive Intelligence Gathering

So far, we have focused on a particular class of material: open source, public domain material that has been made deliberately accessible by someone. What the Internet, on-line services, CD-ROMS, libraries, courthouses, trade associations, and the rest all have in common is that they provide information intentionally to the general public. All of them have organized themselves, to a greater or lesser extent, in such a way as to allow readers to find what they need. In the end, the card catalog and Infoseek serve precisely the same purpose—to allow you to search for information using some formal system of organization.

This relatively organized realm does not by any means constitute all of the public domain. There is a vast amount of information available that was not created with the intention of making it available to the public, but which can be legally and ethically accessed. Some of this material exists in every information domain save, obviously, the innermost domain of proprietary secrets. Some of it is electronic, some paper, some gossip, and some resides in the minds of people. What all of this information has in common is that, while it is available, it needs to be tracked down. Its existence must be guessed at, inferred, logically deduced and so on—but it does not exist with pointers available in any particular card catalog or web search engine.

In fact, we can think of information in the public domain as consisting of a series of networks. In the part we discussed in Chapter 5, the individual works are embedded in systems—catalogs or databases—that point to them and describe them. So, a book on marketing bananas is listed in electronic catalogs under marketing and bananas and any other appropriate descriptor.

There is also information that is not organized this way. Much of this is located in networks of information that don't have external pointers, but which mostly point to each other. For example, specialists in bananas know each other—the banana world is a small one. They also know of information—statistics, studies, specialists on various subjects—that is available. They also personally know a great deal about marketing bananas. There is, however, no database or card catalog listing their names and addresses. They are well known to each other, but are almost invisible to outsiders. You cannot access them passively. You actually have to go out and find them, and that isn't always easy. Yet the payoff, if in nothing else than printed information, can be spectacular.

To give you a sense of just how vast and even exotic this domain can be, consider the following examples.

- A professor, working under a grant from the National Science Foundation, has created a database displaying the consumption and disposal of car batteries. The database is in the public domain, since it was created with federal money, but you need to find out that it exists in the first place in order to ask to see it. There are thousands of databases like this on every possible subject in existence. More are coming into existence every day.

- The Qatar Chamber of Commerce and Industry has produced a computer disk called Commercial and Industrial Directory, which it distributed at the Middle East Economic Conference held in Cairo on November 12–14, 1996. The information is formatted as an Excel file. Over eleven thousand businesses are listed, along with their phone and fax numbers, addresses, and type of business. You'll find everything from A Lady Tailor to the Subarah Shop for Selling Old Equipment, all accessible in various ways.

- The Compound Livestock Feed Manufacturers Association of India has published a handbook that includes detailed statistics on Indian production and consumption of livestock feed, dairy production, egg production, and so on.

- Intersputnik, a Russian-based satellite consortium, publishes a detailed guide to its products, including technical details on its satellites and prices for services. You can lease hemispheric communications coverage from a Russian satellite at $16 a minute. The cost goes down as the frequency of usage increases. Of course, you might prefer a long-term lease. Those numbers are here as well.

- The Belgian Institut de Reescompte et de Garantie issues an annual report detailing its own performance and its read of the Belgian economy—in both French and Walloon.

- The Florida Department of Agriculture and Consumer Services annually publishes *The Source,* a complete directory of Florida seafood suppliers, including what they supply. Three companies supply cigar minnows.

- A downsized engineer we know will provide you with detailed information on selling thermostats to the U.S. Navy for far less than any consulting firm you can hire.

- A retired Israeli government official now living in the United States will tell you more than you probably want to know about doing business in Jordan in exchange for lunch. He's bored and likes to talk.

All of this material—and vast amounts like it and probably more useful—is still in the public domain. All of it is in digital or paper format. All of it is obtainable. But none of it is being tracked in a convenient way. That is the distinction that must be focused on here. The geography of information conforms to the general geography we have been using; all of it exists in recognizable domains. But none of them have been systematically "tagged" and entered into general and accessible databases. These documents and the millions like them are all riches beyond belief. All of them are utterly legal uses of information. Indeed, in many cases, the producers and packagers of the information are eager to have you use them and some may actually go to some effort to bring them to the general public's attention.

THE PRIVATE PUBLIC DOMAIN
AND THE SEMIACTIVE

There are many types of valuable business information that are not to be found in even the best libraries and are rarely included in on-line services. Some kinds of nonarchived, noncataloged material include:

Promotional material: Not brochures and come-ons—although it could include that—this is a whole range of material whose production was motivated by parochial concerns. For example, let's say that a developer wants to build a new shopping mall somewhere and needs to convince the local authorities to permit the development. He creates a substantial study of the area's business environment, including demographic, environmental, and educational data and other factors. In many cases, the study contains the best data available on an area, and huge amounts of money have been spent on it.

Obviously, the developer's motivation in producing the study was promotional—to justify his own project. His conclusions will reflect that. However, the data in the study and much of the analysis are both accurate and priceless; a superb window into a potential market. Now, the study has been distributed to town councils, planning boards, and so on and is fully public, though it probably has not found its way to the Library of Congress or onto a proprietary database. The developer wasn't motivated to do that and the Library of Congress does not go hunting for this material. Nevertheless, if you can find out that it exists and find out who still has a copy, it is probably yours for the asking. Promotional material can include anything from proposals to planning boards to trade organization publications to brokerage reports—vast amounts of material produced by and about business but not readily available. For example, when large chain stores such as Wal-Mart or hotel chains like Hilton decide they want to enter a market, they are frequently required to produce studies for the local governing bodies—town councils, planning boards, zoning commissions—showing their potential impact on the community. Apart from the self-serving aspects of the report, the studies frequently gather some of the best available information on all aspects of the local market—demographics, traffic patterns, income distribution. All of it is in the public domain, all of it is free, and it would cost you tens of thousands of dollars to come close to reproducing it.

Unpublished scientific material: Most scientific research carried out in our universities is never published. Much of it isn't published because it's worthless or someone has reached a conclusion that is worthless—such as it can't be done. But much of it isn't published because its findings weren't deemed significant enough or because the professor was too lazy to whip it into publishable shape. Sometimes it will be published eventually, but currently it is unpublished or has only been presented at conferences. There are real gems here. Things not deemed significant by the scientific community can mean a fortune to an entrepreneur. It is frequently well known in the scholarly community that a given person is working on a project. People constantly pass around drafts of papers. In most fields and among most people, there isn't an extremely high emphasis on security or secrecy. Most scholars are delighted and flattered to find someone taking an interest in their work. The trick is to find out who is doing work that is of interest to you.

People: Which brings us to the most important potential source of knowledge. People are the greatest repository of information, much of it already transformed into knowledge. We have frequently found that speaking to the right person for ten minutes is worth two weeks of reading. If they don't know what you need to know, they frequently know the person, article, book, or database that does. Finding these people is much harder than getting them to talk to you. This is particularly true of the greatest pool of untapped expertise around: government officials. These folks, contrary to popular mythology, know a tremendous amount, but they are buried in a system that makes it hard to track them down. The same can be said to a greater or lesser degree for banks, brokerages, and hockey teams. All contain unexpected expertise alongside expected expertise.

We are talking here about the majority of information and human knowledge: the vast, unorganized soup that surrounds us and is us—like The Force. Special effort needs to be taken to find out about them, locate them, access them. But none of them can be found passively. They won't come to you. You have to go out and find them. This other material requires what we call a semiactive effort.

Information and knowledge are frequently contained among surprisingly small networks of people. Find one, you find them all.

We have already discussed the difference between active and passive search procedures. In the latter, it is not necessary to search out information. The information comes to you via systems that are already organized to be searchable. Therefore, it is not possible to detect the search activity, something that may or may not be important to a business on any given project. In active searches, like the submarine actively pinging its sonar to find other submarines, you go out and find the information and it's extremely likely that you'll be detected. Semiactive searching is an intermediate phase in which the types of information you are looking for are quite similar to those searched for in the passive mode, but in which purely passive techniques won't work. The semiactive search is not passive precisely because it is people dependent. The phone allows you to conduct the search efficiently, but you are constantly dealing with people, and as such, you are subject to detection. At the same time, semiactive techniques don't require you to go to the extreme expense of actually moving very far out of your office—if at all. That holds cost and time down. This is critical for positioning on the knowledge curve.

Obviously, anyone involved in a business is already accessing some of this material. The mere fact that you are in the business means you are on enough mailing lists so that organizations seek you out. And the network you've already developed in your industry—suppliers, customers, bankers, friends—frequently alerts you to interesting information, or yields up the answers you're looking for. But equally obviously, the informal methods you currently use are neither exhaustive nor particularly useful when you go a little farther afield—like looking for potential customers in Qatar, suppliers in Florida, or financing in Belgium.

What we are suggesting is a systematic approach to an activity with which you are fairly familiar. A systematic approach is critical in order to assure you that you have accumulated the critical mass of information needed to make a decision. The key to the system really is to understand it as the opposite side of the natural information accumulation process we discussed in Chapter 4. There, the normal activities of a business gather together large amounts of wide-ranging information, much of it surprising and unpredictable. Here the goal is to use the same informal networks as well as other techniques to seek out, identify, and acquire extremely specific information.

Specificity is the key to semiactive intelligence that should be used only after you have a fairly clear idea of what you're looking for. Sequentially, it must follow a careful review of information already available in the company, as well as a systematic and aggressive accumulation of information from the organized public domain. A careful study of this material should be made to determine whether you have already accumulated the information you need to reach a decision. In many cases, you will find that the cost and effort of gathering additional information may not be worthwhile.

When you have been to all the web sites, downloaded all the articles, ordered all the books and magazine articles—read them! It will also help to think about them before you go off looking for more information.

We have noticed an interesting tendency in our own shop: info lust—a disease that afflicts the industrious. When we begin a project, we start looking for information. Fair enough. We start gathering information. We look at catalogs, bibliographies, old studies, our own databases. We start ordering things. We keep ordering things. Things pile up, higher and higher. We order more things. No one reads anything, they just keep finding more stuff. Then they start calling around looking for more goodies. Finally, they run out of time. They grab a few of the more likely looking pieces and try to fake it. The poor souls who do this are suffering from info lust. Notice, we are not calling it knowledge lust—there is no Faustian legend here. They don't read the stuff, so they don't get any smarter. They just need information. We are gentle with these people, especially after the bills start coming in. Usually, warmth, understanding, and counseling solve the problem. Executions are not usually carried out until the second offense.

You must, absolutely *must*, read the material as it comes in, or at least well before you start your second round of searches. You must *never* pick up the phone to call around until after you have absorbed the surge of passively obtained material. It is not only that you won't know what you're looking for and might be wasting time, but it is also directly harmful. Many times you find people who are pleased to help you the first time you contact them, but they become downright surly when repeatedly pestered. In many cases, people are a wasting asset, at least in the short run—another call in six months may not bother them as much as three calls in two days. You really need to know what you're looking for before you start making phone calls. Thus, a pause should take place at the end of the passive stage—for reading, thinking, figuring out whether you have everything you need, and deciding what it is you don't have.

Let's emphasize this point: The semiactive phase is mission-oriented and task-driven. Its job is to fill in the blanks left over from the passive phase. It is not the place to begin doing research nor is it the place where the bulk of information is to be found. It is knowledge-driven. It should take place only after the information gathered in the first phase has been transformed into knowledge. Otherwise, it is an opportunity for aimless schmoozing. But when it's knowledge-based, it's an extremely powerful phase of intelligence work.

We were once doing a study on the telecommunications industry in the Middle East. Our client was another consulting firm that was putting together an authoritative guide—he hoped—to the region's telecommunications industry for his own clients. He wanted to know how many satellite dish receivers there were in each country at the present time. Simple question, not so simple to answer. We hit all of our databases, but simply couldn't find the answer. It didn't mean that there wasn't an answer, only that the easy ways of finding it were not readily accessible.

We searched through our addled brains to find a way to answer the question. OK, who did we know who knew about the Middle East? Tons of folks. Who did we know who knew about satellite dishes? Tons of folks. Who did we know who were members of both groups? No one. This was turning into one of those killers that cause our accountant to cry and gnash his teeth.

We had to think carefully. Who would we know in the telecommunications group who might be likely to know someone who knew about the Middle East? OK, what group of telecommunications specialists was most likely to know people knowledgeable in the Middle East? Bingo. Members of the U.S. military, people on the staff of places like the Defense Information Systems Agency or the U.S. Army's Communications and Electronic Command. Why? Because the U.S. military spends tons of time in the Middle East. We called a few—and hit pay dirt on our third call. The guy over at the next desk from the person we were speaking to had spent years handling telecommunications for troops deploying in the Middle East. Did he know the numbers? Well, the Defense Department had run a study on telecommunications resources in the region. No, it wasn't classified. Sure, he'd be happy to send me a copy. We didn't tell our client that someone in DOD already had most of the study he was doing sitting on his desk. It wouldn't have mattered, since his clients didn't know about the DOD study and probably never would. We wowed our client. He wowed his clients. Our accountant smiled—a rare event.

PEOPLE: FROM POINTERS TO SOURCES

One way in which semiactive intelligence is used is by finding people who know of the existence of, and can locate, informally published documents. But in semiactive intelligence we begin to reach the point at which people themselves start to become valuable. When dealing with people, we've discovered, we need to increase the care we take to be systematic and focused. This is tough enough when dealing with books and articles, all of them chock full of not particularly useful information. People are even harder. Not only are they interesting in and of themselves, but they will talk about what interests them rather than what interests you—and you can sometimes forget what it is that you called about.

At this point in the process, it is very important to return to some of the basics we discussed in Chapter 3. The process of semiactive intelligence is, of course, unpredictable. Every business, every body of knowledge has a different geography of information, and therefore requires very different actions. But the key in every case is recognizing what is in hand, what remains to be found, and what the most likely procedure is for finding it. It is absolutely essential that the Mission Statement and the Information Inventory, now updated to include information acquired during the passive phase, be studied and that a new Information Requirements sheet be generated.

As you move into the semiactive and active modes, you are moving into a much more undifferentiated information soup. Remain focused or you will find yourself lost faster than you think. Do not stop to smell the roses.

We were once asked by a construction company to check out a mid-sized food-processing company that had asked them to undertake an important construction process for a complex processing plant. The project meant a substantial up-front investment. Question: What was the probability that the food processor would stretch out the payments—or worse, default on them? Legal protections weren't the issue. This was a dynamic construction company, which meant that it was usually one step ahead of creditors. Cash flow was everything and an interruption of cash flow would be catastrophic, regardless of legal remedies two years down the road.

MISSION: DETERMINE THE LIKELIHOOD OF DEFAULT OR STRETCHING OUT OF PAYMENTS

What did we know to begin with:

- Our client was uneasy, having heard rumors that the company liked to play games with its accounts payable.
- Not being in the food-processing field ourselves, we had only a vague idea of who the company was.

During the passive phase we found all sorts of information:

- The food processing company was financing the plant at interest rates of 16 to 18 percent.
- The asset base of the financing was created through a dizzying series of swaps between various companies organized under the chairman and CEO—let's call him Wildman Joe—of the food-processing company.
- The head man loved to sue and was regularly sued. One of the reasons that interest rates were so high was because everyone knew that, regardless of what assets were pledged as collateral, default meant that everyone would spend years in court litigating in the event of failure.
- The CEO of the company was being sued by his own mother over another business deal.

It was clear to us that this company did not play well with others, and that the chairman had been out of school the day sharing was being discussed. Nevertheless, it was a big contract and our client did not want to pass on it if there was any way to ascertain the company's likely course on this particular project. Would it be possible for us to figure out his intentions on this project, separate from his general track record?

Intelligence is a game of probabilities. We cannot look into the hearts of men, and it was unlikely that Wildman Joe himself had any idea what he was going to do with this project. He tended to go with the flow. We didn't doubt that he wanted to build the plant—he wasn't a straight-out rip-off artist—but we did know that if he ran into trouble, the likely outcome would be to stiff everyone involved and let his lawyers sort out the mess. The key, it seemed to us, would be to try to figure out what the likely course of this particular project would be. This, in turn, depended on two different issues. First, how likely was this project to succeed given the climate in the industry? Second, how healthy was this company internally—could it support this project?

Now, the food industry is, in general, a commodity industry. Commodities tend to operate in a near-perfect marketplace. That means that there are few secrets to be found. It is anyone's guess what the weather would be like in Iowa next summer, or whether blight would get into the Russian crop. Indeed, commodities were so perfect a market that a contrarian position is probably the best. Unlike research in a highly technical industry, like computers or pharmaceuticals, where the opinions of the best scientists and analysts are a pretty good gauge to what is likely to happen, specialist opinions in a commodity area are extremely ambiguous indicators. Using semiactive intelligence in this case—contacting key commodities brokers and specialists—would yield interesting information perhaps, but in the end we would not be able to rely on the consensus in determining our own recommendation. If anything, we would tend to go against the consensus. Even the best track record is no guarantee of future results—as the prospectuses tirelessly and accurately tell us. So calling the guy with the best track record won't give us very much that we could rely on. Frankly, if the food market collapsed unexpectedly, all bets would be off. Our client was prepared to live with that risk. What he needed to know was whether Wildman Joe could, under the best of circumstances, pull the project off and whether he had something weird up his sleeve.

We clearly needed to focus in on the company. Some questions emerged. We needed to develop a general read on the internal finances of the company. We needed to figure out what part this particular project played in Wildman Joe's overall plans. We had found what there was to be found in the public domain. It was murky. How could we find some clarity?

In analyzing the project, we focused on the most salient point: Wildman Joe had borrowed a heck of a lot of money at an extremely high interest rate to finance the project. Two questions: (1) Why had he gone that far out on the yield curve? and (2) What would be the general result on his businesses if he did not bring this project home? Now, we could speculate and we could guess, but at the end of the day we had to have the answers to these questions. Indeed, the two questions were really one: What did this project— its success or failure—mean for Wildman Joe's personal fortunes?

So, was this another of the schemes for which he had created thirteen escape hatches in the event that anything went wrong, or was this something that was of substantial importance to him. That would tell us whether he was going to jerk around the contractors— because the one thing we knew beyond any shadow of a doubt was that Wildman Joe took care of Wildman Joe.

In the end, it was all as simple as this. But who would know the answer? Or more precisely, who would know the answer and would also be willing to tell it to us? Yes, we were tempted to call his mother—but after all, a mother who would sue her own son is not necessarily going to be straight with us. This was a life-or-death issue for our client. So where should we turn?

What did we know? First, we knew that Wildman Joe spent his life in court and that he had lots of enemies. Bingo! In the United States, there is a lovely thing called discovery, where people suing each other get to paw through each other's dirty laundry. Some of this finds its way into the public domain, but a lot of it—particularly the impressions drawn from the material—wind up embedded in the heads of litigants and their lawyers. And from our passive work on Lexis, we had a list of litigants and their lawyers a mile long. We were getting somewhere.

Now, lawyers tend to be a closed-mouth lot when they're talking about their clients, but they are not always so circumspect when they are talking about their adversaries. And the litigants themselves—the poor suckers who had been worked over by Wildman Joe—were not only not ethically bound but usually in a mild rage, to say the least. Of course, the list of possible sources was pretty long, so we needed to define what we were looking for:

1. We were looking for people whose litigation would have been directed at Wildman Joe himself, rather than at one of his companies. This was designed to ensure that we would be dealing with people who had glimpsed his personal situation during discovery.

2. We were looking for small businesses rather than multinationals for two reasons. First, in our experience, smaller business people and their attorneys tend to be more garrulous. There is simply a lot more emotion built into a case in which your whole existence is at stake compared to a case whose outcome won't even be noticed on the bottom line. Second, they were more likely to have retained the nuances of the matter in their minds and to have tried to go for the jugular. They would probably know more.

3. We wanted more recent lawsuits, but not so recent that discovery had not yet taken place.

OK, we had a list of cases from LEXIS and Westlaw, the names of clients and their lawyers. It was time to pick a few. We found about twenty and let our fingers do the walking. We were very frank about why we were calling—and very cagey about who we were calling for. Our client did not want Wildman Joe to hear about what he was doing—certainly reasonable. Once we explained what we were doing our only task was to relax and take it all in. The litigants themselves immediately started pouring forth vitriol. The lawyers, having a reputation to live up to, remained totally professional for about ten minutes, and then their own anger started to rise.

Some important things to remember when manning the telephones, probably pretty obvious but worth stating anyway:

- The person to approach is the one with an interest in talking to you. Remember, that interest is not defined as just

financial—psychological interest is at least as important
as financial interest—everything from ego to sympathy
comes out.

- Define the likely mind-set of the listener and play to it. Here,
  a potential victim (your client) is looking for help in not
  being burned and, in turn, you are offering them another
  forum to tell their tale of woe—and maybe do a little harm
  to an enemy.

- Select the appropriate person and/or persona for the phone
  call. Don't send a young kid to call a senior partner at a
  law firm.

- Allow the speaker to unload on you. Act as a bucket to catch
  what comes out and sort it later if necessary. But always keep
  in mind what you are after.

- Allow him to identify with you. You must not identify with
  him. You are playing your game. He is playing his. Remember: Our reason for calling is to find a way to do business
  with Wildman Joe, not merely to celebrate his wickedness.

- In doing semiactive intelligence, the main cost is time. You
  have to debrief your source at his speed. Keep in mind that
  his motivation is not to solve your problem but to satisfy a
  peculiar psychological itch of his own. Patience is the price
  you will have to pay.

But it was Wildman Joe's meanness that was our pay-off. He
had screwed so many people, so royally, that all we had to do was listen and wait. In the end, the details of his personal empire were
clear to us. Wildman Joe was in fact in personal trouble. If this project failed, he was personally finished. When we laid it all side by
side, what we saw was a personal life and personal finances in massive disarray. We were not told this by any one person. Rather, each
of them, in the course of telling us how they had been burned and
what they found out during discovery, painted for us a collective
picture of real financial trouble for Wildman Joe.

The fact was that, unlike most cases, he was personally in more
trouble than his companies were. He had structured the deal in

which our client was involved so that he could personally revive his finances. He needed a home run and this project was it. Now, in most cases, this would be a recommendation to avoid involvement, and had our client been an investor this might well have been our recommendation. But he was only a contractor looking at a potentially lucrative contract. The paradox was that, in this case, Wildman Joe's personal financial problems made this a more secure play. He was using his company's resources to rebuild his personal finances. He needed this project to work. He was far less likely to play games with it during the early phases than in his other projects.

Our recommendation was to go forward with the deal, trading some long-term benefits for short payment schedules to protect against the project getting into financial trouble, but expect Wildman Joe to work hard to get the project done. Moreover, he needs you simply because a lot of other folks are not prepared to do business with him anymore and you are. Our client took our advice, did the deal, and got what was owed him. Better still, Wildman Joe, a born-again nice guy after his brush with disaster, throws as much business to our client as he can handle, since he stuck with him when no one else would. And he could stick because he had the information needed to make an informed, rational decision.

This was a case in which information that we obtained passively—court records—allowed us to determine clearly what we needed to know, and also allowed us to locate individuals who had the information and knowledge we needed to make a recommendation to our client and for him to make a decision. In many, if not most, cases, this is true. Formally published, informally published, and personal knowledge are so intertwined that accessing one part of the information network will allow you access to all other subnetworks—people, unpublished papers, and so on.

There are, of course, places where this doesn't work, particularly in areas that are new to you or in which you have allowed your expertise to atrophy over time. We once had an assignment to produce an ethnic map of Slovakia. This was an intelligence project in the full sense of the term, requiring us to pull together disparate information and merge them together with technology. Our problem: Since this took place right after the collapse of the Soviet empire in Eastern Europe, we didn't know where to start. How could we get the information on ethnicity in a country where all data was a tightly held state secret and in which ethnicity was an explosive subject—and on which very little had been written in the West because of lack of interest and lack of access. Our passive searches hit a blank wall. We didn't even have a Slovakian telephone book, let alone a Rolodex full of numbers.

A new technology proved extremely useful, providing us with a new form of semiactive intelligence—the Internet. As discussed in Chapter 5, this part of the Internet is not the graphically spiffy part that most of us are getting used to, but the newsgroups that have proliferated. Under Slovakia, there were several newsgroups, including one called Alt.Soc.Slovakia. We looked at that and found a rich discussion on Slovakian society. So we posted a question: Does anyone out there know of anyone doing work on mapping ethnic groups in Slovakia? We also posted this on the Hungarian newsgroups, since ethnicity in Slovakia is very much a Hungarian question as well. This not only started off a new thread on both newsgroups, and produced for us manifestos on the injustice of one side or the other, but tapped into a network of Hungarian and Slovakian scholars working on the issue—as well as some government officials wanting to know why we were interested. They turned out to be quite helpful in the end.

Notice the geographical shift involved here. Passive intelligence concentrates on electronic and paper. Semiactive still works these domains, looking for unindexed information. But it also moves in a much murkier domain: gossip and to some extent the gray area between gossip and proprietary information. It is vital to bear in mind that the realm of gossip in information soup is soup—information floating intermixed with other information and even disinformation. The gray area is just that, gray on gray on a foggy day. It is a realm of unclarity and uncertainty, where the motives of all the players are unclear and in which the information you receive is difficult to verify.

The increasing uncertainty inherent in dealing with these interior realms demands increased discipline—a point made over and over. Unlike the internal accumulation system, which is intended to capture and sift lots of gossip, semiactive forays into gossip collection and into the gray area requires a high degree of clarity. In our experience, premature entry into this realm can be disastrous. Without clear grounding in the general area and in the questions you need answered, you will inevitably run into increased rather than decreased confusion. At least as important, you can quickly become a victim of disinformation—being given answers that, were you more sophisticated, you would quickly recognize as, in some sense, false. Without preparation, trading in gossip or semilegitimate data is a nifty way to become a victim.

A step-by-step approach is recommended:

Identify the missing pieces: Study the board. Assess what you have and what question remains to be answered. Determine how valuable, how necessary that information is in giving a final recommendation or making a decision. Decide, beforehand, how much time and money you would be willing to spend on it.

Identify the likely location of the information: In one of our examples, the likeliest location for what we needed was in the heads of lawyers and clients, to be contacted by phone. In our other example, it was in the heads of scholars, to be initially located via the Internet. By the time you have reached the semiactive point in your research, you should know where to access the needed information. If you can't, you have more homework to do. This is a good test as to whether you're ready for transition.

Task-suitable personnel: You may not want to use your most intelligent people here; they may, after all, be social asses. So focus on the most congenial people you have. Indeed, if you are going to do this a lot, you will want to make sure you have a group of diverse personality types for each mission—or at least people with the ability to act. In some cases you want mature adults, male or female, to do the querying. In other cases, you want the young and innocent. It varies by case and context. Remember, you are dealing in gossip—a very personal and even intimate social process. If you need information from the *jefe* of a Guatemalan village and you figure that he responds best to an implicit sense of danger, don't have a nineteen-year-old woman contact him. On the other hand, if you want information from someone who will respond better if he feels he's doing someone needy a favor, don't send an ex-cop to ask questions. Gossip is social in the sense that it is designed to elicit information using socially powerful cues. These cues vary in time and place, and cannot be subject to political correctness. We are in the real world, which is inhabited by some very real and powerful stereotypes. There are still things like pretty girls and tough guys in this realm. That is the way it is—and our apologies to political correctness.

Define means of contact: Today, there is a wide range of mechanisms for contacting people. We have gone from mail to telephone to fax to e-mail and to all of the more exotic emerging means. If you are scoping out things in Silicon Valley, the web is both desirable and logical. But if you want to contact owners of small clothing stores in midwestern towns with populations under 25,000, you will probably want to choose more traditional means. Always bear in mind that as you move deeper and deeper into the information structure, personal contact becomes more and more important.

CONCLUSION: UNRAVELING THE NETWORK

It can begin simply: checking the bibliography of published works to locate publications you haven't found yet or which are not available in libraries. You find out the telephone number of the person who wrote the publication and call him. He turns out to have several other unpublished manuscripts and will send them to you. He also knows two or three other people you really ought to talk to; feel free to mention his name. By the time you're done, you have absorbed an extraordinary amount of information and knowledge for shockingly little money or effort.

We are quite serious in speaking of the compact vastness of networks—and we're not just trying to be cute. Expertise is rare. One of the characteristics of the expert is his comprehensiveness: He knows what he knows and he knows other people who know things as well. His knowledge is vast in relation to the subject, but it is compact in terms of time and utilization. He makes his living by being efficient in utilizing his expertise. In tapping into his expertise, you find vastness and comprehensiveness, but also compact efficiency.

Experts leave tracks; they are never invisible. We made this point when discussing the inside of the company and must repeat it here. They publish papers, give interviews, serve on boards. Now, one problem you have is that the most prominent expert is frequently the least likely to have the time or inclination to help you. But the most prominent is not necessarily the most knowledgeable. Less prominent, younger, hungrier specialists not only know as much but are frequently more motivated to help people in order to build their own unique network and expand their own horizons— plus build their egos. Our strategy is usually to track down a member of the second tier in the profession. He is more likely to be cooperative and quite probably more knowledgeable.

It is the first step that is hardest. Assume that you are entering a field you know nothing about. How should you proceed? Well, assuming that you've finished your passive search—and we assume that because you have absolutely no business doing semiactive research until you have—you must now define what you still need to know. Having done that, go back to the publications and, from what you've read, extract the names of experts in those areas. That will do the trick 90 percent of the time. Certainly, some people won't talk to you, but we have found this to be a surprisingly small percentage. Sometimes you may have to pay for their time to even talk to them—frequently true with lawyers and consultants. Fair enough. Calculate the potential value against the cost and make your decision.

There are cases where publications won't work. Here, unraveling the network becomes more difficult, but not impossible. We favor three approaches at this point:

- Locate a likely unit of government. For example, if you are in the basketball industry, and you are looking for new markets, a logical place to begin is your nation's Education Depart-

ment or Ministry—specializing in physical education. If you
don't know who to ask for, explain what you want to the
receptionist. They will want to get rid of you quickly, and the
best way to do that is to pass you on to someone else. Eventually you will find the one person in the building who worries
about basketballs. He will tell you about all sorts of studies
and meetings and people. The very bloat of government can
work to your advantage. And most government officials—particularly mid-level officials not used to putting up with public
abuse on a daily basis—are actually reasonable, affable
people.

- Locate a semipublic organization, such as a chamber of commerce, trade association, trade union, someone not associated with a particular business but with the industry in
  general. These are superb places for starting to unravel the
  network.

- Universities are useful for more abstract or abstruse areas
  of knowledge, rather than concrete areas of marketing
  or finance. But if you have a question on penetrating the
  Peruvian jelly bean market, you may not find a jelly bean
  expert at the university; however, you will probably find a
  Peruvian expert—and that may begin to unravel the
  network.

One additional point here: The contacts and knowledge accumulated in these forays are remarkably and unexpectedly valuable.
No phone call should ever be made without inputting basic facts
onto a contact sheet—paper or computerized. It is gratifying when
a failed contact turns out to be of extraordinary value.

**Never throw anything away. The effort of saving one hundred
useless contact records is paid for by the use of one
unexpected contact.**

Locating and unraveling the network is usually a fairly easy
process—surprisingly easy given the amount of value embedded in

these networks. Rarely, but sometimes, all of the passive and semi-active intelligence won't do the trick. This is usually a time to hang it up. Sometimes, however, you can't let go. This brings us to the rarest, but for some perverse reason sexiest, aspect of intelligence: the active operation.

7

WHEN YOU ABSOLUTELY, POSITIVELY HAVE TO KNOW

Active Intelligence Gathering

There are times when you desperately need information, times when the normal constraints of cost, time, and even risk don't apply. Times when the normal process of information collection and knowledge production simply can't tell you what you need to know. *These* are the times to use active intelligence collection. Let's say, right from the beginning, that, risk aside, the efforts and costs associated with active intelligence gathering are such that most businesses, in the course of their entire history, will never need to resort to such means. In a sense, what most people see as the heart of intelligence—active means—we see as not only peripheral but rare, usually costing more than it's worth. But rare does not mean never.

Active intelligence involves more than getting out of your chair and out of the office, although it probably means that as well. Active intelligence means going out after information you need once you've determined that it is simply not in the readily accessible domains—or that it is difficult to track down using the tools discussed under passive and semiactive intelligence.

This information is not so much illegal to gather as it is shrouded in secrecy. This is an activity where the borders are more than a little hazy. Put it this way: Information can be owned by someone, and taking it constitutes theft. It is, however, possible to legally pierce the veil of secrecy by observing perfectly legal actions

and inferring from them underlying reasons using other information you have obtained—also legally. If this all sounds a bit cloudy
and you are unclear as to what we are saying, then you are on the
right track, because this area of intelligence is murky and it's never
easy to follow what's going on.

Take some pretty famous examples. During the Cuban Missile
Crisis, reporters noticed limousines coming and going from the
White House. As old hands, they knew this was unusual activity.
From the license plates, they could figure out who was coming and
going. By noticing that the plates belonged to both Defense and
State Department officials, it was clear that a foreign policy crisis
was brewing. It didn't take much to figure out that it concerned
Cuba. The same thing happened during the Gulf War. Reuters
reporter Jacqueline Frank actually wrote a piece entitled "How
Tense Are U.S. War Planners? Just Count the Pizzas." On January
16, 1991, the day before the air campaign began, she noted that on
the previous night, Domino's Pizza had delivered fifty-five pizzas to
the White House between ten P.M. and two A.M. The average White
House order during that time frame was five pizzas. At the Pentagon, just over a hundred pizzas were ordered; at State, seventy-five,
up from one per night. The CIA, using their massive resources to
locate the leak, stopped ordering from Domino's. Frank shrewdly
grasped that the massive increase of pizzas being delivered late at
night meant that the number of people working late had increased.
She also understood that there was probably a reason for this and
that this reason was probably not associated with a study of the
National Park system.

Now, the fact that there was a Cuban Missile Crisis was a secret,
as was the timing of the beginning of the air war on Iraq. Anyone
tapping phone conversations, reading secret documents, or blackmailing participants would be committing a serious crime. What
was not a crime, in the United States, was observing an uncontrolled emission of information—the physical, visible presence of
official limos or of Domino's Pizza delivery cars. Those emissions,
placed into context by individuals possessing highly nuanced information from years of covering the White House, generated knowledge of what was going on that was every bit as clear as if the

president's press secretary had made an official statement. It was possible to penetrate the innermost secrets of the White House perfectly and totally legally. But you literally had to be there to see the limos and delivery trucks—or at least contact Domino's directly and hope they answered your question. More important, you had to have a massive base of information on which to draw to understand the meaning of the limos.

Presence is the key to active intelligence, and what makes it so expensive. Stationing a reporter at the White House is expensive, but it's a no-brainer for a large news organization, a decision that pays for itself in many ways other than the occasional intelligence coup. The White House is an obvious location for a news organization to place a reporter. The problem is much greater for a business since it is not in the intelligence-gathering business and can't cost out the price of an agent over other, profit-making, projects, like the evening news.

But presence is often indispensable. Sometimes the reason for this is to pick up information before it diffuses into the public domain. Other times, this is because the information will not diffuse and will only be available to those present. And then there are the times presence is needed because information has to be coaxed out—in effect, an emission has to be generated. Whatever the reason, active intelligence requires presence by someone who is able to recognize the difference between the significant and insignificant. That's what forces the price up. Expertise doesn't come cheap, especially when it has to go out in the field.

> **In active intelligence, if you have to ask the price, you probably have more sense than to try it.**

It is sometimes possible to find these emissions passively. However, in matters of vital interest, emissions are guarded extremely carefully—particularly those that are likely to move into the electronic domain. Often such emissions show up in the realm of gossip. During mergers and acquisitions, for example, gossip is frequently generated prior to official announcements due to accidental or, at times, deliberate leaks. And there are times when passive intelligence will pick up a nugget that is overlooked by others but from which an experienced hand can draw inferences. But sometimes, the intelligence coup does not derive from a new bit of information available only to you but from the ability to analyze and understand a generally available but neglected bit of information.

At best, active intelligence gets hold of useful bits of information sooner than would otherwise be the case. This is the core issue of active intelligence: positioning yourself on the knowledge curve. Active intelligence can provide you with two advantages. One is simply accessing information that would otherwise be unattainable. The other is accessing information before others have it. The times when the potential payoffs for this kind of information are worth the cost are extremely rare.

The rareness of rational active intelligence in business is made rarer still because active intelligence has the highest probability of failure. As the White House examples show, a good deal depended on luck—noticing the events and understanding them. In many cases, active-intelligence projects are undertaken without a clear goal, which substantially increases the need for luck. After all, sending someone out to find out something—anything—about the competition merely increases the opportunities for trivia while dissipating the energies of the collectors.

Nothing is more important in active intelligence than defining precisely what it is you need to know, how you expect to find it out, and what the financial value to your business will be. Virtually anything can be found out with enough time and enough money. Merely beginning the project starts to run the clock at an exorbitant rate. Our rule is that 90 percent of all information you need can be found through passive and semiactive intelligence. Of the remaining 10 percent, you will find that 90 percent of the desired information is simply not worth it. By the time you get it, it will be too late. By the time you pay for it, it will have destroyed your profit-and-loss sheet rather than having enhanced it. That means that active intelligence will be justified in no more than 1 percent of all cases—and frankly, we think that is a very generous assumption.

THE ACTIVE INTELLIGENCE OPERATION

Assume that you have encountered a business problem that requires information not accessible by passive or semiactive means, and assume further that you have determined that securing this information is of enormous value and you are prepared and able to put substantial resources into the project. Now what?

After you have precisely defined what it is you need to know, the next step is to try to figure out why you haven't been able to find it in the first place. Many times you discover that the reason you haven't found it is because it doesn't exist. At other times you discover that it exists but you just haven't looked in the right place. Sometimes, when you think about it, what you really want is not so much information but analysis. This is a particularly nasty mistake to fall into.

For example, let's say that you want to know if another company is going to produce a product that would compete with one of your own. You know the company is capable of doing it, and you think it would probably benefit them. Many decisions you are about to make depend on their plans. It is something you really need to know. The problem is the information may not exist because the decision makers at the other company have not yet made a decision. That doesn't mean they won't decide to go ahead, so you can't discount it in your planning. But they may decide not to produce the product, so you can't discount that either. You need to generate a Plan A and a Plan B to cover both alternatives. And often you can't wait for a definitive answer to act—by the time the other company's CEO makes his announcement, it will be too late to respond. You need an answer as early as possible.

An active operation that comes up with nothing may not be a good sign. You are now in a classic dilemma of intelligence, one that is particularly painful given the high costs of active intelligence. A negative answer may mean that he is not doing it, or it may mean that your intelligence operation has failed. A positive answer may be a false positive, or intentional or accidental disinformation. This is the classic problem of active intelligence. Any answer you receive may or may not be true. And absolute verification is always difficult. In the end, you are forced to go with probabilities in matters where nothing less than certainty will do. In increasing your information, there is no certainty that active intelligence will increase your knowledge.

The goal, of course, is to minimize this chaos. Before you begin the operation, you must determine what sort of information will satisfy your needs. In this case, what is really needed is analysis. What is the best move for your quarry to make? In the past, was he someone who made the best move or did he tend to screw up? What are the factors that shape his decision-making process? None of these are part of the intelligence-collection process. All of these use intelligence products to carry out analysis, and in the end, all intelligence culminates in analysis. In both government and business there is an ongoing fear of pitting your mind against your competitor's mind. It is much easier to look for more information. The fact is that you may have in hand all the information you're going to need. There is a tendency to push gathering much too far.

However, if it does turn out that additional information is required, then you have to determine several things:

- Where is the information located?
- What is the form of the information? Is it a document? A conversation? An idea in someone's head?
- Is the information you need directly accessible?
- If not, what emissions might permit you to infer the information you need?
- What resources must you allocate and how should they be deployed to capture the information or the emission?

There are two kinds of resources that can be devoted to active-intelligence projects: technical collection systems and human intelligence systems. In the case of active intelligence collection, human intelligence becomes much more important. Most technical collection systems that are used by national intelligence agencies are illegal for use by private citizens. Signal interception, for example, which is done regularly by the U.S. National Security Agency as well as by other intelligence agencies, is not something most companies can legally undertake, outside their own premises at least.

Check out the rules for the specific country in which you are working. Although there are numerous parts of the world where photographing transportation or industrial facilities is illegal, there are just as many countries where whatever can be seen in public can be recorded. Photographic intelligence, while often not very useful, can be extremely rewarding in specific cases. In countries where photography is not a problem, it can open the door to any number of possibilities. Take the following examples:

- A critical issue for business and government alike is the trend in the price of oil. During the early 1980s, a friend was flying us to Long Island, east of New York City, in his private plane. While flying from New Jersey to Long Island, we crossed over the Atlantic approaches to New York harbor. I was startled to see numerous oil tankers, none showing wakes, clearly anchored for scores of miles outside New York harbor. I researched the question and discovered that oil companies frequently ordered tankers to stand at anchor waiting for shifts in the spot market. Looking at that line-up outside the harbor, we realized that the sellers were not entirely happy with the price they were getting and were hoping to see it rise. Also, so many tankers were piling up that it was unlikely that the price would rise. In fact, we were seeing the beginning of the 1980s oil glut. Just looking at what was happening in New York harbor could not justify my going short on oil futures—after all, a temporary breakdown in off-loading facilities could have been the cause. Today, however, it is possible to monitor off-loading activity in all of the world's leading ports—Yokohama, Rotterdam, Houston, and so on. The end of the Cold War has made commercial access to satellite imagery available at surprisingly low prices. For example, Russian Spin-2 satellite imagery with two-meter resolution— you can see cars—costs $300 for a 2km x 2km fragment, supplied on CD-ROM or 8mm tape. The French sell synthetic aperture radar shots at fine resolution for $1,850 for a 100km x 100km swath—just right for tracking shipping. A rush order can be processed in under a week, but costs extra.

- Satellite imagery allows you to monitor large-scale development projects that are inaccessible by other means. Suppose a competitor is building a major new manufacturing facility in China, in direct competition with your company. It is obviously important for you to know how construction on that project is going. A satellite image of the site, taken in various spectra including infrared and visual light, could very well tell you where the project stands—and whether you will have to worry about new products in the next month or next decade.

- An old trick, and one not requiring satellites, is to take regular pictures of the parking lots of competitors. A tremendous amount can be learned by comparing pictures of parking lots over time. Obviously, you can get a real sense of the workforce, and whether the facility is operating at the same level as last year can easily be seen by the number of cars parked at various times of the day. At smaller companies, you can tell something about the relative prosperity of the company: Are there a lot of Porsches in the parking lot or old Chevrolets? This is active, technical intelligence in the best and simplest sense. But just looking isn't enough. Photographs are needed to give you historical context and benchmarks.

The visual is the most legally accessible spectrum in active intelligence and one of the reasons that, for business, much active intelligence is done by humans. Human intelligence, or HUMINT, is generally carried out with the eyes and ears, picking up information that is passed into the public domain and is therefore accessible. Following someone, overhearing a conversation at the next table, staking out the entrance to a building are not illegal. They may not be particularly ethical, but you will probably not be taken away in handcuffs if it's done with common sense.

Technical collection systems are very sexy—rarely useful, but irresistible. Come to think of it, that's what sexy means.

Human intelligence, on the other hand, is more simple than sexy. We once had a case in which we needed to check out a Russian company. The company, whose headquarters was in Moscow, had approached an American firm with a joint venture proposal that was quite intriguing. Obviously, the American company wanted to know more about the Russian company. Passive intelligence, with any degree of detail, on Russian companies is quite difficult. They are about a generation behind us in the information-production industry—meaning that they do not yet use computers for typesetting—which means that most of their reporting is inaccessible electronically. What little we could gather passively on Russia came through Western reporters writing on Russian business, and this tended to focus on the activities of very large Western companies and their Russian allies, not on independent Russian firms.

Phone calls—semiactive collection—would not help either. We needed to know simple things, like the kind of office this company had, who works there, who is their banker, and so on. We needed to see the facility; we needed to talk to people who were unlikely to talk to a stranger over the telephone. In short, we needed someone there to do some legwork. It really didn't take a great deal of skill or even reliability; it just needed a body with a modicum of intelligence. Sending someone to Moscow was extremely expensive and no one on our staff, at that moment, could pass as Russian. This was quite important, for a native gets a different response than a foreigner. We were looking for texture here— how solid was the business? A moderately intelligent and reliable Russian would probably serve us better, and certainly cheaper, than one of our own employees going over there.

This poses the key problem of human intelligence: finding the right person. Sometimes this is an impossible task; other times, such as this one, it appears to be impossible but is really not so hard. Finding what we might call a generic human, Muscovite flavor, while sitting in an office thousands of miles away would daunt many people. Most large companies turn to professional investigative agencies, which charge an arm and a leg—and usually a lung as well. That level of expertise was neither required nor justified for this project.

The point of the play *Six Degrees of Separation,* about a young man claiming to be the son of Sidney Poitier, is simple: No one is ever more than six links away from any person. Everyone knows someone who knows someone who knows someone…until, within six links, you can get to the person you need. Now, as an empirical matter, we don't know if this is true—it certainly sounds good—but it does point to the fact that there are an extraordinary number of linkages at our disposal.

With this in mind, we hit our friends and acquaintances. We asked our staff if they knew anyone who lives in Moscow. Within twenty-four hours we found two U.S. graduate students living in Moscow, a biologist working there, and the in-laws of one of our secretaries who were Russian nationals living in Moscow. Our secretary's in-laws were retirees from one of the ministries who spoke some English. We were on the phone with them within an hour.

They were absolutely delighted to do some work, earn what was for them a fabulous amount of Western currency—and for us, frankly, not a whole lot—and help their daughter-in-law as well. They knew the address well—it was a short distance from their home. They went to it, reported that the "headquarters" was in a shabby apartment house; the telephone and fax numbers were private rather than business exchanges; and no such company was known to the building superintendent. They also noted that there were no foreign private license plates on cars parked around the area—a sure sign that this wasn't an area where internationally connected businesses were established. With a high degree of confidence we were able to report to our client that this company was, like many struggling start-ups in Russia, not more than a name and a P.O. box, and that unless they were willing to get in there, put a lot of money and expertise into the individuals involved—who seemed pretty sharp, we were told—there was not much at the other end to count on. Bad news, but better to hear it early than late.

This was a case of active human intelligence. It was not rocket science. It was not a case that involved great cost or risk. It was simply the only way to handle a case where there was little passive intelligence to hold on to. The hardest part here was finding someone

to do it. However, even small businesses can readily find someone
to check something out so long as it isn't extremely complex,
extremely sensitive, or in some truly godforsaken corner of
the world.

Assuming that your personnel network doesn't turn up someone to do your legwork, here are some suggestions:

- If you can't find someone to check something out in your
  own country, you had better improve your social life fast.

- Universities are tremendous repositories of people who know
  people. This is particularly true of the language and social
  science department. If you want someone in Paraguay, call
  the secretary at the Spanish department, history, anthropol-
  ogy, or political science department. Ask for their Paraguay
  specialist. After they stop laughing, ask for their Latin Ameri-
  canist, any of them. Ask them if they know anyone specializing in Paraguay. They'll know someone. Get a number and
  an introduction. The Paraguayan specialist will know a dozen
  people happy to earn some money. He may be going there
  next month.

- Call the U.S. Commerce Department and ask for the person
  specializing in Paraguayan trade. Call the U.S. State Department and ask for the person on the Paraguayan Desk. In the
  United States and most Western countries, someone in business can readily access even the most senior officials working
  a country. You will be surprised who you can get to speak
  to if you exercise authority, courtesy, and patience. But
  usually, with many requests, lower-level officials will be more
  useful.

- Call the U.S.-Paraguayan friendship association, chamber of
  commerce, or whatever. You can probably find them on the
  web or by calling the nation's embassy. Don't rely on the
  embassy itself for information on particular companies native
  to that country—the con artist might turn out to be the
  ambassador's brother. But you can get quickly plugged into a
  suitable relationship.

Sometimes there are cases that are more sensitive. A client company we were involved with was interested in making acquisitions. One company they were looking at, in New Hampshire, was an old family firm, where the head of the family had recently passed away. A son-in-law was now running the company. Our client badly needed to know the son-in-law's intentions. Was he planning to continue running the company; was he thinking of going public; was he open, eager, or even desperate for a buy-out? We knew that the son-in-law had recently been a senior official at a major computing firm—not at all this company's line—and that he had left his job to handle the family business. He may have been delighted to do so, having waited for decades for the old man to die. Or he might have done it reluctantly, forced into it because there was no one else in the family to take over, and eager to get back to his old job. The facts we gleaned using passive and semiactive means leant themselves to either interpretation. We needed to know for sure.

There were two approaches. The first would be to look at his finances and those of the company. Both were extremely closely held. It was simply not legally possible to see them. The other approach was to get a sense of the guy's thinking. We didn't know him, and we didn't know anyone who knew him—certainly not well enough to tell us something this important. But in one small article we picked up, we found that he was a member of a country club, and a fairly active member at that—on the board and so forth. He would be well known at that country club and organizations like that are hotbeds of gossip.

The question we now had was: Did we know anyone who might be active in that particular country club? Given the focus of our attention, our needs were pretty well defined: We needed someone, fairly well-to-do, who lived in or around that New Hampshire town. The odds were excellent that if he didn't know the guy, he would know someone who did, and if he didn't belong to the club, a good friend of his probably did. So we needed someone who was geographically positioned to help us out and located in the appropriate social stratum. And we needed to maintain security. We couldn't let our target know he was being tracked, since this would give away our client's intentions. In effect, what we needed to do was access the gossip domain to see what was being emitted into that sphere by the new CEO, and we needed a collector in place who would also serve as a screen over our activity—a fancy way of saying we needed to hear the gossip and the country club was a great place to listen if we could recruit a member.

Again, we asked our staff: Did anyone know anyone who lived in that particular town in New Hampshire? Not surprisingly, no one did. We extended our query to some of our outside professional supports, whom we frequently used as extended parts of our network. A partner in our accountant's firm came from that town. We explained to our accountant, under the seal of professional confidentiality, what we were after and why. We made it clear that we were not seeking anything illegal or even vaguely unethical. All we wanted was information that was already public, if unpublished, in that town. We made it clear to him that we did not want to be connected with the query in any way, but we did want to know what the word was in that country club about our man's intentions. We wanted no confidentialities violated, no secrets stolen. We merely wanted a report back on what was being said publicly.

Our accountant agreed to serve as go-between—he liked being our accountant and this was a service that would enhance his value to us. Also—and this is important—there is a mystique in covert intelligence gathering that excites the Walter Mitty in many people. It is something that can be taken advantage of. Anyway, he spoke to his partner, explaining what was needed. We had asked him not to tell his partner about us, but this was a fairly empty request. First, his partner could probably infer which of their clients being handled by our accountant would make such a weird request. Second, our accountant's loyalty to his own firm probably transcended his loyalty to us.

As soon as you tell someone that something is a secret, their brains go into overdrive trying to figure out what the secret is.

In going to our accountant, we were making a conscious decision to accept a calculated risk of leak. Face it: Every time you take a matter to another human being, you run the risk of some degree of betrayal, intended or otherwise. This is one of the great disadvantages of human intelligence. It is far easier to control security breeches during technical intelligence projects than in human intelligence. The very thing that gives human intelligence its strength—context and nuance—also allows agents to see and understand far more than you want them to or hope they do. It also makes them unpredictable. Would our accountant tell his partner who we were? Would the accountant guess? Would he guess who our client was? Would he tell his wife? Would she tell her mother? Would her mother tell his mother, who still lived in that town. Would unexpected friendships or loyalties compromise our operation? Would he let all this slip unintentionally—or for personal profit?

This was the hard part. We most emphatically did not want this guy to know that we were investigating him. We were afraid of two leaks. First, that anyone we approached in the club would tell him what we were up to. Second, we were afraid that a leak would occur during the course of our investigation, while questions were being asked. We needed to proceed with maximum stealth. It was a risk we hated—but had—to take. At each step—the query to our accountant, his query to his partner, and the partner's search for access to country club gossip—the risk of leak and exposure grew.

The fewer the links, the more likely the operations will be traced back to you. The more links, the more likely a leak will occur somewhere.

In sensitive human intelligence matters, therefore, it is imperative to keep the number of links to the actual agent to a minimum consistent with the need to shield yourself. One main reason is security. The agent, the person actually gathering the information, obviously must know what he's after. As with all collection systems, context and nuance are essential. Transmitting that context to the collector means transmitting it through each and every link. This increases the knowledge embedded in the pipeline and increases the damage caused by a leak. Thus, on the whole, the fewer links the better.

Another reason for keeping links to a minimum involves the reliability of transmissions. As a kid, you probably played a game called telephone. Seven or eight kids would line up. Someone would tell a simple story into the first kid's ear, and they would successively whisper it to each other. It was amazing to see what came out at the other end, after retelling by seven or eight people. By the time you were done, the story was unrecognizable. That is the problem of transmitting through too many links. In handling agents, two-way communication is needed, which doubles the possibility of transmission error, massively multiplying the possibilities of miscommunication. This means that, from a transmission-quality standpoint, minimizing the number of links is essential.

From a security standpoint, however, it cuts both ways. On one side, there is the risk of leaks and betrayal; on the other side, there is the need to shield the questioner. In this particular project, we decided that the priority was on security—it would be better to have a distorted answer than to have the questions traced back to us. That decision was situational. There was no principle involved beyond the nature of the case.

In the end, this relatively simple query produced a query structure looking something like that shown on page 179.

Our accountant's partner contacted five people he knew from his hometown. We asked him, through our accountant, not to ask any questions at this point, nor even to ask about the guy we were tracking. All we were interested in at this point was someone who belonged to the country club. We really did not want someone who knew our CEO intimately. Quite the contrary. An intimate friend would almost certainly have alerted the CEO to our interest—the worst outcome. Our reasoning was that given his prominence at the country club, given the recent death of his father-in-law and his new position, and given the fact that in addition to interest, there was no perceived need on their side for security, there was an extremely high probability that country club gossip would be both rich with information and, on the whole, accurate. So we were obviously hoping to avoid his best friend. What we were looking for was an active member of the club—someone who hung out, played golf, had some drinks, and went to parties.

PROBING THE COUNTRY CLUB

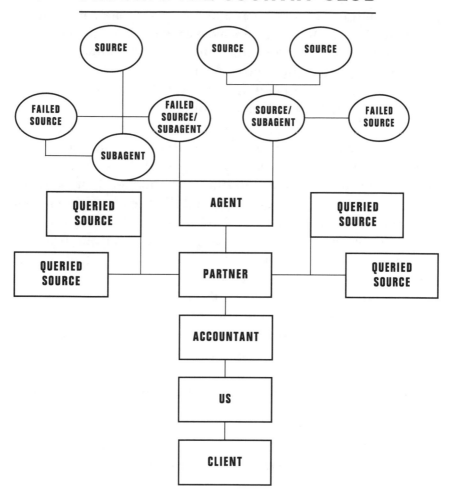

Our accountant's partner sequentially contacted people, beginning with those he knew best and therefore provided the least security risk. It took five calls before he found someone he was confident was well connected to the crowd. This guy became the agent. We had now reached the critical point in the operation. The agent, whom we never met and never would meet, had to be fed the question, and there was no way of being cute. He needed to know that someone was interested in finding out how the new CEO felt about the company. What were his plans? Had he sold his house? Had his family moved? What had he been saying? Ideally, our accountant's partner could have worked this into a casual phone conversation, saying that he had heard that So-and-so had died and turn the matter into idle gossip. Had he found someone in the know in the first few tries, it might have worked. Unfortunately, he was down to number five on the list before hitting pay dirt. This guy was someone he never called casually, so it had to be turned into a purposeful call.

We were now facing a dilemma. What's in it for the guy he's calling? Those involved to this point—us, our client, our accountant, and even the accountant's partner—all had financial motivations of one sort or another to pursue the matter. Our potential agent had no such motivation. We could provide him with one—by paying him—but a member of that country club would not be a poor man. Everyone has a price, or so we hear, but the price for turning a well-to-do man into a spy is usually substantially higher than the project is worth. Moreover, in approaching someone with a money offer, you already shape the relationship. It is extremely difficult to offer someone money for spying and then, when he gets insulted, ask him to do it for free. Our policy is simple: We almost never offer money to a potential agent unless it is a completely impersonal job. We try to find a plausible way to make it sound like help for a friend and then let him ask for money if he's going to.

Offering money is a big step. The deal is no longer casual, no longer minor. It increases your own vulnerability.

The partner was dealing with an old friend from high school, someone he hadn't seen in years. There was no use in faking sudden nostalgia. The key was to determine if the friend was on intimate terms with the CEO. If he was, then we instructed our accountant to have him back off. If he knew him at a distance, we asked him to explain that he, as an accountant, was involved with some people who were interested in the status of the firm now that the founder was dead—something both true and not particularly revealing. He was wondering if his friend had heard any gossip about what the new CEO's plans were.

The fat was now in the fire. But it was in the fire in such a way that we probably weren't going to get splattered. There was no reason for the accountant's partner's friend to feel used, nothing to be ashamed of, nothing illegal or unethical involved. The old friend said that he would ask around. The accountant asked that the matter not be traced to him because he did not want to appear to be stalking or harassing the guy—plausible, reasonable, and surely something a friend could do for an old friend. They talked about family, reminisced, and swore that they had to get together soon. We had our agent in the country club.

Now things were no longer in our control. This was not an agent who could be controlled by us. We had to rely on him to actually ask around, ask the right questions, ask the questions with delicacy, understand the answers, and communicate them back to his friend, our accountant's partner. But we had enough cutoffs—breaks between ourselves and the agent—that we had traded minimal control for maximum distance. Fair trade, under the circumstances.

The old friend started to ask around. He had heard gossip but had not paid much attention. In the information soup of the country club, this was not a matter of interest to him before. Out golfing one Friday afternoon, he asked a golf partner if he knew the CEO and if he knew what his plans were. His golf buddy said that he didn't know him but he would ask around. No big deal. That night at dinner, he asked another friend if he knew the story. He did. He had heard that the CEO was extremely unhappy about having to leave his job, because he felt he had a shot at becoming the CEO there—a much bigger company in his own area of interest—but pressure from his wife and her family forced him to take the job. But, he said, that was a few months ago, he might have adjusted to the new situation. He'd ask around. His wife, hearing this, said that she knew his sister well. She was going shopping with her next week and would let him know what she found out.

Our agent now had two subagents without any direct knowledge working on the case, and a subagent with knowledge. One subagent never panned out. He asked someone who didn't know anything and gave up. The friend's wife asked the CEO's sister and hit pay dirt. His dinner companion asked three people, two of whom had information.

All of this came back to our agent as follows: One person said the CEO was pretty happy with his new position while two other sources, including his sister, said that he was desperately unhappy. The agent, without consulting us, dropped out the odd story and gave us only the unnuanced tale: The CEO was unhappy, primarily because the finances were a shambles and he was afraid that his reputation was going to go down with the company. He wanted out.

This came from the agent, through the accounting partner, our accountant, to us, to our client. And it turned out that part of it was true and part false. The CEO wanted out because he was ambitious. But the finances of the company were not in shambles. He was simply unhappy with his position and trying to build himself up by bad-mouthing his father-in-law's managerial skills. But we had our report.

Problem: How did we know this report was accurate? Answer: We didn't. We could have mounted another separate operation to see what was confirmed, but we didn't have the resources. Moreover, in dealing with gossip, the problem is that the soup itself might be false, and reentering the soup would not have improved the quality of data. We could have hired a private investigator, for ridiculous amounts of money, but he would merely have done what we did, or tipped our hand.

After all the work and effort, we needed to sit down and think through whether the information we had was reliable. In the end, it was our client's decision. It was his call because it was his risk. He wanted us to be more certain than we could possibly be. We could have faked a false certainty, but the fact was that there were too many links, too many agents, too many of them collecting without a real motivation to be accurate—too much chance for error. But the core report was that the man was unhappy. A buyout was possible. An approach was made. A buyout did take place. We were heroes.

Now, this scenario was obviously case-specific. That's the nature of active intelligence. Unlike passive intelligence, where you can pretty much go down a checklist, in active intelligence things change with each case. Nevertheless, certain things are constant. The most important is this: Know what you want and figure out where you're likely to find it. In this case, we decided that a country club was the best place. The possibilities are endless, and some are obvious: trade shows, which are like huge bowls of ice cream begging to be eaten; charity functions with concentrations from the relevant industry; bars frequented by company employees. Virtually any persistent gathering of people is a potential intelligence gathering site, so long as you know what you are looking for.

Then there is the question of how to approach the site. Sometimes you can be blunt. We love calling a company, asking for a given department, and just asking a question. Cold calling works, if only because the guy at the other end is taken by surprise—and it's open and honest. Sometimes, though, you can't be open, honest, or blunt, so calling and pretending to be a customer works. On rare occasions, hiring an investigator to follow someone around works— but only if you're interested in who he's meeting with. Otherwise, it's pretty pointless.

Know what you want; have a good idea where to find it; find the right person to go after it.

CONCLUSION: THE USES AND LIMITS OF ACTIVE INTELLIGENCE

The key to active intelligence is the clear identification of the information being sought and a rigorous definition of where that information is likely to be found. In our operation, we knew what we wanted to know and identified a location where that information was to be found. With that clearly in hand, we figured out a way to get someone into position to hear what we needed to hear. Once we heard what we needed to know, we terminated the project.

When you've got what you want, go home while you're still ahead.

This can often be the most important rule to follow, the most important part of the operation. Open-ended active collection operations can get very expensive and very hairy. In this operation we were very careful to "stay on the sidewalk." By this we mean that the sidewalk is public property. If, while walking down the street, you pick up something on the ground or see something taking place, even on private property, you are still clearly within the law. Staying on the sidewalk means staying within the public domain. Widely circulating gossip is within the public domain. Finding out what was being said in a social circle is perfectly legal, even if it was rigorously planned and carefully targeted. And it can be cost effective, precisely because it ended when we found out what we needed.

Long-term, unending operations, in our experience, have a nasty and frequently unintended consequence of going off the side-walk—into private property. Let's say that you want to find out more about what a competitor is doing. A neat way of doing this is to have someone answer one of his help-wanted ads. Initial interviews can be very revealing. You're OK since they are publicly broadcast, and hopefully the interviewee is not being asked to sign confidentiality agreements, but is openly stating that he's happy where he is but wants to hear more about what this company is doing. But let's assume that he's called for another interview or that he's offered a job. You're on a slippery slope filled with temptation—to mix metaphors. You now have the opportunity to plant an agent directly in the belly of the beast—the monster competing with you. Is there any situation that would justify this?

It might help to remember a famous case in the world of inves-tigative reporting. Two "Prime Time Live" producers applied for and accepted jobs with Food Lion, a food-handling company, on the basis of false employment records and references, then pro-ceeded to tape and film the inside workings of the company using hidden cameras and microphones. What did they get? A good story. What did it cost them? When discovered, they were sued for fraud, trespass, and breach of loyalty for their falsification of records to obtain the jobs. Note: They were not sued for libel, so the informa-tion they obtained was probably accurate. Maybe their case wasn't long term or unending, but it was certainly off the sidewalk. The jury awarded Food Lion $5.5 million.

What are you going to get from using these methods? Your fantasy is that you'll get everything, but that's not likely, any more than someone working for you is likely to get "everything" about you. Are you going to get more than if you have someone hang out at the coffeehouse where your competitor's employees go? Could the "Prime Time Live" producers have accumulated the desired information any other way? Maybe not, but was it enough to justify the cost and the risk? Well, if you are as vague as most people are about what they are after, almost anything can be justified. But if you are as focused and specific as you need to be, then you'll probably realize that the risk isn't worth it.

Focus and specificity can save you from the worst thing in intelligence work: the unlikely outcome. Even with the best security you can never tell how something will leak, how some extremely unlikely coincidence will blow up in your face. We cherish the story of one of our friends who lived in a small town in Pennsylvania. A respectable fellow in most ways, he did have a lover. Once, on a business trip to Los Angeles, he arranged to take her along. He followed security procedures in every way. She traveled on a different day on a different airline. He checked into the hotel room only under his name and she never answered the phone. Thousands of miles from home, they were anonymous, secure, safe. They went walking down the street in Century City, hand in hand, very much in love. Sitting on a bench, ten feet away from them, was his minister's wife, attending a convention for minister's wives in Century City. What were the odds of that happening? In our experience, too darn high.

Ongoing intelligence operations are going to blow up in your face. Count on it. In a world governed by Murphy's Law—where anything that can go wrong will go wrong—extended and interminable intelligence operations are accidents waiting to happen. The longer they go on, the more likely they'll go wrong. The broader they are, the more likely they'll bump into something. You may think you don't care if people find out that you are spooking around, but you do. By being known as a spook, people will throw up barriers to your most routine, passive, and semiactive questions.

Denied easy access to the public domain, you will find that, in the long run, you will know less than you did before and at much higher prices. Promiscuous active intelligence just doesn't pay. And that goes triple for illegal active intelligence—also known as espionage.

8

LUCKY GUESSES

The Art of Analysis

Analysis is where the rubber meets the road. The interpretation of information—analysis—is the tissue that connects business intelligence with business operations. All of the intelligence gathering in the world, no matter how subtle and effective, is merely the raw material that allows the analyst to cook up his brew. Remember our example of the first business intelligence operative? When Joseph helped the Pharaoh corner the Middle Eastern grain markets he was more of an analyst than an intelligence gatherer. After all, it was his ability to interpret the Pharaoh's dreams—to analyze them—and produce an action plan that allowed him to be so effective. Without this ability the operation would never have gotten off the ground. The point of gathering tea leaves is to read them. Without being able to read them, all the gathered tea leaves will constitute nothing more than a giant mess on the table.

The product the analyst produces is advice, and it can take many forms—from regular briefings to formal newsletters to web sites with fancy interactives. No matter how complex the delivery system becomes, the analyst serves his customer—the decision makers in the company. Now his analysis can be distributed to other employees, and even to customers or the entire industry. But the focus of the analyst is, and must be, the corporate decision makers.

This is an important part of analysis that is frequently forgotten until the analyst is sacked. Business-intelligence analysis is not an academic study, a search for truth that will withstand the test of the ages. The sole purpose of business analysis is to provide the specific customer in the specific company what he needs in order to make decisions. Please notice that we said "needs" rather than wants. That is and always will be the crisis of the intelligence analyst—as it is the crisis of the doctor, lawyer, or accountant. What the customer needs is not always what he wants. But an intelligence analyst who doesn't have the confidence of his customer is useless, and the one who wins that confidence by giving his boss only what he wants to hear is equally useless.

The intelligence analyst is only as good as his customer: This is where the ultimate responsibility rests. Unfortunately, as lawyers know only too well, it is easier for the customer to blame the analyst than himself. And that, as we say, is life.

Every businessman is also an analyst. One of his jobs is trying to figure out what is going to happen next, and to position his company to take advantage of it. So one of the first decisions in creating an intelligence system is to define the manager's role in the overall process. In a small business, where the entrepreneur is already acting as CEO and janitor, he or she will continue in the role of analyst—hopefully with some new insights about that role and the process of collecting intelligence. But in larger companies, even though it is prudent to minimize the cost of intelligence by dual-tasking collection with normal business functions, separating analysis from operations remains an important thing to consider. We have already touched on some of the reasons for such a separation, as well as some of the arguments against it. In order to go into the question in more depth, we need to think about what is involved in analysis and then consider the necessary functions and skills of an analyst.

THE ART AND CRAFT OF ANALYSIS

What do we mean by analysis? Does simply thinking about one's job constitute analysis? In a general sense, it is obviously necessary for every employee to spend time thinking about his or her job—God help the company where this does not happen! However, when we talk about intelligence analysis, we mean something a bit different than ordinary thought. It must be more self-conscious and self-aware than the ordinary, necessary process of thinking about doing a job. Intelligence analysis must have a different and much clearer purpose, focus, and method.

The foremost purpose of analysis is to translate information into a particular type of knowledge, which, in our introduction, we called situational awareness. Situational awareness is a term we borrowed from fighter pilots, who live in a world in which the collection of information tends to outstrip the ability to absorb and analyze it in the time frame in which decisions have to be made. Fighter pilots are moving at near, or even above, the speed of sound and dealing with other, potentially hostile, aircraft doing the same thing. Sensors are gathering information about everything from the temperature of the turbines to the location of friendly and enemy fighters. The pilot must absorb all of this information *and* make decisions. He can't spend a great deal of time reading each dial, looking at each digital readout, or studying a radar screen. He doesn't need any one piece of information nearly as much as he needs an intimate, intuitive grasp of the *entire* situation around him in one comprehensive gulp—what psychologists call Gestalt. Military aircraft designers are spending a great deal of money trying to solve the problem of "information overload."

Information overload is simply excessive information, information that has not and probably cannot be digested. A pilot cannot afford to spend too much time interpreting or analyzing information. He needs to have information delivered to him as knowledge, in a predigested form, so that he can, with minimal effort and distraction, absorb it and turn it into situational awareness. Situational awareness, then, is a knowledge of the whole situation, constructed out of the pieces of information that are surging toward him, and fused into a synthesis that is readily understandable and can provide the pilot with the knowledge needed to make decisions in the next tenth of a second.

Given enough time, the pilot is quite capable of understanding every bit of information provided to him. Indeed, if he did have time to study every bit of information coming into his cockpit, he would undoubtedly have a superior situational awareness. But trying to do so would paralyze him, making it impossible for him to fly and fight his aircraft. So he has become increasingly dependent on systems that analyze the information for him, fusing it into a single, comprehensible, real-time situational awareness. The push for virtual reality in the cockpit is an attempt to force computerized analysis to its limits, creating an automated analogue of reality, which fuses all incoming information into one useful, if not fully true, picture of what is happening out there.

Effective decision making requires that situational awareness be effortless. Achieving an effortless sense of reality takes a lot of work.

The fighter pilot requires someone or something else to do his analysis for him, since the decision point passes well before he can absorb the material. Left to his own devices, the pilot is too far behind the knowledge curve.

What has happened in the cockpit, we would argue, is also happening in the executive suite—if not in quite as dramatic a fashion. The time needed to fuse information into a knowledge of the situational awareness is expanding dramatically. Obviously, business executives would be substantially better off if this were not the case. The optimal situation is always one in which the decision maker is intimately familiar with every morsel of information before acting on it. However, what is optimal is not always possible, both in the head office and in the cockpit.

Just as the pilot needs tools to fuse information into a comprehensive situational awareness, so does the businessman, who, in a sense, lives in a much more complex, less orderly, and unpredictable environment. The variables that are matters of life and death for the pilot are fairly well defined, more predictable, and mostly physical. While engaging a MiG fighter, it is unlikely that he will be seriously effected by Japan's new import regulations.

The businessman, however, can be affected by virtually anything. Information on so many potentially important things are constantly flowing into his business. Most of these things are irrelevant; some hint at wonderful opportunities; still others point to deadly danger for his business. This is where analysis must extract from this information soup those things that are of real significance to the business, identify variables that are both changing and likely to require decisions, and present them in an efficient manner. The direction and nature of threats and opportunities for the businessman are highly unpredictable in location and type. They are also rarely physical. Usually, a businessman can't spot it on a radar screen; his screen is much more complex and subtle. The collection process is of no value if it overloads the executive—the last thing he needs is more data dumped on his desk. As with the fighter pilot, excessive, undigested information can retard the decision-making process. The executive and the fighter pilot both need intelligence—knowledge at the right point on the curve—rather than more information.

The purpose of analysis in business intelligence is to present the decision maker with a full and comprehensive awareness of what is going on around him, in such a way that he can make a decision or request and receive additional, detailed information quickly and efficiently. Some day, as with the fighter pilot, microprocessors might exist that can produce this situational awareness. But today, while microprocessor support might be available, it takes a human being to turn information into knowledge. The analyst is the microchip that processes and fuses the incoming information quickly enough to alert the executive to impending shifts in his surroundings. The executive may have time to do this himself, or he may hire someone to do it for him. This is where the focus of analysis and the role of the analyst overlap and need to be considered together.

THE ANALYST

The analyst needs to be comprehensive, but also focused, in his work. That is a tall order. A soap manufacturer needs to know about

much more than the manufacturing of soap. Everything from the
latest fashions in Brazil to European Union environmental regulations to information on interest rates in Japan are of potential interest to him. Indeed, since the unanticipated is the most dangerous,
it is literally impossible for him to circumscribe his universe of information. That universe is usually circumscribed by available time
and resources; so inevitably, some event will take him by surprise.
Had he been able to anticipate it, he could have dealt with it far
more effectively. Context and nuance, as discussed in Chapter 3, are
indispensable if the significance and relationships of facts to each
other are to be recognized.

This is one of the central problems in going outside your own
organization to do intelligence work. A business analyst drawn from
a consulting firm can certainly carry out excellent research on a
detailed question, but he cannot provide the kind of situational
awareness required unless he is intimately familiar with the business
realities a decision maker is dealing with. A company having an
inventory problem is going to be watching short-term interest rates
much more carefully than a company whose concern is a new
emerging competitive technology. At the same time, the intelligence analyst must know what is of *potential* interest to the business,
so that he can provide timely warnings of dangers and opportunities.

The analyst must be given access to a company's strategic
thinking as well as to operational details. That is why, in one sense,
the ideal analyst would be the head of the business. Leaving aside
the important question of self-criticism, no one knows—or ought to
know—the company better than its CEO. That means no one is a
better analyst. This is one of the great advantages small companies
have over large ones. While large companies have more room to
maneuver and greater economies of scale, small companies have
superior situational awareness, because strategy, operations, and
analysis are all located in the brains of one or a handful of people.

Second, the analyst must be intimately familiar with the types
of information available. He must know what information has to be
gathered and absorbed to provide baseline situational awareness
and what must be available to deal with specialized queries. He

must be familiar with the strengths and weaknesses of all his sources, know what he can ask for, where he can ask for it, and how much trust he can place in it. The intelligence analyst must, therefore, be both a trusted member of the company's management team, with ready access to the decision-making process as an observer, and intimately familiar with the information flowing into the company, or that might be brought in.

An analyst without access to the secrets of the executive suite is like a doctor who can't examine the patient. All you'll get from him are the bills.

The analyst must also be a magician, a soothsayer. Like Joseph, the intelligence analyst is a fortune-teller. The ultimate value of intelligence is prediction, which, after all, is the difference between intelligence and journalism. A journalist tells you what has happened; the intelligence analyst tells you what is going to happen. If an intelligence analyst can't tell you what will happen, then all you need is a subscription to the *Financial Times*. Now, obviously, there are very few fortune-tellers among us with the skill of Joseph, who could turn the Pharaoh's neurotic nightmares into a business plan. And this is the crisis that every intelligence analyst faces. Lacking Joseph's skills, most analysts can't risk categorical declarations. The guy who said that talkies were a passing fad and silent movies would continue to reign probably had trouble getting anyone's attention with his prediction that TV would never work.

In order to achieve even these modest goals, a good analyst needs to have certain moral and intellectual qualities. The most important of these are honesty and courage. The foundation of intelligence analysis is a willingness to be wrong, wrong in two senses. First, it is the willingness to change your mind when the facts demand it—not to fall in love with your own analysis, not to let your own ego get in the way of recognizing error. Second, it is the willingness to stand alone, against the crowd when necessary, even if it turns out you were wrong.

The intelligence analyst must have an ego so large that he is genuinely more concerned about what he thinks of himself than what others think of him. This allows him to stand free of trends. It also frees him from the need to be an iconoclast—allowing him to go with the trend when that seems reasonable to him. Honesty and courage are the critical elements, along with deep-seated ambition. There are many businessmen whose driving ambition is to be average, to do as well as everyone else. They would rather be wrong than alone. The real intelligence analyst is different: He has to be indifferent to whether he is alone or in good company. He has to be more obsessed with whether he is right than with whether his boss likes him.

> **Intelligence analysts are strange people. You may invite them to the office party, but it is doubtful that you want one marrying your brother or sister.**

Intellectually, the intelligence analyst is caught in a two-dimensional struggle. On one hand, situational awareness requires that he be a generalist; on the other hand, mastering specifics requires that he master narrow areas of expertise as well. That is one dimension of the struggle. The other is a struggle between the discipline of believing only what he knows to be true and the need to be intuitive, or guessing successfully at the parts he doesn't or can't know. The intelligence analyst's mind must be synthetic: It is an artifact that the analyst has to craft for himself, as if he were crafting any other tool of the trade. It is also synthetic because its task is to synthesize, to pull together all the diverse strands that constitute the situation.

The best analysts we know try very hard to be stupid and simpleminded. Sophisticated, well-connected people are bad analysts because, being well connected, they start to think like the people around them. Bright and sophisticated people believe they know a great deal: They are intimately connected with highly placed friends, they go to meetings, get invited to give talks. They are in the know, so to speak. They know what Henry Kissinger and Alan Greenspan are saying at cocktail parties. They attend conferences at the Harvard Business School. They speak with partners at Goldman Sachs. They even speak with people at Microsoft. They are the best and the brightest.

From Henry Kissinger, they learned in 1977 that Iran would be a tremendous place to invest on the international scene. Alan Greenspan told them in 1982 that the economy could not recover unless the budget deficit was brought under control. At Harvard in 1990, they learned that Gorbachev was the man, and that Boris Yeltsin was a loudmouth bumpkin. They also learned that the Soviet Union, whatever its problems, would survive. At Goldman Sachs, in 1992, they heard how the Japanese economy would overtake the United States. From Microsoft in 1992, they learned that the Internet was not something that had to be taken seriously.

The assumption that is frequently made is that because these sophisticated, well-connected people are privy to the inner thoughts of powerful decision makers, they know what is going to happen and that their worldview, if properly understood, will create a map of the future that will guide the analyst. However, being sophisticated has more to do with blending in with a mind-set, going with the crowd—albeit an exalted and sophisticated crowd—than it has with being right.

All those who predicted that Arab petrodollars would rule the world in the twenty-first century were replaced by others who believed that Japan would rule the twenty-first century; they were then replaced by people who believed that China would rule the twenty-first century. The best and the brightest were wrong. An intelligence analyst following their thinking ought to be working on the editorial page of the *New York Times,* and not for your company.

Analysts should not be afraid to stand alone. The danger of casual assumptions of well-connected sophisticates is twofold: It is not simply that conventional elite opinion and expectations are frequently wrong, it is also a fact that accepting basic assumptions from anywhere limits the analyst's imagination and causes the analyst not to question and examine issues that must be examined.

The history of national intelligence is littered with such universally accepted assumptions that proved to be utterly wrong. Just consider one incredible error with tremendous consequences for business. In 1973, the Arab oil embargo raised the price of oil dramatically and caused gasoline shortages in the West. Sophisticated opinion—ranging from such places as the World Bank to Harvard to the Club of Rome to the Kremlin—combined with the growing power of the Arab world and with basic assumptions about the ecology to reach a basic consensus: We were entering an epoch of permanent oil shortage. It was agreed that with demand growing, spaceship earth (they really talked that way) had a fixed amount of crude oil available. Therefore, the price of oil would continue to rise indefinitely. Indeed, the argument went, this applied not only to oil but to all sorts of primary commodities like food and ores. The age of expansionary industrial economies was over.

It followed, therefore, that investment in an industrial plant put you on the short end of the stick. People producing cars were at the mercy of people producing oil. It made sense to put your money into extractive industry and farmland, and avoid investing in industrial infrastructure. Since most undeveloped raw materials were to be found in the third world, it made more sense to invest in the third world than to invest in advanced industrial countries.

An analyst who uses the phrase "as everybody knows" ought to look for a new career, probably in the food-service industry as a party planner.

So, during the 1970s, huge amounts of money were invested in Mexican, Nigerian, and Indonesian oil and other commodities, while the Arabs seemed about to gobble up the West's industries. If you wanted to build a plant in the United States, you went to Riyadh or Dubai.

The problem was that the consensus was wrong in a fundamental way. The assumption was that we had discovered all the oil there was to discover. With the price of crude soaring, the world went crazy hunting for oil. And they found it. By the early 1980s, the price of oil, and of all other commodities, was plunging. Oil-tanker owners and third-world refineries built on the assumption that oil would be selling for over $40 a barrel and up to $100 a barrel went bankrupt as the price of oil plunged. And third-world governments, which had borrowed huge amounts on the assumption that the loans would be paid back from oil and other mineral revenues, defaulted on billions of dollars' worth of loans. People who bought Iowa farmland in the 1970s were bankrupt in 1985.

Anyone following the consensus in 1975 would have invested in Mexican oil, Iowa farmland, and Filipino government bonds. They certainly wouldn't have invested in Chrysler, which, as everyone knew, was finished, along with Detroit. And it would never have occurred to anyone that what they ought to be looking at had nothing to do with the industrial/mineral relationship with which everyone was obsessed but instead should be looking at start-ups with weird names like Intel, Apple, or Microsoft. The consensus in this case was not only wrong, it didn't even understand the issue.

Most people tend to think in straight lines. They figure that if China's economy grew by 8 percent for the past five years, then this will undoubtedly continue into the future, and by 2020, China's economy will be larger than the American economy. Or if Microsoft continues to grow the way it is growing, by 2020, everyone in the world will work for Microsoft. This is obviously nonsense. The fact that China has grown as fast as it has means that it probably won't continue to grow that fast. The same for Microsoft. Good analysts always remember that what goes up must come down. They therefore tend to think in terms of curves rather than in terms of lines. The hard part is predicting the shape of the curve. But convincing most people in 1975 that the petrodollar was a passing blip would have been hard enough. People who believe in curves tend to lead lonely lives.

There are two types of analysts. The first type wants to be right. The second type wants to have company. One of the hardest things in analysis is saying things that no one else believes to be true. No one can be an analyst who is at root a conformist. This is obviously true in stock-market analysis, where being a contrarian is embedded in the entire system, under the theory that if everyone believes the market will go up, it can't, since everyone will have already invested their money in anticipation of the move. That contrarian spirit must be extended to all sorts of intelligence analysis. It is the only way things can be ruthlessly and rigorously analyzed.

METHODS OF ANALYSIS

We use something called zero-based reasoning in our work. Like zero-based budgeting, this is an approach which says that every bit of what we assume to be the case must be reexamined and justified on a regular basis. In part this is a mind-set. It is the thing that is most obviously true, the thing that everyone knows to be the case, that must be examined most carefully—and that is something that requires a powerful will not to believe. But it is also a matter of method. In Chapter 3, we discussed developing an information inventory. Here, we would suggest a careful, written inventory of assumptions.

An assumption inventory simply means defining the basic worldview with which you are dealing. In Chapter 5, we discussed someone looking to buy a pager. What assumptions does he believe as he begins his research? Arbitrarily, a list might include:

- People will increasingly want to be reachable wherever they go.
- The price of cellular phones will remain dramatically higher than pagers.
- The FCC will continue to permit pager operations at the current level.
- The marketing of pagers and of pager connectivity will continue to include small businesses.

Any or all of these might be true. Most experts in the field would argue that they are in fact true and will remain true. But if you put your hard-earned money into a business, it is no comfort that you, along with the experts, were wrong. Your goal is to be right.

Therefore, the beginning of any analytical work consists of gathering together all of the information that has been found, and trying to extract from it the common, stable assumptions that most people appear to share. These assumptions shape the literature, the research, the arguments—everything including many of the facts.

The analyst begins by extracting these core assumptions, identifying them, and making them the focus of the research. The most obvious, reasonable assumptions should worry you the most, for example: Do people really want to be reachable wherever they go? Are they going to become tired of being reachable? We don't know, but that is, after all, the core issue in an industry selling perpetual availability.

People who don't constantly reexamine basic premises are people who say things like: Why would anyone want a computer at home? What would you do with it?

Zero-base analysis carries with it a cost. You are, in effect, continually reinventing the wheel. By taking nothing for granted, the analyst winds up constantly reexamining everything. In essence, this is what the analyst *should* be doing. It's the nature of the job. But in practice, this gums up the works tremendously. We recommend two solutions. Systematically, periodic assumption reviews should be carried out. Existentially, one part of the analyst's brain should always be studying the assumptions.

One solution, used in the defense community as well as the intelligence community, is the Red Team or B Team approach. On a major project, or on an issue of ongoing importance, teams are assembled outside the group that normally deals with the problem. Their job is to take a look at everything the Blue Team or A Team has been working on—in particular the assumptions—and tear them apart. Obviously, this is a pretty expensive way to approach the problem. We suggest, for small businesses in particular, that the approach should be periodic, rigorous reviews.

Part of the issue here is how the intelligence process is approached. Analysis drives, or ought to drive, collection. That the collector needs to be guided in his collection is obvious. But in order to do that, the analyst must translate a business's needs into information requirements. This requires the analyst to have an intimate understanding of the strategic problem facing the business. In turn, that understanding will guide the system. Strategic understanding allows the analyst to prioritize. He knows what is important and when it will be important. He can also focus particular tasks into a coherent whole. Most important, the analyst will be in a position to examine the premises driving the strategy, revealing shortcomings and redefining the strategy as needed. As part of the assumption inventory, we would strongly urge periodic strategic reviews. Obviously, these are already being done regularly in healthy businesses. Regularizing these reviews, turning them into the equivalent of strategic audits, provides everyone with an opportunity to rethink the basic issues facing the business. More important, by linking the strategic review to the intelligence process, there is an increased probability that the review will not be carried out in an information vacuum. An intelligence-based strategic review does not consist simply of reevaluating the assumptions behind strategy, but on reexamining the information in hand and collecting new information. Strategic review without intelligence gathering frequently means reinforcing existing beliefs, which may or may not continue to be valid. Intelligence-based strategic review becomes a tool for evaluation in the context of new information.

The ongoing task of the intelligence analyst can be divided into three parts:

- Issue-driven projects—specific projects designed to solve immediate problems. Where shall we build a new facility? Will the city council pass a new zoning ordinance that will affect us? Would a new product be made obsolete in two years because of new technologies? Each of these projects shares certain characteristics: They are limited in scope and finite in duration. In addition, while they all may require complex analysis and massive information, they all produce fairly specific and limited answers. The vast majority of business intelligence projects, although not necessarily the most important ones, take this form. They are by far the easiest to analyze precisely because they are finite.

- Ongoing analysis of the operating environment—examination of the immediate competitive environment of a business. This is the type most closely associated with "competitive intelligence." The task here is to define the environment—

what companies must be monitored, what products, what governmental bodies, and so on. What variables must be monitored—such as prices, technology, particular people. Having specified scope and timing, systems must be designed to monitor at the frequency desired.

- Tours of the horizon—searching for the unanticipated. This is the most difficult, the most necessary, and the most neglected aspect of business research. Most businesses operate over extended periods of time in fairly constrained operating environments. Competitiors, personalities, technologies in this environment are fairly predictable and change occurs incrementally. Sometimes, change crashes in from the outside. A new technology makes your particular product obsolete; a new personality goes on a buyout binge; a new competitor enters the field. The difficulty with this sort of challenge is its unpredictability. Who could predict that electric calculator companies would be forced out of business by a chip invented for NASA. Who could predict that a new environmental regulation would push the auto battery business against the wall? Who could predict that Rupert Murdoch would decide to enter the TV production business and create an entire new network? Well, these were predictable if you were looking in the right place. This is the analyst's most demanding task: knowing what to be concerned about while it is still a distant problem, and taking it seriously.

No one, including the CIA, has the resources to do completely satisfactory work in all three areas. Therefore, the task of the analyst is to decide how much time and resources should be devoted to each task. This has to be done by the analyst, because this hierarchy can only be created by someone with a full sense of the problems associated with both the business's position and the difficulties of the collection process.

The problem facing the analyst is the tension between the need to complete short-term, finite projections and the need to do long-term monitoring. Murphy's Law, that work expands to fill available time, needs to be amended:

Work with deadlines attached take priority over work without deadlines. That means that people will flounder around with a $10,000 project on a deadline while neglecting a potential billion-dollar deal without a deadline.

The analyst has a particularly acute case of this problem. As work piles up, his ability to think and read in the long range declines. As long-range judgment declines, so does his ability to evaluate short-term projects. Retail-site selection that ignores a new set of potential planning ordinances or the arrival of a megastore in the region is not likely to yield the necessary results—profits. Analysts must be ruthless in reserving a proportion of their time for monitoring the immediate environment and even more ruthless in making certain that a careful watch is kept on the horizon. There are no hard-and-fast rules for how many resources ought to be allocated nor how much time—so an arbitrary rule ought to be 50 percent/40 percent/10 percent of time and resources, with some of the best intellectual power reserved for the third. It is in this final 10 percent that the great dangers and opportunities lie. It is also the most unruly and unpredictable realm; the realm that requires the most judgment.

ISSUES FACING THE ANALYST

Judgment is at the heart and craft of intelligence. Everyone else can process things, but the analyst must go beyond the process, stop, and judge the meaning of what has been found. There are two problems at the root of the analyst's dilemma:

- The analyst lives in a world of imperfect and incomplete information. No matter how much work is put into gathering the best available information, it will remain flawed. The analyst nevertheless must make the best practical judgment possible in spite of this inherent weakness. "I don't know" may be honest, but it is hardly useful to a manager who *must* make a decision.

■ The analyst can never be certain that he has all the information available. By definition, it is impossible to know what you don't know. And since what you don't know could very well kill you, the analyst is always inclined to continue the search for more information, always afraid that the next report will contain information invalidating everything. Putting off reporting out of fear of surprise is an occupational hazard.

The analyst is caught up in a continual interplay between information gatherers and decision makers. Decision makers want answers and they want correct answers. The analyst in turn puts pressure on gatherers to collect more and better information. The point at which the analyst has all the information he can reasonably expect to collect arrives long before he has gathered all the information that it was cost effective to gather. But how can the analyst know that he has reached this point?

We have a simple, if not always reliable, rule of thumb. Most research refers to other research and almost all business information refers to other business information. We reach a point in our work where we are familiar with all the references being made. The bibliography in an article refers to other articles we've already read. Most experts refer to other experts—experts we contact refer us to experts we already talked to. Reaching this point seems to happen quite suddenly: One day we realize we have exhausted the accessible information.

It does not mean that there isn't anything else to know, nor that this material might not be useful. But it does mean that the common network of discourse has been exhausted. From here on out, we are in no-man's-land, where even the experts with whom we've been dealing haven't gone. There may be some important information that hasn't been networked into the publications and expertise of people, but it is unlikely. This is the analyst's decision point: Move ahead, or let it slide. There is no science to this point— it is the art of analysis.

Part of the problem here is the extent to which an analyst will rely on expertise. Do the experts in a field really know what is going on in that field? A distinction must be made here between expertise in a finite area of existing information—such as a technology—and the broader area of prediction. A genuine expert on magnetic media in computers is probably a reliable source on the boundaries of the field. Get a few of these together and, between them, they probably know everything going on in the field. That does not mean that they can predict where the field will be in five years. So distinguish between expertise in an existing area and expertise in prediction. This is perhaps clearest in a field like economics. If you were interested in a small, technical area of economics, tracking the expert would do the job. But all of the experts in economics together could not tell you where the global economy was going to be in ten years.

Expertise does not necessarily extend to fortune-telling—the thing in which an analyst is most interested. Analysts who rely on experts to predict future trends are being sophisticated—and they'll get nailed. The forces that are shaping the economy are thoroughly impersonal. The richest and most powerful financier has little control over and minimal knowledge about where we will be in the future. Here it is absolutely essential to capture the impersonal essence of the forces that are shaping the world.

The distinction between the sphere where personal expertise is valid and the sphere where impersonal forces can explain what is about to happen, is the primordial mud of intelligence analysis. This is even true in predicting people's behavior. A given politician or businessman may not be the best source to consult on what he will be doing in five years. He may not have anticipated the forces that will come to bear on him and he may not have insight into his own probable reactions to those forces. President Richard Nixon did not think he would have to resign, but a good intelligence analyst could have predicted the forces likely to develop over time and predict his actions—well before he did.

Do you really think Hoffa knew he was going to be whacked? The insider knows what he hopes will happen. Sometimes it does.

Knowing what people will do before they themselves know it is, after all, what intelligence analysis is all about. Lest this appear to be impossible or absurd, let's consider a group of intelligence analysts who already do this on a daily basis: financial analysts predicting which stocks will go up or down.

FINANCIAL ANALYSTS AS INTELLIGENCE ANALYSTS

The financial analyst is a natural generalist who derives his vision of the future by creating a stylized construct of the present, consisting of financial statements, press releases, gossip, briefings, and the like. Financial analysts who survey the broad markets for investors are forced to take extremely wide, synthesizing views of reality. Even here there is pressure to specialize in particular industries, but good financial analysts look at their specialty industries from very broad perspectives. Financial analysts are intelligence analysts, serving a specialized but extremely large segment of business—the financial markets. A significant source of information about any company listed on pretty well any stock exchange is the reports produced for security houses and stockbrokers by their teams of financial analysts. Ostensibly, these reports are produced for the benefit of major clients of brokerage firms so that they may decide if they wish to invest in a corporation. But most stockbrokers make their reports available to the serious media, which means newspapers like the *Financial Times* and the *Wall Street Journal;* financial news agencies like AFX, Bloomberg, and Reuters, or business television networks like CNBC. The reports can usually be located through the archives of these organizations and obtained directly from the brokers.

The principal objective of the financial analyst is to assess the value of the companies he studies, and to assess future potential profits and share value—basically to try to predict the future. To get this kind of price-sensitive information he needs to probe deeply, and get as much inside information as possible. So a successful analyst will spend part of his time in the office poring over company accounts, reading official filings to stock exchanges and bodies like the Securities and Exchange Commission (SEC), and teasing out the numbers. But then the analyst will want to visit the company, meet as many people as possible, and also meet the company's competitors. The best analysts will also want to visit at least some of the company's operations or factories to make an assessment of their efficiency. Herein lies the danger. The financial analyst has to make sure he is not suborned by a new breed of flack, known as the investment relations consultant. The job of this person is to put a favorable spin on a corporation's financials, to try and ensure that the analyst only meets the "right" people, and to keep the share price as high as possible.

Investor relations managers tend to have generous expense accounts. They are at their most active in Wall Street and in the financial capitals of Europe, and they spend considerable energy and charm in courting the analysts. This is the financial analyst's equivalent of the sophisticated, well-connected source. Both those close to the decision makers and the investor relations manager types have a definite personal interest in presenting the best picture about their organization or country.

Financial analysts are both role models and sources. But beware. Contrary to their self-image, they are still human and fall in love with their own advice.

The lesson here for those gathering business intelligence about subsidiary companies or overseas operations that are secretive about their activities is to look at analyst's reports on their major business partners, especially if these partners are based in Europe or the United States, where analysts are most active and where reporting requirements from the share markets are rigorous.

PROJECTING THE FUTURE

In any attempt to project the future, the key question that must be asked is: What will determine the future? Answering that question will, in turn, determine what information will be required to get a sense of the future. We can divide the factors determining the future course of events into two categories: personal and impersonal.

There are events that basically depend on the will of people. For example, whether this person or that person will be hired for a job depends to a great degree on the will of the hirer. Whether a new product will or won't be invented depends on what is going on inside the mind of the inventor, investors, and so on. Whether a particular company will attempt to buy out another company is, at least in part, a matter of will—and therefore you need to know what certain people are thinking in order to predict the future.

There are other matters that really don't depend on will, that are highly impersonal matters. For example, whether the stock market will rise next year is not in the hands of any one man or even group of men—paranoid fantasies not withstanding. The path the market will take depends on a wide variety of impersonal forces. We can and do debate which forces are more or less important—indeed, that debate and the different perceptions and theories is one of the forces that shapes the market—but you cannot predict the course of the stock market by having a long talk with any one person. If it can be predicted at all, its course will be determined by very public forces, data about which is widely available. In business, a large part of the future is determined by market forces that, by definition, are not under anyone's control.

The first task that any analyst has, the foundation of all of his work, is to determine the extent to which his company's situation and future are defined by personal and impersonal forces. Consider: You are the owner of an independent but prosperous bookstore in a small town. You are aware of a major trend in your industry—giant bookstores. You are doing pretty well but doubt that you can survive if a giant moves into your area. Your lease is up for a two-year renewal. If a giant is going to move in, it would be rational for you to close operations now. If a giant is not going to move in, then you certainly should sign up. Question: What will the giants do?

At first glance, this is a very personal decision. There is obviously a team in place at each of the giants that has identified the markets into which they would like to move, and there are clearly plans in existence for at least the coming year, and probably more, for new openings. So, at first glance, an analyst would decide that this project is dependent on personal inclinations and focus on penetrating the planning cell, which may or may not be possible.

If you look at the matter a little more carefully, however, you can see that there are two types of impersonal forces at work. First, while planners have the power to select, the selections are clearly going to be made not arbitrarily but by some predefined criteria. Now, you can try to steal the document that contains those criteria, or you can reverse engineer the document. You know where the giants have opened stores in the past and you have an awful lot of statistics available on those locations. You can take a look at where they have gone and deduce the criteria they must be looking at. Then it is a matter of looking at your own market and seeing if it fits those criteria. This isn't foolproof, and, obviously, you cannot absolutely predict the future, but past performance is a pretty good indicator in this case.

There is a second set of impersonal categories you might look at. The giants have been expanding heavily. This fact alone does not mean that they will continue to expand at the same rate. They might become more or less aggressive. To a very large extent, this will not depend on them. More precisely, all businesses live in a world of constraints, and they make decisions within the context of those constraints. What does the company's balance sheet look like? Expansion requires borrowing. How much more can they borrow? They've had a massive expansion. Is their management holding up or are they having problems? What does the retail book environment look like? Are computer games, the Internet, and other things cutting into the market, ruining some of the projections they were operating under? Are they going to be able to carry out any more expansions?

In other words, an analyst, trying to figure out what all of the information means, can go after the intentions or the capabilities of the subject. This is the oldest dilemma in intelligence analysis and one that will never be solved. If you focus on capabilities, you find out what the other side *can* do, not what they *will* do. If you focus on intentions, you are focusing on what they would *like* to do, not what they *can* do. Obviously, the answer is to focus on both. Still, even in this simple case, you can get tripped up. Here are some possibilities:

- The giant's management is ignorant of its own limitations and overexpands. Yes, they wind up in Chapter XI eighteen months from now, but not before they expand into your market, wrecking your bookstore. The argument to focus on capabilities assumes that your subject reads his capabilities the same way you do. This is, then, a case where management's personal defect meant that they would be misreading constraints and acting in a less than optimal fashion.

- The giant's management has concluded that rather than putting all their eggs in one basket, they would rein in their bookstore expansion and diversify in sushi bars. This is a personal decision based on impersonal analysis. However, the analyst's own impersonal analysis wasn't extended to include the entire universe of options—it never occurred to him to study the relative rate of return on investments in bookstores versus sushi bars. The bookstore closed and no giant bookstore ever showed up. We have here a case where personal information controlled the area of impersonal knowledge that had to be mastered.

- The giant has generated more accurate data than the analyst has available and is aware of that fact. The analyst's data shows that the community is unsuited for a giant bookstore. However, the data the analyst is working from is drawn from a census area that is defined too narrowly. With better data showing that shopping patterns in the region justify a much broader geography, they have decided to move into the region. So this is a case where the best available data, defined by the depth of the business's pockets, simply isn't good enough.

- The giant has been growing at a rate of 20 percent increases in square footage for three years. Everyone inside and outside the company expects that to continue indefinitely. The analyst expects it to continue. Everyone forgets that no retail sector has ever increased by that rate for more than three years (not true, but we're writing this book). Sloppy thinking on all sides, yours included, decides to draw a straight line instead of the inevitable curve. The store is announced, ground is broken, but it is never completed due to a massive slowdown in the industry. So here was a case where everyone can agree on something and it still won't be the way things turn out.

We could go on. The point we are making is that the interplay between personal and impersonal forces, choice and constraint—ultimately the interplay between business and its environment—cannot be tracked with scientific precision. In a world filled with unintended consequences, unexpected by-products, knowing whether to look at a company's plans and internal thinking or at its external reality is a matter of art rather than science.

In general, our experience has been that personal contacts are too overrated in generating information. This runs counter to the experience of most businessmen, but that is because for most businessmen, the core experience of doing business is selling—themselves, their product, or their company. And in selling, nothing can replace the personal relationship. There is a tendency to extrapolate from what you know, to reason by analogy. In selling, the personal relationship is the key. It seems to follow that, in intelligence, these personal relationships will give you a window into the mind of your subject, which in turn tells you what he is going to do, if not precisely what will happen.

We all have our reasons. Any insider has his reasons for talking to you. Those reasons affect truthfulness. Use your contacts. Don't worship them.

Consider what happened to Western businessmen in Iran during the reign of the shah. Everyone doing business in Iran had close contacts with Iranians, many of whom were relatives of the shah, friends of relatives of the shah, and so forth. Every one of these FOS (friends of the shah) advised their Western contacts to stay in Iran—everything was fine. Then the shah fell and these businesses were wiped out. How could all these contacts have been so wrong?

Well, think about it. First, what makes you think that an FOS knows if there's going to be a revolution? If an American were approached in 1997 and asked who would be president in 2001.... well, he could have an opinion, but just because he was rich and famous and an FOB (friend of Bill), how much would that count toward his ability to predict who will be president? What makes us think that a well-connected Iranian really knows what's going to take place?

Second, and more important, what makes you think that he'll tell you even if he knew? A friend of the shah makes his living by being a friend of the shah—and by getting you to do business with him in Iran. If he were to advise you that the shah was going to fall, would you invest in Iran? He wouldn't make money that way. Moreover, if the shah falls, then you can't make money being his friend, right? So you aren't likely to tell your Western "friends," who keep you rich, to stay out. Quite the contrary, you'll urge him to come on in *before* the shah falls.

> **There are some things nobody can know; just because someone is related to someone powerful doesn't mean they can predict the future. Look what happened to businessmen who were close personal friends with the shah himself? Better still, look what happened to the shah!**

Listening to well-placed individuals is useful in giving you a sense of what they are thinking. But many businessmen, who like to be "in the know," get hooked on the idea that they've got a contact who is telling him what is really going on. The only thing he is telling you is what he *thinks* is going on, and that only if it's in his interest to do so.

There is nothing wrong with using personal relationships to gather additional information, so long as you don't fall into the fallacy that these insights will be definitive. It is absolutely vital to remember that (a) people lie, (b) people frequently don't know their own minds and can't predict what they themselves will do, (c) the best-laid plans of mice and men…, and (d) some people are idiots—even CEOs of major companies.

For all these reasons and more, we are major advocates of impersonal studies of capabilities. While never definitive, they tell us more about what people can do than about the fantasies in which people indulge. And they give us a sense of the limitations that are imposed on people by reality.

In the end, it comes down to this. If having lunch with a CEO would tell you what his company's stock is going to do, we'd all be rich. CEOs themselves don't know what is going to happen to their stock or even their industry. If they did, none of them would ever be fired. Since they don't know, talking to them is useful only if they are treated as indicators—frequently as contrarians.

Analysis is the art of the probable: What will probably happen and when will it happen? It is not a game of certainties. Neither being a CEO's best friend nor spotting a pattern repeating itself for the eighty-third time in history guarantees that, on the eighty-fourth time, you will be able to figure out what you are doing. The very best you can achieve is something the trade calls the weight of evidence. When everything is laid side by side, every fact is culled, and you've sent out for all the information you need and have gotten it, the best you can do is take a walk, weigh everything, see where most of the evidence lies, and try—more often than not—to be right. If you can be right, at least more often than others, you will have done your business a great service and justified your existence and salary.

CONCLUSION

The art of analysis requires detachment and disinterest. It requires honest, utter self-confidence, and a total lack of ambition. What is needed and what we have are, of course, two different things. But some things are indispensable. One is that the analyst have access to the executive suite—and to the entire company—so that he has the context and nuance needed to do his work. Another is that he be respected enough to be listened to. In some ways, the second is harder to achieve than the first.

This is why there is a strong argument to be made that the CEO ought to be his own intelligence analyst—at least he'll listen to himself, and if he fails, he'll have no one else to blame. That is attractive, no doubt about it. But it misses the practical realities. First, the sheer quantity of material that must be assimilated makes analysis a full-time job. The CEO will just miss too much of the unexpected because he is too busy doing other things. Second, the CEO needs a critic, a B Team.

During the 1980s, there was tremendous debate in the U.S. intelligence community about the level of Soviet spending on defense. The CIA had an official estimate but it was controversial. President Reagan appointed a group of outsiders—a B Team—to take a look at the CIA's information and see what conclusion they drew from it. The conclusion was quite different, and an extremely healthy and edifying debate was kicked off.

Businesses desperately need B Teams, particularly those with strong, charismatic leaders. This does not apply only to large companies but to small ones as well. Someone needs to occasionally impose a reality check on the CEO. Reality checking is the specialty of the intelligence analyst, perhaps his most precious gift to the company. That is why we recommend, wherever possible, that the role of intelligence analyst be carried out by someone other than the CEO. Let us further suggest that the analyst be independently wealthy, doing this work as a hobby. It will make those Friday afternoon meetings, where he tells the executive committee that an Indian company is about to put out a product identical to their Product X—the savior of the company and brainchild of the CEO—and that it will sell for 35 percent of the price Product X will sell for when it hits the market next year.

9

TAKING COVER

Counterintelligence

Security and counterintelligence are not, properly speaking, part of the intelligence suite. But propriety aside, it is obviously a matter we need to address. This is particularly the case when you realize how revolutions in digitizing information have increased your own access to information about the world—and about competitors. We have been discussing all the ways you can access information. The other side of that coin is the equivalent ease with which others can access information about you. Now, some of the threats are very old: disloyal employees, careless and loose talk, physical break-ins, and the like. But some of the threats are radically new and unprecedented. You are used to locking your doors physically. But new technologies have created new doors, and you have to keep those locked as well. Even more important, you need to keep critical information from wafting out through unseen cracks—to be sniffed at by competitors as cagey in the intelligence game as you've become.

Securing a company's secrets is expensive, but so is losing those secrets. IBM is just one American company to claim to have lost billions of dollars through the theft of its proprietary information. Marshall C. Phelps, Jr., the vice president for commercial and industry relations, says that "the theft of corporate proprietary assets has occurred from many quarters: competitors, governments seeking to bolster national industry champions, even employees—we have been the target of each."

When Phelps told this to a congressional committee in 1992 he was stopped in his tracks by the chairman, who asked him to repeat the sentence for the record. Phelps replied:

> These activities have resulted in losses to IBM in the *billions*. Settlement agreements, judicial mandates, and commitments to third parties preclude us from discussing the specifics of many of these cases, which include the theft of personal computer–related technologies, theft of trade secrets critical to our mainframe systems, theft of information by governments for their own use and by their indigenous hardware and software suppliers, and counterfeiting of our trademark on hardware and software.
>
> One of the most critical IBM proprietary elements of our PC technology is software known as the Basic Input/Output System, or BIOS. The BIOS controls key output operations, such as interactions between the computer and diskette drives, fixed disk drives and the keyboard. This copyrighted software has been deliberately and repetitively misappropriated by many domestic and foreign companies seeking to manufacture inexpensive copies—or clones—of the IBM PC.

Confirmation that Russia has been one of the countries stealing proprietary information came in testimony to the same committee from Stanislav Levchenko, a former KGB intelligence officer from Moscow whose previous jobs included planting forgeries of foreign government documents. He said that far from the end of the Cold War meaning the end of espionage, there was a new target: American industrial corporations:

> The remnants of the secret police are still there.... [F]or decades political intelligence was the number one priority. Now high-tech intelligence and economic intelligence is the most important priority of the headquarters and of the residences abroad. The economic situation of Russia

and the surrounding states is severe. They do not have the resources nor the time for expensive research and development efforts necessary to compete in international markets. To survive, they will steal the proprietary secrets of foreign companies. It will be naive to hope that President Yeltsin will decide to cut Russian intelligence substantially. In addition, practically all the new countries, the former republics of the USSR, can be expected to conduct intelligence on their own with U.S. technology as a prime target. Allegedly the Ukraine already has hundreds of intelligence officers and is training the younger generation. The intelligence services of the former republics will almost assuredly coordinate their work. An important part of it will be industrial espionage.

The former Soviet Union was by no means the only villain in the theft of American corporate secrets. After the hearing, the chairman, Congressman Jack Brooks of Texas, said testimonies from U.S. industry representatives and government witnesses had "painted a dark and sinister picture of just how foreign economic espionage activities by countries such as France and Japan have cost American companies billions of dollars and hurt U.S. competitiveness."

Governments remain the first threat to your information. Former governments are the second.

Nor, as Microsoft's Dr. Nathan Myhrvold reminded us, is the issue only "about super computers for Uncle Sam, or paranoid management information systems personnel at a bank."

It goes far beyond the issue of foreign economic espionage. Instead it ultimately is about every PC. It is about doctors protecting the confidentiality of medical records that they store in computers rather than on paper. It is about preparing tax forms on a home computer and then transmitting them electronically to the IRS—without fear that the government or a hacker may obtain access to your financial records or any other information you have stored in your computer.

Myhrvold joined other leaders of the computer industry in calling for a strengthening of encryption, and for the U.S. government to relax restrictions on the export of powerful encryption software. Encryption is based on a simple idea that can be traced back to antiquity: transforming a message into a form that cannot be understood by anyone without access to the encryption formula. Julius Caesar was known to have used a crude form of encryption in which he changed every letter in a message to the one that occurred three letters later in the alphabet. Thus "attack at dawn" became "dwwdfj dw gdzq."

We have been talking about the migration of intelligence techniques from the national security arena to the business world. Along with the migration, we are seeing the movement of espionage techniques as well. That means, obviously, that national security techniques for counterintelligence and security will migrate as well. In the end, this will pose a substantial cost to business. Securing the knowledge that is the underlying capital of modern industrial society will not be an easy task. The very digitization of data that has proven such a boon to mining data will become the Achilles' heel of business.

At this moment, the threat to business still comes from the national intelligence agencies. French and Chinese intelligence services are reputed to be particularly aggressive in trying to get hold of strategic technologies. Recently, several members of the CIA station in Paris were expelled by the French, officially for engaging in industrial espionage. Whether the charge was true or merely retaliation against similar charges made by the United States against French intelligence is less relevant than the obvious fact that national intelligence agencies, looking for a role beyond the politicomilitary sphere in which they operated during the Cold War, have focused on accessing key emerging technologies in foreign countries.

In a sense, this provides a degree of security for most businesses. Consider this: A highly centralized intelligence agency, controlled by a government, is going to focus on matters of the highest national priority. Now, even if that no longer means focusing on plans for weapons systems, it does mean focusing on technologies critically important to the nation as a whole in its international competition. The United States and France are locked in a bitter competition in the passenger aircraft industry. That means that French and American intelligence, tasked with supporting their respective aircraft industries, will focus their attention there. Relatively little will be left over for the countless other secrets in the countless other industries.

National economic espionage will therefore focus on big-ticket items, simply because that is the only cost-effective way to operate, and because the political and bureaucratic realities dictate that sort of approach. At this time, therefore, the focus of industrial espionage, from the state level, is on the top of the pyramid, and people operating in less salient, less exposed industries are safe from the concerted and effective intentions of professional espionage organizations. But they should not feel comforted by this.

The intelligence industry, worldwide, is experiencing a massive downturn. Two factors have come together to create a massive economic crisis and layoffs. One is the general tendency to downsize governments worldwide. The other is that the end of the Cold War and growing peace in the Middle East have thrown countless sophisticated, top-of-the-line spooks out on the streets. Former KGB agents, agents formerly employed by Eastern European Communist states, now frequently outcasts at home; retired Israeli military and foreign intelligence officials; CIA and DIA agents taking early retirement or being RIFed (reduction in force), have created an army of unemployed spooks. All of them have one thing to sell—their expertise.

And in most cases, their expertise is not in the modern areas of passive intelligence in the electronic domain but in the older, Cold War crafts of breaking and entering, wiretapping, tailing, videotaping, and so on. Indeed, those who specialized in computer espionage, information management and analysis, and such are the ones most likely to remain employed. They are needed far more than those with older skills. So, since 1991, the world has had hordes of nasties released on it. And all of them are looking for work.

If a Ukrainian national comes to you with a deal and he speaks perfect English, and his résumé says that he worked for the Soviet Ministry of Agriculture as agricultural attaché in Cairo, you could do worse than pass on the deal. A lot worse.

We were involved in a couple of cases recently pointing in this direction. In one, a Ukrainian national approached a client looking to purchase some technology. It turned out that he was less interested in purchasing it than in stealing it. In another, similar case, some Hungarians were looking to sell some chemicals in the West. It turned out that they were dealing on the come: If they got an order, they'd then go out and steal it. In both cases, we were clearly dealing with former spooks, out of a job, trying to hustle a living for themselves in the New World Order.

In many, if not most, cases these people live on the edge—or over the edge—of the law. They work with and frequently become part of organized crime. In a sense, they are not nearly as dangerous as they appear, simply because their approach is not particularly subtle; they have become thieves and extortionists more than intelligence agents. The threat here is less industrial espionage than the increasing threat of organized crime on a global basis. The downsizing of intelligence services coupled with massive social instability in the former Communist world has generated an entirely new, increasingly global organized crime system. Less integrated into the culture of international business than the old Italian Mafia has become, they pose real, physical danger. But it is simple criminality more than espionage.

The average businessman rarely faces a threat from a national intelligence agency, and most mobsters are less interested in stealing intellectual property than in making you an offer you can't refuse. The real threat that most businessmen face comes from the same forces that have given them, in our opinion, their tremendous intelligence opportunity. Digitization of information has allowed them to tap into information resources previously unimaginable. That same digitization inside their company opens the door not only to intentional theft but, even more serious, the unintended emission of important information generated by the business into the public domain.

SECURITY AND SECRECY

In thinking about security and counterintelligence, it is important to begin with Napoleon's famous dictum: He who would defend everything, defends nothing. There are two important sides to this truth. The first, more obvious one, is the simple recognition that no one has the resources to genuinely secure everything he holds. Security has a price, and not everything you possess is worth that price. Someone who tries to secure everything equally will, inevitably, be allocating equal resources to protecting things that have no value to protecting things on which the future of the company rests. That sort of policy obviously makes no sense. Somehow, a hierarchy must be created that frankly recognizes the relative importance of information.

There is another, somewhat more subtle and complex side to this as well. The foundation of information security is secrecy. The more people who know a piece of information, the more likely that information is to leak. That's obvious. And the solution would appear to be equally obvious: Make sure that as few people as possible are familiar with critical information—the old "need to know" principle. Now, in many cases, need to know works, but it also has costs and risks.

Secrecy is extremely expensive. One cost, obviously, is the cost of securing information physically. But the deeper cost of secrecy is inefficiency. In many large companies, research and development projects, client lists, profit and loss statements are closely held. As a result, one division might be developing at substantial cost a gadget that another division had already developed but not yet released; one division might be spending large amounts of money developing contacts with a potential customer that is already a loyal cus-

tomer of another division; one division might be undertaking a project identical to one another division undertook—with disastrous
results.

Secrecy protects information by limiting information's mobil-
ity. Sometimes it's simply confined to use by a few people. In other,
more extreme cases, it's broken up, compartmentalized, as the jar-
gon would have it. In compartmentalization, the information itself
is broken up into pieces so that even those with access don't get to
see the whole. These moves work. They decrease the chance that
anyone outside the company will find out what is going on inside.
Secrecy also increases the probability that people inside the company don't find out what's going on.

Secrecy and security are costly. The major cost is inefficiency.
Duplicated effort, insufficiently exploited capabilities, and lack of
synergy in carefully compartmentalized projects dramatically
increase costs for businesses. Part of the cost is the sheer expense of
physical security systems, from those on computers to those on
doors. Part of the expense is time—time spent accessing information. And part of the expense is the cost of failing to squeeze the last
ounce of utility out of a piece of information. The classic example
of all of this was the old Soviet Union. It had superb security yet
collapsed into inefficiency. The right hand didn't know what
the left hand was doing, because they weren't cleared to see the
information. The United States leaked like a sieve. Yet connections
were made between bits of information that generated entire
industries—precisely because the information was not compartmentalized.

Secrecy and security carry with them another danger. When
information is held tightly, that means that fewer people know
what's going on. It also, therefore, means that those fewer people
are in a much more powerful position both within that organization
and in being able to betray the organization. By concentrating
information at certain points—not necessarily at the top of the
pyramid, with the chairman or even the CEO, but at the top of the
functional pyramid, in the hands of those individuals controlling
operations—secrecy increases the cost of security failures.

The digitization of information increases the possibility of leakage simply because the efficient packaging of information makes transfers easier. Consider the now classic case of GM, Volkswagen, and Jose Ignacio Lopez de Arriortua, whose defection from the world's largest auto manufacturer, General Motors, to Europe's top carmaker, Volkswagen, paved the way for the most bitter public wrangle over industrial espionage in a generation. The row involved criminal and civil court proceedings and politicians, diplomats, and leading businessmen in both Europe and the United States.

Lopez, a devout Catholic who often publicly carries a rosary, was born in the Basque region of northern Spain and pursued a career in purchasing, rising to the position of head of purchasing for General Motors's European subsidiary, Adam Opel. There he had won accolades for the way he had revolutionized the car producer's relationship with suppliers, allowing Opel to cut costs. As a ranking and highly rated GM executive, Lopez was fully involved in the corporation's plans for the future.

One of these came to be known as Project X—hardly an original description in a world where thousands of corporations have concepts or ideas carrying this name—which involved the creation of a new car production plant in the Basque country. Project X called for the techniques that Lopez had instituted to be fully developed in the new plant. The regional government was keen to bring new industry to an area of high unemployment, and wanted to emulate Ford's success a decade earlier when it had built a successful facility in Valencia, another area of Spain. The Basques offered GM strong financial incentives to build the plant in their state; after serious consideration the Detroit-based company turned the idea down.

What happened in the ensuing months is a matter for speculation and the subject of $1 billion in lawsuits still pending. What is known is that on January 1993, in a hotel in the German city of Hannover, well away from Opel's headquarters in Rüsselsheim or from Volkswagen's home base in Wolfsburg, Lopez sat down to breakfast with Ferdinand Piech, who had not long before taken over as chairman of VW. Also present was Gerhard Schröder, a former German foreign minister who had become the premier of the state of Lower Saxony. At fifty-nine, Lopez could have been contemplating a peaceful and lucrative retirement. Instead, as the breakfast ended, he was handed a contract. According to *The European* newspaper, there was a blank space left for Lopez to enter his own salary.

Within days, Lopez and three GM colleagues were established in Wolfsburg with the mission to plan a new VW assembly plant codenamed "B" in the Spanish Basque country. The plant was to be the embodiment of the principles Lopez had followed at GM. Autos were to be slotted together like a child's Lego set from prepackaged modules rather than from hundreds of small components. The workers engaged to slot these modules together would be supplied from outside contractors at lower rates than those normally paid to employees on an assembly line. The concept was remarkably similar to GM's aborted Project X.

Three months later, GM began a legal action against Lopez alleging industrial espionage, its Opel unit in Germany claiming that Lopez and the members of his team who had defected with him had carried away crates of secret information that was copied and entered into VW computers. So serious were the charges that the German government began its own investigation, which led, three years later, on December 13, 1996, to Lopez being formally indicted. Charged along with him for industrial espionage, in a fifty-eight-page indictment, were colleagues Jorge Alvarez, Jose Manuel Gutierrez, and Rosario Piazza.

When a top executive moves over to his competitor, having someone sort of watch while he packs his office is not being too pushy.

This was in many ways a classic case. An executive at one company moves to another company. He takes not only his know-how and experience but also documents. Hard to protect against under any circumstance, how do you keep your purchasing head in the dark about what's going on? One way for GM to have protected itself was to compartmentalize information, to keep Lopez from knowing everything there was to know about what was going on.

The price for that, of course, would have been a secure, but paralyzed, GM. You just can't do that.

Lopez's crime was made easier, and much more damaging than it would have been twenty years ago, by the invention of the floppy disk. Assume that you had taken a filing cabinet full of documents. No matter how important they might be, a filing cabinet could not possibly contain the totality of Project X, in all of its complexity and subtlety. But digitized data...well, a briefcase could easily contain the keys to the kingdom.

SECURITY AND THE DIGITAL AGE

The Lopez case represents a classic problem of espionage by betrayal, for which classic solutions are available. These problems must be handled by the standard security procedures of a company. But companies today have a new emerging set of security problems that have not been anticipated and for which classic solutions will not do.

A friend of ours in South Africa runs a merchant banking house. He's had his ups and downs but, on the whole, has done quite well. About a year ago, the South African government agency that deals with securities firms investigated a merger of which he was part. As frequently happens, stories of the investigation leaked into the press and his name was tangentially mentioned. The newspaper in which it was mentioned implied that in some way he was under investigation. That wasn't true, but it was, after all, one of many stories about him, and while upset, he was only mildly concerned. Unfortunately, he had a problem that he hadn't anticipated and that wouldn't have been a problem just a few years ago.

It happened that the newspaper that mentioned the investigation is one that is monitored by Reuters, the British news service that frequently runs stories from newspapers around the world on its international service. These newspapers are not necessarily the most influential or important. They just happen to be the ones with which Reuters has agreements. Nor is it run on the standard wire that most global media pick up, but on a specialized wire that does not have very deep penetration. So it was a pity, from our friend's point of view, but no major cause for concern. It would all be forgotten shortly.

Unfortunately, this was not the case. This particular wire was archived on several major on-line databases, including Lexis-Nexis and FT Profile. This meant that every time someone put our friend's name into one of these databases, this story, with the implication of wrongdoing, would come up. Since it was a minor story, and basically inaccurate as well, there would be no follow-up. But for as long as on-line services carried Reuters—which is to say for at least our friend's lifetime—there would be a story in there, along with all his successes and awards, clearly implying that our friend may well be a bit of a scoundrel.

Ever since Gutenberg laid the groundwork for mass media, one solace has been paper's short legs and memory. Not only would a newspaper story in South Africa not be known outside the circulation area of that newspaper, but would usually not even be remembered in South Africa. And if it was vaguely remembered by someone, who could possibly find it, even a few months after publication? There was a comforting element of forgetfulness about the media. You could live things down.

This was no longer the case. Our friend came to the United States trying to arrange financing for a new project. He was approaching some major American banks where he wasn't well known. He had good introductions, so he was being taken seriously, but naturally, his hosts wanted to know a little more about him, so they checked his name in some on-line services. The last story on him—it was the most recent and therefore the first to come up—was the story about the investigation. Plus, it turned out that another British newspaper, picking up on the Reuters story, had mentioned his name in another obscure, but archived, publication. It appeared to his hosts, not knowing any better, that he had recently run into some serious regulatory problems back home that hadn't yet been cleared up. Fortunately for him, one of the bankers he was meeting with had the courtesy to mention the problem to him, allowing him to not only explain it but to call his office and arrange for his attorneys to gather some exculpatory material. But the fact remained, except for the opportunity to explain himself, the new public record of on-line services would forever carry that information. Every time someone checked him out, those stories would be there, on-line, coming up every time his name or firm's name was put into the query field.

In effect, this was a case of unintended disinformation—electronic domain style. Absolutely no one had planned to harm his reputation, but there it was. Information that's emitted no longer dissipates. It congeals. That means that our friend could not treat that story indifferently. It could and did come back to haunt him. The real division of the media today, from an intelligence point of view, is the archived and the unarchived media. Information that is released and archived becomes part of the permanent record. Information that is unarchived does not. In the electronic archives, it is extremely important to note, major publications like the *London Times* and minor publications like the *Baton Rouge Advocate* are both available and have equal weight. If they carry someone's name, they will come up not in order of prestige but with last publication first. And we have noted that, psychologically, these electronic archives are great democratizers—we read press releases with the same care that we read *New York Times* columnists.

Now, if something accidental could cause harm, imagine what deliberate misinformation, targeted at archived media, could do. Imagine what unintended releases of information from your own company can do. Today, the first line of counterintelligence is not the secretary stealing documents from the filing cabinet to give to her KGB lover, but enemies deliberately releasing information into strategic, archived publications, there to haunt you forever. What is said about your company and what your company says about itself today has taken on massive significance. Where previously new reports would have to reach a level of notoriety rarely achieved in order not to be forgotten, today it has become impossible to live anything down.

Business must take control of this electronic environment. In the case of our South African friend, our advice was to issue a press release. That sounds fairly trivial but it isn't. Today, press release organizations, like Business Wire and PR Wire, exist, and for a few hundred dollars they'll process and distribute press releases. Almost all on-line databases archive these releases, right alongside major newspapers. Many browsers aren't even aware that Business Wire is a paid press release service—a vanity press, if you will. By issuing a press release via Business Wire, our friend guaranteed that he would control the first story that came up. He would also be in a position to counter the impression left.

This seems an odd thing to discuss in the context of counter-intelligence, but everything that we have been saying in this book leads to the conclusion that the emerging information battle-ground is the electronic domain, where the very laws of information are being rewritten. This is where attacks will be made and this is where they will have to be defended against. And ultimately, this is where leaks will occur.

Consider this tragic tale: A computer scientist had been working on a breakthrough piece of software for several years, and had been coming close to success. His company was getting ready to go into high gear on his work. He attended a conference in Cologne, West Germany, where he was on a panel as a commentator. He was among friends; it was a small gathering; he was far from home; and he was relaxed. He spoke a bit too openly about his work—but then, really, who would know?

The conference was being transcribed by a company that transcribed conferences and sold the transcriptions to an American technical publisher who then sold the transcriptions at absurdly high prices. As part of its strategy, it also published some technical magazines and frequently ran teasers from conferences. Fairly casually, the transcription editor selected an interchange involving the computer scientist in the monthly magazine, which also was archived on Lexis-Nexis. In short order, whether keying in the type of software, the scientist's name, or his company, the most recent thing to come up were his comments—highly revealing to the competition. The competition, also working in the same direction, rapidly shifted plans and sped up its own work, beating the scientist's company into the marketplace by months. Disaster.

The first step in contemporary counterintelligence is a dramatic shift in the psychology of employees concerning information.

This is infinitely more important than nifty badges dangling from the neck on chains or keypads on the door. An awareness that nothing is casual any longer. The recognition that emissions of information no longer dissipate as they once did has taken a long time to penetrate corporate culture. The emphasis there has been on traditional security.

- Making sure that only authorized personnel enter the premises.
- Making certain that critically important documents are seen only by those authorized to see them.
- Making certain that copying machines and secret spaces are kept separate.
- Sweeping the building for bugs.
- Checking the briefcases of people entering or exiting buildings or areas.
- Maintaining the integrity of computer systems.

All of these remain extremely useful. But the basic modern threat does not come, in our estimation, from hackers breaking into your network. While that can happen, it can also be guarded against. The basic threat to the security of your information comes from uncontrolled and unguarded emissions from your own company.

This has always been a problem. As the Lopez story points out, one of the major vectors of illicit emissions is people motivated to betray. But the real threat today comes from the loyal employee, doing his best at his job. The weak point is the casual comment to a reporter, an indiscreet response at a professional conference, a professional paper not clearly thought through.

Nothing dissipates. You must learn to live with every indiscretion as long as electrons remain electrons.

One of the interesting phenomena we have noted has been the proliferation of local business papers. Even relatively small towns have spawned business journals and their imitators. These newspapers carry tremendously detailed, friendly stories on local businesses. Executives, speaking to a friendly audience in the editor and reporter, tend to let their hair down and speak frankly to their community. These local journals are gold mines for us, carrying detailed information on companies and people we could never find out about from the national media—and they are on-line alongside the *Wall Street Journal*. The speed with which information congeals on-line creates a real-time threat to your company. Almost before you know it, an indiscreet remark is embedded in databases.

BASIC SECURITY IN THE DIGITAL AGE

In the olden days—about ten years ago—most companies maintained safes in which vital and sensitive documents were stored. Today, the most valuable information in a company exists in endless, unlocked little cubicles called hard drives. What is amazing about our hard drives is not only how much utterly invaluable information these drives contain, but how little most managements know of what is contained on them or where. The only thing more amazing is how utterly insecure these drives are.

Any effective security and counterintelligence system must begin with the hard drive. First, companies must, once and for all, develop systems for finding out what employees are keeping on their drives. This is not a matter of making certain that employees are not playing Doom on company time, but of developing an effective inventory of a company's knowledge base, increasingly present on the hard drive more than anywhere else. Tools are now becoming available to allow managers to access hard drives. Windows 95, for example, provides connectivity between the hard drives. One result is that, for the first time since personal computers swept into offices, it has become possible to take inventory. It also becomes easier to tap into other people's hard drives and make off with what they have.

The hard drive isn't a stockroom. You can't take physical

inventory and be certain that nothing has been taken because it is easy to copy information without the copying being noted: You can put files on a floppy, you can send it via e-mail, or you can just pick up the hard drive, take it home, and copy the material to another hard drive—duplicating valuable information infinitely. Indeed, the hard drive's vulnerability rests in the fact that it can simply be stolen—physically taken, with or without the rest of the computer. A hard drive is extraordinarily small for the value it might contain. So we are in a situation in which a majority of a company's information rests on what is probably the least secure part of the computing system.

There are three basic solutions to hard-drive security:

1. Passwords
2. Encryption
3. Scrubbing the disk

None of these solutions, by itself, will suffice. Passwords protecting access to either files or to the computer system itself certainly will stop the untrained and may slow down the experts, but they can be broken. The passwords systems protecting major word-processing software files can and have been broken. The same is true for encryption. Encryption can always be broken, given enough time and enough money. Encryption can be so complex that it would take the National Security Agency twenty thousand man-hours to break the code—or it can be so easy that a fourteen-year-old hacker can get past it in an hour. Encryption does not absolutely protect anything. What it does is increase the amount of time and the resources required to break into the file. Obviously, this means that the more valuable the prize inside, the more likely that someone— competitor or law enforcement agency—will go to the trouble of breaking the encryption seal.

In the end, the best protection for files is removing them physically from the hard drive and storing them in a safe place that no one knows about. While it certainly defeats one of the reasons for having the hard drive—convenience—it does secure vital information. But even deleting a file is not quite as easy as it sounds. The act of deleting a file does not erase it. The data is still there and can still be read, sometimes by simple utilities designed to undelete and sometimes by more sophisticated means. All deleting a file does is tell the operating system that the space occupied by the file is now available for use. Until the space is actually used, the file is still there.

Consider this: While you are clicking away in Microsoft Word or Corel Word Perfect, backups are taking place. Every fifteen minutes or so, whatever you are working on is backed up. Fifteen minutes later, the backup file is deleted and another one is created. Every time you print the file, a print file is created on your hard drive. In the course of writing a fifteen-page proposal, literally hundreds of copies of that file have been created and deleted. That means that for weeks or even months after you have mailed out the proposal, deleted it from your drive, and forgotten about it, enough copies of that proposal remain on your drive that it can be reconstructed with not very sophisticated means. The larger your hard drive, the more free space it has, the more likely past secrets and indiscretions are still sitting on your hard drive—everything from e-mail to secret sketches of your newest project.

First off, tie down your central processing units (CPUs) and put strong, serious locks on them so that your computers can't take a walk or have a hard drive lifted out of them. Second, put in place a systematic scrubbing approach. Using software like "defraggers," which consolidate files on hard drives, it is possible to overwrite all unused sectors, thereby eliminating old files. But bear in mind that recent thinking is that a single overwrite will still allow sophisticated systems to "read" your files. Plan to overwrite several times. This is a bit time consuming, but it will mean that even a stolen computer won't yield your most valuable or dangerous secrets.

The network is the next problem. Again, the very way in which it has made life easier also makes information more vulnerable. An unscrupulous employee, for example, can e-mail your secret business plan to your competitor, going into the server drive where it is stored and shipping it out. Some simple rules are essential:

- Access to server drives is a great convenience. Creating multiple real or virtual drives and controlling and limiting access

to them is vital. Everyone should not have access to everything.

■ Password protection and encryption will slow down most
thieves. They will also provide you with hints of hacking. Logs
of failed passworded log-ins are extremely valuable. If someone tried to get into your account or a file twenty-four times
yesterday, it probably wasn't an accident. Protect.

■ Firewalls between your Internet site and the rest of the network are essential. The best firewall: no connection at all.
Use a separate computer off the network to serve the Internet. Seal the rest of the system off from the world, except of
course for e-mail.

■ Set rigid rules on not downloading software from the outside
to any computer on the net without using virus-scanning
software. Enforcing this rule by monitoring incoming and
outgoing files by size also has the advantage of warning you
when someone is trying to ship out large amounts of information.

Data transfers of all kinds must be monitored. Routine e-mail
is not the problem—or at least not the major problem. The major
problem occurs when a multimegabyte document is shipped out.
Make it clear that the export of files larger than a certain size will
not be supported by your e-mail system and will require technical
support from the system manager. This will mean that whenever a
really humongous file is going to be shipped, someone else is
alerted and can examine it.

But what is going to kill you are the floppies—those miserable
3.5-inch disks that can contain an entire book. And this is the heart
of the matter—there is never a foolproof security or counterintelligence system. Neither the Borgias nor Microsoft can defeat human
cupidity. What can be done is increase the time and cost of these
efforts. The goal can never be to make industrial espionage impossible. What it should be is to increase costs and risks beyond the
potential value of the information. That can be done, albeit with
cost to your business as well.

CONCLUSION

In our view, businesses are threatened far less by the theft of their information than by their own people giving that information away. A casual remark in the hands of an analyst with context and nuance is more dangerous to your business plan than fifty former Mossad agents. And no amount of legal protection—not copyrights, patents, or confidentiality agreements—will protect you from the careful collector and the meticulous listener.

This is the shift that is taking place in business intelligence. The threat does not come from espionage but from intelligence; not from breaking and entering as from leaking and gossiping; not from unscrupulous former employees as much as from loyal current employees. And it poses a fundamental challenge—and opportunity—to modern business. The challenge is to protect your own material and the opportunity is to see what your competitor is doing.

The problem here is that the solution—strict controls on the movement of information within a company—poses a tremendous price for business. Inefficiency grows out of secrecy, and inefficiency can destroy a company. The problem facing business today is securing information without capitulating to secrecy. It is a far graver challenge than the KGB ever posed.

The solution is twofold. First, it is cultural, recognizing that loose lips do indeed sink ships. Imposing a culture is difficult, but less difficult than imposing secrecy. Second, the solution is technological. Emerging, but not yet present, technologies will allow us to tag information and know who has seen it and what they have done with it. As information grows more precious, tracking its movements will become the solution to a problem that cannot help but grow.

10

AND NOW A WORD FROM OUR LAWYER

Intelligence and the Law

Well, it's that time again—time to visit with the lawyer. Always an interesting experience. Notice how he starts; the very first line: " 'Is it legal?' That's the basic question people have about law and corporate intelligence." How do we convince him that this is most emphatically not the basic question? The basic question is how can I find out what I need to know and not get into trouble? There's a world of difference between the two questions.

The world of intelligence is a world of ambiguity and risk—you are never quite sure what the rules are but you've got to act anyway. In the world of law, you never act until you are sure of your ground. But how can anyone be sure of his ground on a project involving Somali and Chinese oil? What ground—we're in a swamp! The lawyer's solution: Wait while he researches the legal aspects. Our answer: Do it and let the lawyers sort it out later. Visits from legal counsel are, in our world, exciting moments indeed.

We don't have contempt for the law. What we have is a real problem! At any moment the law can shut anything down, and we can't afford to be shut down. In a world where there are countries in which asking about rice production can get you put in jail, we need to find a way to do what we have to do without going away in handcuffs. So the legal question is important but, from our point of view, ultimately subsidiary. It's something that you need to ask to be a responsible citizen, even if you get a long, convoluted answer that basically says: "Maybe, but don't hold me to that."

Notice the little disclaimer in the third paragraph: "Without here providing legal advice, we can offer some useful guidance to the reader first by pursuing some clarifying questions." Is there someone out there who can tell us what that's supposed to mean? We guess it means that he doesn't want to be held to anything he says.

But we're in the real world. So while our accountant has been sweating bullets by our side through this whole thing, now our lawyer comes in to get the last word—and leave it to us to figure out what that word is.

We can't wait to see the bill.

THE LEGAL CONTEXT
BY JOHN S. BAKER, JR.

"Is it legal?" That's the basic question people have about law and corporate intelligence. The question can be asked in a way that implies criminality: "Isn't corporate *espionage* a crime?" However the question is phrased, though, a competent, cautious lawyer typically might answer: "Each situation is different, depending on the facts. In many areas, the law is unclear. You should consult an attorney with your specific questions."

There you have it: an answer that is perfectly accurate...and completely useless! Worse than useless, however, is the answer of the less-than-competent lawyer who, like many accountants, simply says: "Just don't do it!" That way, of course, the lawyer cannot be blamed if anything goes wrong.

Without here providing legal advice, we can offer some useful guidance to the reader first by pursuing some clarifying questions: (1) Is intelligence gathering the same as criminal espionage? (2) Even if not criminal, is intelligence gathering a legitimate corporate activity? (3) How does one recognize a criminal or illegal corporate practice? Intertwined with these questions is another one: Are we talking about American law, the law of some other country, or both?

The terms *intelligence gathering* and *espionage* suggest that the main legal issues involve criminal law, when actually the most significant issues involve intellectual property and trade secret law. The United States, in particular, has focused on protecting innovation and preventing what is deemed to be unfair competition. Among its many firsts, the U.S. Constitution authorizes Congress to grant exclusive rights to authors and inventors. Congress has long given patent and copyright protection for intellectual property and more recently has protected trade secrets that were already generally protected under state laws.

The Economic Espionage Act of 1996 criminalizes the theft of trade secrets. What makes either intelligence gathering or espionage criminal under this law is the misuse of trade secrets. If the crime is an act committed on behalf of a foreign government, it is labeled *economic espionage.* Otherwise, the crime is theft of trade secrets. If trade secrets are not involved, someone who employs "espionage" techniques does not commit the crime of economic espionage—even though the person is "spying" on economic activity. Thus, in the United States, "espionage" and intelligence gathering need not be criminal nor illegal.

Few countries, besides the United States, protect trade secrets as such. Of course, a foreign government might charge theft or embezzlement in a case involving trade secrets, as was filed in Germany against former General Motors executive Jose Ignacio Lopez de Arriortua. Nevertheless, outside the United States, the secrets of a *private* corporation do not have the same protection as they do within the United States. Taking economic "secrets" from a foreign government or a *government-owned corporation* will, however, very likely be considered not merely theft but criminal espionage.

In less free countries, the scope of espionage is quite broad. A country may treat as state secrets matters which in the United States would be public information. Basic statistics about a country, such as population and industrial output, are still technically illegal to obtain in many areas of the world. In former Soviet bloc countries, such laws may or may not be enforced. A practical way of gauging a country's interpretation and enforcement of criminal espionage as to basic economic data may be to assess the degree of freedom afforded journalists and lawyers to practice their professions. A country such as China, which has had very few lawyers and whose government greatly restricts and sometimes arrests journalists, is not a hospitable place to conduct private intelligence gathering—at least on the ground.

Lawyers, as well as reporters, around the world routinely engage in intelligence gathering. American trial lawyers call such fact-finding or investigation "discovery," a process governed by rules and enforced by courts. Any lawyer or reporter who does not adequately investigate before making allegations acts irresponsibly. For lawyers and journalists, intelligence gathering must be considered obligatory.

If intelligence gathering is permissible when done lawfully by lawyers and journalists, should it be any less so when done by corporations? If there seems to be a difference, the explanation may lie in the labeling rather than in any analysis. Legal and journalistic research may seem more legitimate than corporate espionage because lawyers and journalists, although acting in a private capacity, claim to advance the public interest. Is there really any difference, though, in what these professions in fact do and what businesses do when it comes to intelligence gathering?

What is the difference, actually, between some forms of research and espionage? Is it research or spying (or both) when an insurance company investigator videotapes the physical activities of a person who has made a claim for injuries allegedly resulting in permanent disability? Is it research if directed by the lawyer but spying if done by the corporation? Are the labels at all meaningful? Cannot the intelligence gathering done by a corporation benefit the public, just as it can when done by a lawyer or journalist?

Intelligence gathering, practiced legally, is part of the competitive enterprise. A person or corporation that is the object of intelligence gathering may call it corporate espionage. But what if that corporation takes defensive security measures? Aren't both corporations then gathering intelligence on each other? Are they both engaged in corporate espionage? Is one or both of them engaged merely in market or competitive research? The answer given at the beginning of this chapter by "the competent, cautious lawyer"—that is, "it all depends"—has this virtue: It resists the tyranny of labels. Some forms of intelligence gathering, such as trial-related discovery, are not only legal but legally enforceable. At the other end of the spectrum, some forms of intelligence gathering, such as theft, are not only illegal but criminal. The legality and criminality of most intelligence gathering, however, does "depend"...namely on the rights to the information, the means of obtaining it, and the use to which it is put.

Illegality and criminality are often inaccurately equated. Not everything illegal is criminal. The fact that an act is not criminal does not mean it is legal. Many "wrongs," such as personal injuries, are not legal or right, but they may not be criminal. Personal injuries are most often "righted" by civil remedies, usually monetary damage awards. It is, however, more difficult to distinguish the criminal from the merely wrongful or illegal—and even from the innocent—with business-related offenses than it is in personal injury cases.

LEGAL RISKS IN PASSIVE INTELLIGENCE

Passive intelligence gathering involves the lowest level of legal risk. Legal issues revolve around rights in information. Legal issues can arise at each point of the passive research process: reading, copying, and manipulating. Most commonly they arise in the context of copying materials.

Basic Copyright

Just think about how many people have ever made a photocopy of a copyrighted document. It need not have been a secret document—a newspaper article qualifies. Such copying is prohibited by U.S. federal law and, by treaty, must be prohibited by signatory countries. Even a single instance of copying copyrighted material, unless it falls within the "fair use" exception (determined by four factors, including the amount of material and the impact on the economic benefit to which the copyright holder is entitled), is illegal. Under U.S. law, it also becomes criminal if done "willfully and for purposes of commercial advantage or private financial gain" (17 USC Sec. 506 [a]).

Even civil enforcement, which is relatively rare, of noncriminal violators has been most likely when financial gain is involved. Kinko's, a nationwide and now international copy service, was sued by several publishers for copyright infringement for copying and printing, without permission or payment, selections from copyrighted books that were collected into anthologies and sold to students for use in college courses. In 1991, a federal court rejected Kinko's claim that the copying constituted "fair use" and found that Kinko's had committed copyright infringement. The court also stated: "Kinko's has failed to prove it was an innocent infringer by failing to show its good faith. Kinko's should have known that it was infringing plaintiffs' copyrights."

The practice at issue in the Kinko's case involved publishing rather than intelligence gathering. Yet the case has had an impact on all commercial photocopying practices. Since losing the lawsuit, Kinko's will not copy a single newspaper article or more than one page of a book (deemed to be within "fair use") without a written copyright permission. The civil lawsuit it lost does not dictate that policy. The copyright statute itself imposes that obligation. As a result of the lawsuit, obviously, Kinko's has become more sensitive to its statutory obligations. As a commercial "gatekeeper," Kinko's has become an effective enforcer of federal copyright law against others who use its services. If Kinko's did not now do so, it would not only risk civil suits but would become a more likely target for a criminal prosecution. Its personnel can no longer claim ignorance that its prior business practices violated the law. The litigation eliminated any arguable legal ambiguity as to certain business practices and prompted greater caution as to other practices.

Electronic Copies

Transforming data and other information into intelligence requires copying. As long as manual, typed, and photocopying were the only widely available ways of copying information, intelligence gathering outside government was limited. As in so many matters, computers have changed the landscape. The same computers both make private intelligence gathering cost effective and also make illegal copying much more costly to the owners of information. One does not imply the other, however. Intelligence gathering does not require illegal copying.

Normally, mere reading of (at least, nonclassified) information raises no legal issues. Certainly this holds true when reading a book or other printed publication. Unless you have stolen the publication, you need no legal permission to read and thereby obtain information. Stating the obvious would not serve any point, but for the fact that the same treatment almost did not apply to electronic materials.

In December 1996, treaty negotiators reached two new international agreements on changes in copyright protection. Negotiators rejected attempts to make reading copyrighted material on a computer screen a violation of copyright law. Few people would think it should be. But there were those who would have made anyone—including schoolchildren at their library—copyright infringers for even looking at the copyrighted material on a computer screen.

What makes research done on-line different from that drawn from a book? With a book, the acts of publishing, reading, and copying are clearly distinguishable. The publishing of a book is complete before the ordinary reader has the opportunity to read it. If the reader copies part or all of the book by hand or using a copy machine, he clearly must make the decision to do so—regardless of whether the act of copying is or is not permissible.

In electronic publishing, the lines separating publishing, reading, and copying are blurred. If you access a commercial on-line service such as LEXIS-NEXIS, you pay a fee that may include only reading, both reading and copying ("downloading"), or separate fees for each. You may be paying to read materials that you might otherwise read without cost in hard copy, but it may be difficult or time-consuming to get the information. So you pay for instant access. Paying the service provider effectively satisfies whatever financial obligations are due the copyright holder (or other owner if the material cannot be copyrighted). The provider pays the copyright holder.

The openness of the Internet invites copyright infringement. Internet-service providers, through which users access the Internet, have no affirmative obligation to screen out illegal copies posted on the Internet. As a result, in the absence of the 1996 international treaty, users of the Internet arguably are routinely violating copyright. Browsing the world wide web necessarily involves producing a temporary copy of the material to be read by the user. Thus electronic publishing, reading, and copying are not neatly distinguishable. While the treaty exempts the temporary copying inherent in basic electronic viewing from infringement, it leaves vague the distinction between a temporary and a permanent copy.

Software and Databases

Electronic copying, as already indicated, does not basically differ from other kinds of copying as a matter of copyright law. Because of the amounts of revenue lost to software producers, what differs is the enforcement of the law. Software piracy violates both the copyright law and the trade secrets law, as discussed below.

Any business using computers has to be concerned about its employees using illegally copied software for any business purpose. It does not matter that the use of illegal software was unauthorized, unless the copying or use was contrary to clearly established employer policy. If the business is not selling illegal copies, it might seem it has nothing to worry about. Not true. Unlike photocopying, relatively small-scale illegal software copying does receive vigorous enforcement due to the intelligence gathering of the Software Publishers Association (SPA). To protect themselves, businesses need to implement their own internal security to prevent being the object of enforcement.

The rarity of enforcement actions for illegal photocopying as well as the legality of personal-use-only video-copying (e.g., recording a televised movie on a home VCR) seem to have misled many into casually making illegal copies of software. Like the music industry trade associations that have engaged in enforcement for years, the SPA directs an aggressive effort to identify, punish, and deter software copyright infringers. In doing so, the SPA effectively employs passive, semiactive, and active intelligence gathering. As of

1995, the SPA's toll-free telephone line has been receiving a hundred tips per week, generally from disgruntled employees, identifying use of illegally copied software. The SPA verifies reports by checking whether the targeted company has registered with the software publisher. If the company has not, the SPA will seek a voluntary audit in which the company agrees to allow the SPA to inspect its computers for pirated copies. In doing its audit, the SPA uses special software that can detect whether any software has been deleted.

Why would any company allow the SPA such access? It's quite simple. As a result of amendments to the copyright act in 1992, the burden of proof rests on the software user. The user must, by receipts and/or other records, prove its right to use the software. If the company does not agree to a voluntary audit, the SPA can seek a court order for an involuntary audit. When that occurs, the SPA arrives with federal marshals to execute a search warrant to inspect the computers. Either way, if the company is using illegally copied software, it will pay fines. If the company resists, officers and/or managers may suffer criminal prosecution.

Intelligence gathering involves the use and creation of databases. Copyright protection does not cover facts, only the manner in which they are compiled. The user would prefer that databases not be copyrighted, and courts have traditionally restricted severely the scope of database copyright. That allows users of data more freedom to create new databases. When the user creates a new database that has commercial value, however, the user-turned-creator may now have second thoughts about copyright coverage.

The 1996 Geneva conference on copyright failed to expand copyright protection to databases. Compilers of databases would like the same protection for their work product as is currently provided only for creative materials. Like software producers, database owners can and do charge for access. Without copyright protection for a database, however, the user is not barred from copying, manipulating, and/or redistributing the data—unless restricted by agreement.

Database creators may be able to restrict their use by contract, but the protection may still be lacking for some. Market conditions and the database owner's marketing strategy will determine its ability contractually to impose the conditions. The distribution requirements of certain databases preclude charging fees, much less imposing other conditions. Obviously, for example, the New York Stock Exchange must continue to distribute its information to millions without charge and therefore cannot contractually impose restrictions on those who read its quotes in newspapers. With copyright protection it could continue to distribute to the same audience without charge, but the law would impose a restriction on copying, manipulation, and redistribution without permission of the copyright holder, which presumably would involve a charge.

Theoretically, copyright protection and the ability to charge should stimulate the creation of more databases, thereby increasing the sources from which to gather intelligence. Increased supply and competition supposedly should more than compensate for the fact that some currently available free sources of information would carry a charge. On the other hand, with or without a charge, databases would become less generally accessible. Although lawfully obtained, databases, like stock exchange statistics, would no longer automatically be available for incorporation into newly created databases. The ease and cost of accessing and creating databases is central to passive intelligence gathering.

LEGAL RISKS OF THE SEMIACTIVE AND ACTIVE MODES

Semiactive intelligence gathering, like telephone market research, does not involve any particular legal risks in free countries as long as fraud or bribery is not involved. Active intelligence gathering can simulate and may supplement or substitute for law enforcement. Naturally, it carries the greatest legal risks. As exemplified by the theft of trade secrets, the legal issues involve overlapping questions related to rights in information, the means of obtaining it, and its use.

The problem of trade secrets demonstrates that at least for defensive purposes, corporations with valuable proprietary information must undertake security measures that, in themselves, amount to active intelligence gathering. Moreover, if certain corporations examine their policies related to security they will realize they are pursuing inconsistent goals. On the one hand, computer-related as well as other corporations are resisting federal proposals to limit encryption. Federal law enforcement and intelligence agencies want access to encryption software in order to subject electronic communication to court-ordered surveillance. Simultaneously, the same industry has pushed for new federal criminal laws on trade secrets and computer crimes. The obvious argument by federal agencies is that it has been given more responsibility to solve computer-related crimes without commensurate ability to do so. The solution for corporations may be to rely more on prevention than on federal criminal enforcement.

Requesting Information

The semiactive mode—for example, making telephone calls or conducting face-to-face interviews for information—does not itself ordinarily involve any particular legal risks, at least in free countries. In China, on the other hand, asking routine questions about business activity may be deemed a subversive act and therefore criminal activity. A Western businessman attempting to track down the source of piracy of his product may find himself accused of espionage simply for asking. Even within liberal democracies, laws do protect the secrecy of information stamped "classified" or "state secrets." No country is more open than the United States and yet the shear size of our federal government means that more information is classified than the total amount of information many countries have. As a result of the end of the Cold War, as well as the simple passage of time, which eliminates all but the historical value of most information, the reasons for classifying much information have been lost. Federal agencies are currently undergoing a complete review to declassify information that no longer needs to be classified, but the process is expected to take a number of years.

In the United States, the presumption favors disclosure of information. Government information may be classified, but it cannot be copyrighted. Once disclosed it becomes freely available. Moreover, any citizen can request nonpublished information from almost any federal agency following the relatively simple procedures provided by the Freedom of Information Act (FOIA). Such requests produce a great deal of information that agencies would not have volunteered to release, if only for reasons of inertia.

What about paying for information? What's the difference between paying for information and bribery? Paying another's employee in order to gain business from the employer may constitute commercial bribery in the United States. If the transaction includes the transfer of proprietary information, theft of trade secrets may also be involved. The original meaning of bribery, which applied only to payments made to government officials, has expanded in the United States to commercial situations. Definitions of commercial bribery are quite broad, but fortunately the crime does not generally get applied to exchanges of gifts and favors among businesspeople, which, according to prevailing custom, are normal and acceptable. Otherwise, under the wording of some American commercial bribery statutes, a salesperson who, as part of a sales call, buys lunch for a corporation's purchasing manager, *literally* could be guilty of commercial bribery.

American corporations conducting business outside the United States have greater cause for concern about "bribery," in the traditional sense of payments to government officials. In many countries—such as Mexico, where the governments have substantial control over the economy—"customary" payments are expected. The antibribery provisions of the Foreign Corrupt Practices Act, however, make it a crime for U.S. businesses or their agents directly or indirectly to pay or to give anything of value to a foreign government official, any person acting on behalf of a foreign government, any foreign political party, or candidate for office in a foreign country. The statute does not prohibit payments to others unless some or all of the payment is going to a covered person or entity. The prohibition applies to payments for "influencing any act or decision of such foreign official in his official capacity." Those words standing alone, however, include not only clear cases of bribery but other kinds of "customary payments."

Recognizing problems with the statute, in 1988, Congress amended it to clarify that payments "for routine governmental action" are not prohibited. These include "any facilitating or expediting payment" for such services as obtaining work permits, processing visas and work orders, providing police and other government services, as well as phone service and other utilities. The exception for such "facilitating" payments does not solve the basic competitive disadvantage American companies face against companies willing to pay genuine bribes. The exception, however, does distinguish and permit customary "grease" payments.

Tape Recording and Wiretapping

Among the familiar techniques common to intelligence gathering and other purposes is the recording of telephone conversations. Such recordings may be routine or for a special purpose. As the Nixon tapes prove, their impact can be for posterity.

The legal treatment of recording telephone conversations generally turns on whether one party consents to the recording and whether it fits within the expanded notion of a "wiretap." Government wiretapping is easiest to pin down. Both the U.S. Supreme Court, under the Fourth Amendment of the Constitution, and the European Court of Human Rights, under Article 8 of the European Convention on Human Rights, have ruled that government wiretaps must proceed according to written regulations that restrict their operation and require advance approval by a judicial officer.

In the United States, it is a crime for anyone other than a properly authorized government official to engage in wiretapping. Federal law does allow (although some states make it a crime) for one party to record the other's conversation without the second party's knowledge. Federal *constitutional* law treats consensual and nonconsensual recording differently; the distinction turns on the notion of "reasonable expectation of privacy." When neither party consents to the recording, they both have a reasonable expectation of privacy. At the same time, in speaking with others, we each run the risk that the other will record the conversation and therefore have no unilateral expectation of privacy.

Federal statutory law, however, has been expanded beyond "reasonable expectations of privacy" to prohibit recording a cellular or portable telephone conversation. Even though courts have ruled that persons do not have "reasonable expectation of privacy" in such over-the-air conversations, the federal wiretap law prohibits intercepting a cellular telephone conversation. Had it not been for the publication of a recorded cellular conversation involving House Speaker Newt Gingrich, relatively few people would be aware that such nonconsensual recordings violate federal law.

In the United Kingdom, the law on electronic eavesdropping has been the recent subject of debate. In January 1997, the government failed in an attempt to allow wiretaps without judicial approval. Also, reaction to interception and publication of embarrassing cellular telephone conversations by Prince Charles and Lady Diana has prompted calls for greater restriction on various types of surveillance by nongovernment snoopers. In the meantime, private surveillance in the United Kingdom may involve relatively minor civil or criminal violations that appear to go largely unenforced. All kinds of private surveillance equipment are widely available in the United Kingdom.

According to a major supplier of private security and intelligence technology, Quark Research Group, most countries in the world (other than the United States) either do not have or do not enforce restrictions against use of private surveillance equipment. The Persian Gulf countries, however, are an exception at least in that such equipment is not generally obtainable there.

Taking and Securing Information

Breaking into private or government property and stealing are crimes around the world. The case of the Watergate break-in (done for the purpose of obtaining information) attests that in the United States even an illegal entry directed by government officials is a crime.

Increasingly, corporations have to be concerned about "break-ins" searching for information from computers and employees. As noted above, few countries other than the United States legally protect trade secrets. Whether inside or outside the United States, however, the protection requires a corporation to defend any information it wishes to keep secret. Outside the United States, "stealing" trade secrets may not be stealing at all. Until recently, even in the United States, theft has involved the taking of tangible, movable property. Such property can only be in one place at one time. When taken, the owner or possessor has clearly lost something. With the taking of intellectual property, nothing tangible need be taken. Lost is the exclusiveness to the information. The loss is the decline in market or potential market value. Those who take may not think they are depriving the owner of anything, even though the taker obviously realizes a gain of something.

The treatment of trade secrets is changing. Until recently, legal enforcement in the United States was under state law and generally through a private civil action. The increasing importance of intellectual property as a significant source of wealth has increased the incidence and consequences of trade secret theft. As a result, in 1996, the U.S. Congress passed and the president signed the Economic Espionage Act, previously mentioned, which makes trade secret theft a federal crime but does not provide a private right of action for damages. The new statute will mean that large-scale incidence of trade secret theft will likely result in indictments.

The new federal statute presents some problems of definition. Although it utilizes the definition from the Uniform Trade Secrets Act, the fact that the act is criminal and federal raises the uncertainties about enforcement. The statute defines trade secrets as follows:

> all forms and types of financial, business, scientific, technical, economic, or engineering information, including patterns, plans, compilations, program devices, formulas, designs, prototypes, methods, techniques, processes, procedures, programs, or codes, whether tangible or intangible, and whether or how stored, compiled, or memorialized physically, electronically, graphically, photographically, or in writing if—

A. the owner thereof has taken reasonable measures to keep such information secret; and

B. the information derives independent economic value, actual or potential, from not being known to, and not being readily ascertainable through proper means by, the public....

Under the definition, the information *need not actually be secret.* It is only necessary for the owner to have taken "reasonable steps" and that the information have economic value "from not being generally known or being readily ascertainable through proper means by the public."

Every good employee doing interesting work will "gain valuable learning experience." If every employee in a corporation routinely must sign a nondisclosure agreement, which is good practice at least in technology companies, does that mean that everything learned on the job by every employee falls within the definition of a "trade secret" for purposes of this criminal statute? No employer would have previously thought to sue an employee for walking away with the valuable training provided by the employer, no matter how ungrateful or disloyal the employer thought the former employee. It would have been costly to do so and the suit would have been deemed frivolous. Even with an employee nondisclosure agreement, the former employer would rarely sue the new employer for benefiting from what the employee learned with the former employer unless it was clearly well-guarded proprietary information.

The increasing ease with which information is moved has inspired greater concern for security precautions to avoid having one's communication "overheard" or "secret" information copied or stolen. Connecting computers to the Internet facilitates illegal copying and other crimes, especially fraud. These crimes and the general desire for secure communication have created a demand for copy avoidance. This requires encryption, which in turn has alarmed federal law enforcement that their own intelligence gathering will suffer as a result of perfect, private security. Given the enormous consequences of electronic copying and encryption, they have received considerable attention in terms of legal enforcement.

Using Information Transnationally

Growing international commerce and electronic communication have propelled the revival of an international law of commerce. This development updates the *lex mercatoria,* or "law merchant," that was a medieval body of customary rules used by merchants to supplement the commercial law of states. The practice never died out completely. As modern nation-states rose in power, however, such customary law was not viewed as "real law," which was deemed to emerge only from legislative bodies. Today, the creation of an international commercial law has been proceeding largely, but not exclusively, by multilateral treaties. The World Trade Organization and also recent treaties on intellectual property designed to facilitate commercial development of the Internet are both products of and creators of such international commercial law. Other sources of the growing international commercial law derive from assertion of extraterritorial jurisdiction by one nation, namely the United States, and by contract, which is a method the European Union may use to protect data transfers.

The U.S. contribution to shaping this international law of commerce has not only been by treaty. Whether or not consciously intended for this, the extraterritorial assertion of jurisdiction over financial crimes and drug-related offenses has brought tremendous influence globally. Outside of extradition and the limited area of war crimes and genocide, criminal law has not been the subject of common or reciprocal international enforcement. Nevertheless, through the federal crime of money-laundering, the United States directly asserts broad jurisdiction over nonresident, non-U.S. citizens, thereby affecting the practices of financial institutions around the world. Such influence will only increase because, since 1990, the Financial Crimes Enforcement Network of the U.S. Treasury Department has been using and building the ultimate intelligence-gathering tool ("A hybrid between a data base and a focused surveillance tool, it combines qualities of many surveillance technologies." See Steven Bercu, "Toward Universal Surveillance in an Information Age Economy: Can We Handle Treasury's New Police Technology?," *Jurimetrics Journal,* Summer 1994, p. 5), which, in cooperation with Interpol, "will consolidate, analyze and disseminate data concerning financial crimes throughout the world."*

The American assertion of extraterritorial antitrust jurisdiction, even of a noncriminal nature, has been a source of conflict with other countries. The European Union also claims extraterritorial jurisdiction over competition issues. Nevertheless, the competition laws of the European Union as well as Japan are neither as strong nor privately enforceable as are American antitrust laws.

Both the United States and Great Britain are free-trade nations. Nevertheless, the two countries have had serious conflicts as a result of the assertion of American antitrust jurisdiction. Antitrust conflicts between the United States and Great Britain have largely, but not exclusively, concerned airline service. Both countries have been protecting the interest of their dominant airlines. The two governments have had a bilateral agreement regulating the amount of airline traffic between the two countries. The United States has long pushed for an "open skies" agreement that would let market forces determine the access of airlines to each other's markets. Since the late 1970s, when airfares were deregulated in the United States, competition from American airlines and pressure from the U.S. government have prodded gradual deregulation in Europe.

The British airline Virgin Atlantic has from its beginning battled with British Airways. Virgin was formed after an earlier British low-fare airline, Laker Airways, went into bankruptcy. In the early 1980s, the U.S. Justice Department launched an antitrust investigation to determine whether British Airways and other competing airlines in the United States and abroad colluded to put Laker out of business. Also, Laker's British liquidator in bankruptcy filed an antitrust lawsuit in an American federal court.

As a result of diplomatic negotiations, the Justice Department dropped its Laker investigation in 1984. That did not end the Amer-

*N. Brady., 1/12/93

ican lawsuit by the British liquidator, even though the litigation was blocked in part by a British court. Also in 1984, in order to avoid an antitrust lawsuit from the newly launched, privately owned Virgin Atlantic Airways, the then-government-owned British Airways asked for and received a letter of assurance from the Justice Department that certain proposed fares did not pose a possible antitrust violation. Since being privatized in 1987, British Airways has been sued by Virgin Atlantic Airways in a New York federal court. The court rejected various legal arguments by British Airways that it should decline jurisdiction and send Virgin Atlantic to a court in the United Kingdom. Certainly, the American airline industry has had a significant impact on the British airline industry not merely due to the market but due to enforcement of American antitrust law.

The European Union (EU) may soon be exerting a strong influence on American practices regarding the use of data *not* through criminal law but through contracts necessitated by the EU's privacy rules. Countries in Europe have adopted "data-protection laws" designed to restrict the disclosure of personal information. As a result, several countries have begun restricting the export of data to persons or entities in countries that do not have sufficient protection for personal data. The United States is not considered as having sufficient privacy protection for personal data. A recent study of U.S. law prepared for the Commission of the European Communities recommends solving the problem of inadequate and inconsistent standards in the United States not by blocking the flow of data to the United States but by strict liability on European companies for adherence to the European standards.

In summary, whether you are doing business in your local community or overseas, intelligence is a necessity. Wherever you do business, law is a reality. To the question "Is intelligence gathering legal?," the answer is "Yes, depending..."—depending on what you are trying to find out, where you are looking for it, and how you plan to get it. In general, passive techniques in the advanced industrial countries are going to be legal. Passive techniques in some less developed countries may be illegal, but as long as what you do is passive, you're probably going to be safe from retribution. Legal problems develop as you become increasingly active. First, you face dangers because you must act rather than simply absorb. Second, you come into direct conflict with others who may use the law as an instrument to stop you. This is particularly true in the United States, the most litigious nation on earth. The legality of intelligence gathering intersects with the likelihood of a lawsuit merely to deter you from pursuing the truth. So, intelligence gathering is legal, but… Consult your attorney.

CONCLUSION

OK, is everything clear now? We thought so.

Actually, there are several important things to take away from this discusssion. First, there is not a separate area we might call business intelligence law. Since business intelligence touches on everything, all aspects of law impinge. The obvious areas—copyright, privacy, wiretap—are there. But so are antitrust laws and virtually any other area businesses are interested in.

Second, Anglo-American law takes itself seriously. Legal systems in other parts of the world do not. The fact that Albania has a law on the books does not mean that Albania intends that law to be enforced. Conversely, the fact that Albania doesn't have a law on the books doesn't mean that law enforcement agents won't nail you for doing something they don't like. The problem is, of course, that a citizen of the United Kingdom or the United States is dealing with a government at home that expects businesses to obey laws overseas, even if the natives know that the law is a joke. Even obeying the laws of friendly, legally and culturally compatible countries like the United Kingdom and the United States is difficult.

Third, the growing power of multinational organizations like the European Union and the World Trade Organization place businesses in a difficult position, particularly in areas like intellectual property law, where the rules are not only not yet clear but actually contradictory.

Fourth, with the emergence of the electronic domain, any comfortable assumptions you may have about the law should be discarded. The law of passive, electronic domain intelligence doesn't exist. Unfortunately, you can't wait for the law to define itself in order to do your business. Your work goes on regardless of ambiguity.

This is the ultimate problem faced in dealing with the law. The fact that business intelligence techniques are at the cutting edge of a technological change that the law has not yet caught up with; the new global nature of business intelligence; the intersection of business intelligence with fundamental international disputes and fault lines—all mean that the law is not a particularly faithful guide.

No matter what you do, somewhere, somehow, it may be illegal. And yet you must gather information or die.

Where neither law nor custom is a guide, we urge common sense.

- Be aware of the ambiguous position you are in.
- In collecting information, try to make sure that you really need it.
- In collecting information, try to make certain that you are not stepping on the toes of people who are extremely powerful in countries where the law isn't taken seriously, and where you have no choice but to visit.
- Try, for as long as possible, to stay with passive techniques in the electronic and paper domain.

Not a very strong position, but the best available at this point in time.

APPENDIX

TOOLS FOR FINDING PEOPLE

There are two extremely valuable sources for directories of business, government, and associations. These are Gale Research and U.S. West Direct, both with catalogs on the web. If you can't find a directory pertaining to your search from either of these sources, it probably doesn't exist. U.S. West even offers to find a relevant directory for you if they don't already carry it.

THE DIRECTORY SOURCE
U.S. West Direct
c/o PDC
13100 East 39th Avenue, Unit U
Denver, CO 80239-3527
U.S. and Canada, phone: 1-800-422-8793, Ext. 160
Other countries dial international access code, then: 1-303-375-0707, Ext. 160
U.S. and Canada, fax: 1-800-522-8793
Other countries fax by dialing your international access code, then: 1-303-373-9878
http://www.w3.uswest.com/directorysource/usw_directory. html
Call for pricing and availability as both are subject to change.

GALE RESEARCH
835 Penobscot Building
645 Griswold Street
Detroit, MI 48226
Phone: 313-961-2242 or 800-877-GALE
Fax: 313-961-6815
http://www.gale.com/
http://www.thomson.com/gale/default.html

The *Yellow Book* Leadership Directories are another excellent series of directories of key personnel in the U.S. federal, state, and local government; foreign business and government representation in the U.S.; and U.S. corporate, legal, financial, association, and news media fields.

YELLOW BOOK LEADERSHIP DIRECTORIES SERIES
Leadership Directories, Inc.
104 Fifth Avenue, 2nd Floor
New York, NY, 10011
Phone: 212-627-4140
Fax: 212-645-0931
$190–$265 each; $1,460–$1,600 complete library

A couple of good collections of web-based phone and fax listings are Kapitol and the Reference Shelf. Kapitol includes a number of more obscure links—such as the fax directory of Sierra Leone—and rates all their links by ease of use, completeness, and reliability.

KAPITOL
31 Rue E. Gossart
B-1180 Brussels - Belgium
Phone: +32-2-344-42-42
Fax: +32-2-344-22-96
E-mail: kapitol@infobel.be

THE REFERENCE SHELF
http://www.synapse.net/~radio/referenc.htm
Kapitol—International Directories
http://www.infobel.be/infobel/infobelworld.html

Most military contacts can be located through two sources: the U.S. military's
Defense Link on the web, or Jane's annuals, available in print or on CD-ROM.

DEFENSELINK http://www.dtic.dla.mil:80/defenselink/index.html
Links to nearly all publicly accessible U.S. military web sites

JANE'S ANNUALS AND JOURNALS
http://www.janes.com/janes.html
http://www.thomson.com/ janes/default.html

> JANE'S CANADA
> Vanwell Publishing, Ltd.
> 1 Northrup Crescent
> P.O. Box 2131, Station B
> St. Catherines, Ontario L2M 6P5
> Canada
> Phone: 905-937-3100
> Fax: 905-937-1760

> JANE'S UK
> Sentinel House
> 163 Brighton Road
> Coulsdon, Surrey
> CR5 2NH
> UK
> Phone: 44-181-700-3700
> Fax: 44-181-763-1006

> JANE'S U.S.
> 1340 Braddock Place, Suite 300
> Alexandria, VA 22314-1651
> Phone: 703-683-3700
> Fax: 800-836-0297

> JANE'S WEST COAST
> 17310 Redhill Avenue, Suite 370
> Irvine, CA 92714
> Phone: 714-724-0868
> Fax: 714-724-1576

Besides the information available from the directory clearinghouses listed above,
the U.S. government is well represented on the web. A comprehensive starting

point can be found at the FedWorld site, while the individual branches of government have excellent sites of their own.

FEDWORLD http://www.fedworld.gov/

OFFICE OF THE PRESIDENT http://www.whitehouse.gov/

U.S. HOUSE OF REPRESENTATIVES http://www.house.gov/

U.S. SENATE http://www.senate.gov/

The Foundation Center is an excellent source of directories and information about U.S. and international foundations.

THE FOUNDATION CENTER
79 Fifth Avenue, 8th Floor
New York, NY 10003-3076
Tel: 212-620-4230
Fax: 212-691-1828
http://fdncenter.org/

In addition to the directories available through Gale Research and U.S. West, contact information for foreign governments, businesses, finances, and associations can be found at the sources listed below.

EUROPEAN UNION
Delegation of the European Commission to the United States
2300 M Street, NW
Washington, DC 20037
Phone: 202-862-9500
Fax: 202-429-1766
http://www.eurunion.org/

INTERNATIONAL MONETARY FUND (IMF)
External Relations Department
Washington, DC 20431
Phone: 202-623-7300
Fax: 202-623-6278
http://www.imf.org/

KR ONDISC Worldwide Government and Defense Directory on CD-ROM
$2,900 (includes 4 quarterly updates)
(Includes: *Worldwide Government Directory, Worldwide Directory of Defense Authorities,* and *Profiles of Worldwide Government Leaders.*)
Knight-Ridder Information, Inc.
2440 El Camino Real
Mountain View, CA 94040
Phone: 415-254-8800
Fax: 415-254-8123
E-mail if you are located in the United States: customer@corp.dialog.com
E-mail if you are outside the United States: intl@corp.dialog.com

UNION OF INTERNATIONAL ASSOCIATIONS (UIA)
Rue Washington 40
B-1050 Brussels

Belgium
Fax: 32-2-646.05.25.
E-mail: weblist@uia.be.
http://www.uia.org/
Tens of thousands of organizations listed on-line, with contact points. The UIA
also offers the four-volume *Yearbook of International Organizations* in print and
CD-ROM versions. Print version: US$ 875.

THE UNITED NATIONS
New York, NY 10017
Phone: 212-963-1234
http://www.un.org/

THE WORLD BANK GROUP
1818 H Street, NW
Washington, DC 20433
http://www.worldbank.org/
Web site contains contact phone numbers by topic.

WORLDWIDE GOVERNMENT DIRECTORIES, INC.
7979 Old Georgetown Road
Bethesda, MD 20814
Phone: 301-718-8770 or 800-332-3535
Fax: 301-718-8494
http://www.wgd.com/
1,450 pages, $347

There are a large number of trade and business directories available in print and
electronic form. Many of these are available from Gale Research or U.S. West.
Other excellent sources of information include Dun & Bradstreet's large number
of publications and services and the Thomas Register. International Thomson
Publishing, which owns Jane's and Gale Research, also offers a large number of
CD-ROM, on-line, and diskette directories related to international business.

DUN & BRADSTREET INFORMATION SERVICES
3 Sylvan Way
Parsippany, NJ 07054-3896
Phone: 201-605-6000 or 800-234-3867
Fax: 201-605-6930
http://www.dnbcorp.com/

DUN & BRADSTREET, LTD.
Holmers Farm Way
High Wycombe
Buckinghamshire HP12 4UL
England
Phone: 44-494-423-600
Fax: 44-494-423-595

DUN & BRADSTREET ONLINE SOLUTIONS http://www.dbisna.com/

INTERNATIONAL THOMSON PUBLISHING
Information/Reference Group
835 Penobscot Building

645 Griswold Street
Detroit, MI 48226
Phone: 313-961-2242 or 800-877-4253
Fax: 313-961-6083
http://www.thomson.com/

THOMAS PUBLISHING CO.
5 Penn Plaza
New York, NY 10001
Phone (US/Canada): 212-290-7277 or 800-699-9822, ext. 444
Fax (US/Canada): 212-290-7365
Phone (International): 212-290-7279
Fax (International): 212-290-8825
http://www.thomasregister.com/

The Thomas Register of American Manufacturers, Products, and Services (33 volume set;
annual)
Includes subsets on Products and Services, Company Profiles, and Catalog File.
Price range for set from $255.80 (in U.S.) to $495 (in Central/South America)
Thomas Register is also available on CD-ROM
Price for CD-ROM from $402 (in U.S.) to $490 (International)

INTERNET SEARCH ENGINES

We regard Internet search engines as a vitally important part of searching the net.
For that reason we are providing this list, which describes and evaluates each major
engine. We are giving you name and address, whether it searches usenet groups as
well as the web, whether it has advanced search features that allow you to tailor
your search request, and are evaluating ease, content, and speed on a 1 to 10 scale,
with 10 being the best. The evaluations are subjective, and reasonable people can
quarrel with them, but it is our call and this is how we see it.

SEARCH ENGINE NAME, TYPE, ADDRESS	USENET?	ADVANCED SEARCH?	EASE	CONTENT	SPEED	INPUT	COMMENTS
Ahoy! (personal web page) http://ahoy.cs.washington.edu:6060	n/a	N	7	4	7	Names.	First and last name must be entered. Missing data that can be found in other locations.
Alta Vista (general) http://www.altavista.digital.com	Y	Y	8	7	8	Keyword. Boolean for advanced search.	Good information source; large number of responses makes retrieving specific information difficult.
American Directory Assistance (people finder) http://www.abii.com/lookupusa/ada/ada.htm	n/a	N	6	7	8	Names.	Provides street maps. Entering specific state does not allow for large searches.
Bigbook (business/company finder) http://www.bigbook.com	n/a	N	7	8	7	Names.	Comprehensive listing for businesses. Does not provide exact search option.
Bigfoot (people finder) http://www.bigfoot.com	n/a	N	6	6	4	Names, regions, states, etc.	Major difficulty is accessing homepage and search engine; sometimes is not available.
Cosmix Insane Search (meta) http://www.cosmix.com/motherload/insane	Y	N	8	9	6	Boolean. Menu-driven function.	User chooses how to search. Results are compiled and relevancy is better than most "meta" search engines.
Deja News Service (newsgroup) http://www.dejanews.com	Y	Y	6	6	8	Keyword or newsgroup classification.	Nice, updated directory of newsgroup postings.
Dogpile (meta) http://www.dogpile.com	Y	Y	6	8	6	Keyword. Boolean searching.	Handy time delimiter gives user some control. User must search within individual engines.
Excite (general) http://www.excite.com	Y	Y	8	8	8	Keyword. Boolean for advanced searching.	Advanced search capabilities are tough to learn but are extremely powerful.

Four11 Directory Services (people finder) http://www.four11.com	n/a	N	8	7	9	Names, countries, states, cities, domains.	E-mail search is very good. Phone number list is not as comprehensive.
GTE Yellow Pages (business finder) http://superpages.gte.net	n/a	N	7	5	5	Keyword. Boolean and menu-driven.	Lots of graphics makes loading very slow. Often returned no matches.
Galaxy (general) http://galaxy.tradewave.com/galaxy.html motherload/insane	N	Y	8	7	8	Keyword. Boolean is clickable option.	Allows Gopher and Telnet searching as options. Provides a fairly lengthy excerpt from page.
Highway 61 (meta) http://www.highway61.com	N	N	6	8	6	Boolean is menu-driven function.	Aims at being humorous; could be more straightforward and well defined.
HotBot (general) http://www.hotbot.com	N	N	8	8	7	Boolean is menu-driven function.	Nifty searching options. User can search for people, phrases, etc. Also a good date delimiter.
Infohiway (general) Http://www.infohiway.com	N	N	4	5	6	Keyword.	Confusing search interface will frustrate novice web users. Irrelevant hits sometimes result.
Infoseek (general) http://www.infoseek.com	Y	Y	8	8	8	Natural language or keyword.	Subject searching is available. Natural language functions are a nice frill but of little use.
Infospace People Search (people finder) http://in-101.infospace.com/iui/people.htm	n/a	N	8	6	8	Names, addresses.	Comprehensive, versatile people finder with phone, address, and e-mail capability.
Internet Address Finder (people finder) http://www.iaf.net	n/a	N	7	5	7	Names, organizations, domain name, or e-mail address.	Allows searching for user by e-mail address and by name. Available in Dutch, French, German, Italian, Portuguese, and English.

SEARCH ENGINE NAME, TYPE, ADDRESS	USENET?	ADVANCED SEARCH?	EASE	CONTENT	SPEED	INPUT	COMMENTS
Linkstar (people finder) http://www.linkstar.com	n/a	N	7	7	5	Keyword with menu-driven functions for search refining.	Hits are comprehensive and informative. However, speed is not impressive.
Looksmart (general) http://www.looksmart.com	N	N	6	7	5	Category search drives hits.	Java applets make loading the page and search slow. Must search by category.
Lycos (general) http://www.lycos.com	N	N	7	7	8	Keyword.	Sounds and pictures are searchable. Irrelevant hits sometimes retrieved.
Magellan (general) http://www.mckinley.com	N	Y	7	5	7	Keyword. Boolean with menu-driven search.	Allows subject searching; particularly low on content for a general search engine. Good advanced options.
Metacrawler (meta) http://www.metacrawler.com	N	Y	7	9	7	Keyword and menu-driven options.	Combined hits are pooled together, though relevancy is well below average.
Open Text (general) http://index.opentext.net	Y	Y	7	7	7	Keyword. Boolean	One of the more relevant search engines. Allows refining of search after search is made to find more specific items on the web.
Pathfinder (general) http://www.pathfinder.com	N	N	5	4	6	Keyword with clickable options.	Graphics on search interface make load time slow.
Reference (newsgroup) http://www.reference.com	Y	Y	7	5	6	Keyword with Boolean searches.	Relevance very poor. Updated often, but hits are very erratic.

Resource						Search method	Comments
SavvySearch (meta) http://guaraldi.cs.colostate.edu:2000/form	N	N	7	9	6	Keyword. Boolean is menu-driven.	Results are categorized by search engine. No relevancy ranking, but integration is an option. Retrievals available in 23 languages.
Switchboard: Find a person (people finder) http://www.switchboard.com	n/a	Y	7	6	7	Name and category driven.	Allows user to find business by category and people (latter listing is not well updated).
Tilenet (newsgroup) http://tile.net/news/search.html	Y	N	6	2	7	Keyword. Boolean.	Primitive searching capabilities search from a small number of newsgroup postings.
WWW Worm (general) http://wwww.cs.colorado.edu/wwww	N	N	7	5	6	Keyword. Boolean is menu-driven.	Limited capabilities; content does not match other general engines.
Web Crawler (general) www.webcrawler.com	N	N	8	7	8	Boolean, keyword searching.	Easy-to-use general search engine. Well laid out and user-friendly. Relevancy is suspect.
WhoWhere (people finder) http://www.whowhere.com	n/a	Y	6	6	7	Names.	Good e-mail finder with one weakness: Only identification is through e-mail. Refers user to other services to find people.
Worldpages Power Find (people finder) http://www.worldpages.com	n/a	N	7	7	7	Keyword or location search.	Business, people, and government searches are allowed. U.S. locations must include state entry.
Yahoo! (general) http://www.yahoo.com	N	Y	8	8	7	Keyword.	Allows subject/category searching and people search. Extensive list of city maps.
555-1212 (people finder) http://www.555-1212.com	n/a	N	7	7	7	Name, location, domain name.	Allows searching of e-mail addresses, telephone numbers, and web sites by area code.

MULTIPURPOSE	INTERNET ADDRESS	CUSTOMER SERVICE
America Online	http://www.aol.com	800-827-6364
CompuServe	http://www.compuserve.com	800-848-8990
Microsoft Network	http://www.msn.com	800-373-3676
Prodigy	http://www.prodigy.com	800-776-3449, Ext. 717
BUSINESS		
Dialog	http://www.dialog.com	415-254-7000
Dow Jones	http://bis.dowjones.com/online-lib/index.html	214-951-7171
E Library	http://www.infonautics.com/cnsm.htm	610-971-8840
Eye Q	http://www.datatimes.com/products.html	800-642-2525
FT Profile	http://www.info.ft.com/online/profile	44-(0)-171-825-7905
LEXIS/NEXIS	http://www.lexisnexis.com	800-544-7390
Profound	http://www.profound.com	800-213-0648
Proquest Direct	http://www.umi.com	800-521-0600

Every company will use a different mix of services. Our expectation is that subscriptions to two or three services will suffice for most users. But mastery of the choices is a critical step in developing an intelligence capability.

MONTHLY ON-LINE USAGE COST

Based on 10 hours of on-line time, 100 search queries, and 100 document downloads or prints.

LOW-END ON-LINE SERVICES	TIME (includes document downloads, prints, etc.)
America Online	$19.95 flat rate
CompuServe	$24.95, $1.95 per hour after first 20
E Library	$9.94 flat rate
Microsoft Network	$19.95 flat rate

HIGH-END ON-LINE SERVICES	TIME	DOWNLOADS/SEARCHES	TOTAL
Dialog*	$530	$407	$937
Dow Jones*	free	$1121	$1121
Eye Q	$39	$450**	$489
FT Profile	$240	£500	£740
Lexis-Nexis (per use)	$360	$4000	$4360
Lexis-Nexis (flat rate)	$4250 (flat rate)	$200	$4450
Profound	$898	free	$898
Proquest Direct*	—	$383	—

*Service charges vary depending on source accessed. Estimates are based on averages taken from a representative sampling of sources.

**Includes charges on full-text documents viewed but not downloaded.

LIBRARIES WORTH VISITING ON-LINE

The sample below was determined on ease of use, content, and updates of information. When dealing with foreign libraries, most especially in Europe, there is a serious lag problem that reduces the site's usefulness. These are libraries that we like to use.

United States

BRIGHAM YOUNG UNIVERSITY
Telnet: library.byu.edu
128.187.11.10
NOTE: Select vt100 terminal and select "a" on Gateway menu.
Has unlimited number of returns, plus full citation.

GEORGETOWN UNIVERSITY
Telnet: library.lausys.georgetown.edu
141.161.93.5
NOTE: Log-in is george.
Access law and medical library, but limited display of information.

HARVARD UNIVERSITY
Telnet: hollis.harvard.edu
128.103.60.31
NOTE: At prompt, type hollis.
One of the best—plus you can e-mail your results back to yourself.

JOHNS HOPKINS UNIVERSITY
Telnet: janus-gate.mse.jhu.edu
128.220.8.2
NOTE: Log-in is janus.
Access the Woodrow Wilson Collection and the American Psychology Association database. Full display of records.

MASSACHUSETTS INSTITUTE OF TECHNOLOGY
Telnet: Library.mit.edu
18.92.0.26
NOTE: Log-in is library, Password you press enter.
Clumsy search but great library.

PRINCETON UNIVERSITY:
Telnet: Catalog.princeton.edu
128.112.204.71

PURDUE UNIVERSITY
Telnet: thorplus.lib.purdue.edu
128.210.21.22
NOTE: Log-in is catnet.
Access to other regional libraries.

RICE UNIVERSITY
Telnet: alexandria.rice.edu
128.42.74.100
NOTE: Log-in as Guest.

U.S. NAVAL ACADEMY
Telnet: Library.nadn.navy.mil
131.121.1881
NOTE: Log-in is library.

UNIVERSITY OF CALIFORNIA
Telnet: melvyl.ucop.edu
192.35.222.222
NOTE: Set vt100 or Help when prompted.
Access the California system. Some subject area databases are useful to businesses. Sends result to you via e-mail.

UNIVERSITY OF NOTRE DAME
Telnet: irishmvs.cc.nd.edu
129.74.4.5
NOTE: At Enter command or Help prompt enter library.

UNIVERSITY OF TEXAS AT AUSTIN
Telnet: utxuts.dp.utexas.edu
128.83.216.12
NOTE: Log-in is utcat.

Australia

UNIVERSITY OF SYDNEY
Telnet: lib7.fisher.su.oz.au
129.78.72.7
NOTE: Log-in is library.
Lots of Pacific basin material.

Hong Kong

CHINESE UNIVERSITY OF HONG KONG
Telnet: library.cuhk.edu.hk
202.40.216.17

United Kingdom

CAMBRIDGE UNIVERSITY
Telnet: ul.cam.ac.uk
131.111.164.59

OXFORD UNIVERSITY
Telnet: library.ox.ac.uk
129.67.1.46
NOTE: At the terminal type enter vt100.

INDEX